NATURE GUIDE
ROCKS
AND MINERALS

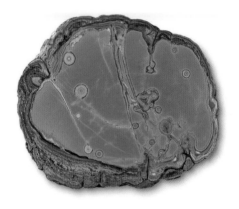

SMITHSONIAN

NATUREGUIDE

ROCKS

AND MINERALS

Ronald Louis Bonewitz

**LONDON, NEW YORK, MELBOURNE,
MUNICH, AND DELHI**

DORLING KINDERSLEY

Senior Editor
Peter Frances

US Editors
Jill Hamilton
Rebecca Warren

Jacket Editor
Manisha Majithia

Jacket Designer
Laura Brim

Managing Editor
Camilla Hallinan

**Associate
Publishing Director**
Liz Wheeler

Publishing Director
Jonathan Metcalf

Senior Art Editor
Spencer Holbrook

Production Editor
Rebekah Parsons-King

Production Controller
Erika Pepe

DK Picture Library
Rose Horridge

Picture Researchers
Jo Walton, Julia Harris-Voss

Managing Art Editor
Michelle Baxter

Publisher
Sarah Larter

Art Director
Philip Ormerod

DK INDIA

Managing Editor
Rohan Sinha

Deputy Managing Editor
Alka Thakur Hazarika

Senior Editor
Soma B. Chowdhury

Editors
Pragati Nagpal, Neha Pande, Priyaneet Singh

DTP Designers
Sourabh Challariya, Arvind Kumar,
Arjinder Singh, Jagtar Singh, Rajesh Singh,
Bimlesh Tiwary, Tanveer Zaidi

Production Manager
Pankaj Sharma

Deputy Managing Art Editor
Mitun Banerjee

Senior Designer
Ivy Roy

Designers
Arijit Ganguly, Mahua Mandal, Tanveer Zaidi

Assistant Designer
Sanjay Chauhan

Consultant Art Director
Shefali Upadhyay

Picture Researcher
Sakshi Saluja

DTP Manager
Balwant Singh

CONSULTANT

Dr. Jeffrey E. Post, Geologist, Curator-in-Charge, National Gem and Mineral Collection,
National Museum of Natural History, Smithsonian Institution

First American Edition, 2012
Published in the United States by DK Publishing
375 Hudson Street, New York, New York, 10014
13 14   10 9 8 7 6 5
006–181829–Jul/2012

Published in Great Britain by Dorling Kindersley Limited

A catalog record for this book is available from the Library of Congress.

ISBN 978-0-7566-9042-7

DK books are available at special discounts when purchased in bulk for sales promotions, premiums,
fund-raising, or educational use. For details, contact: DK Publishing Special Markets, 375 Hudson Street,
New York, New York, 10014 or SpecialSales@dk.com

Reproduced by Bright Arts, China, and MDP, UK
Printed and bound in China by Leo Paper Products

Discover more at
www.dk.com

CONTENTS

HOW THE ROCK AND MINERAL PROFILES WORK

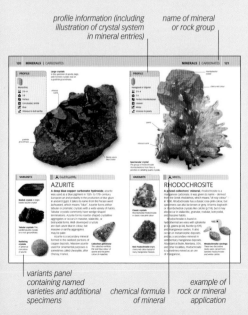

profile information (including illustration of crystal system in mineral entries)

name of mineral or rock group

variants panel containing named varieties and additional specimens

chemical formula of mineral

example of rock or mineral application

KEY

☒	Hardness
♥	Specific gravity
▨	Cleavage
⬗	Fracture
▱	Streak
⬈	Luster
▲	Type
⊕	Origin
♦	Temperature of formation
⬙	Pressure of formation
⊞	Structure
⊙	Grain size
■	Major minerals
⬓	Minor minerals
❋	Color
◀◀	Precursor rock
⊛	Fossils

INTRODUCTION

WHAT IS A MINERAL?

A mineral is a naturally occurring solid with a specific chemical composition and a distinctive internal crystal structure. Most minerals are formed inorganically but some, such as those found in bone, are formed organically (by living organisms).

WHAT MINERALS ARE MADE OF

Most minerals are chemical compounds composed of two or more chemical elements. However, copper, sulfur, gold, silver, and a few others occur as single "native" elements. A mineral is defined by its chemical formula and by the arrangement of atoms within its crystals. For example, iron sulfide has the chemical formula FeS_2 (where Fe is iron and S is sulfur). Iron sulfide can crystallize in two different ways. When it crystallizes in the cubic system (pp.22–23), it is called

copper cast into artifact

COPPER DUCK

Native elements
Native copper was probably the first metal used by humans. This duck's head was made in North Africa about 1,900 years ago.

brassy yellow color

cubic habit

PYRITE

Same composition but different structure
Though pyrite and marcasite have the same chemical composition and are both iron sulfide, their differing crystal structures make them different minerals.

rosette-shaped aggregate

metallic lustre

MARACASITE CRYSTALS

pyrite; when it crystallizes in the orthorhombic system, it becomes the mineral marcasite. Minerals are classified by their chemical content: for example, those containing oxygen ions are called oxides and those having carbon and oxygen ions are called carbonates.

Native sulfur
Sulfur is mined at Kawah Ijen, Java. Volcanic gases escaping from small openings in the ground (fumaroles) carry sulfur vapors to the surface, where it is deposited as a yellow crust.

Volcanic rhyolite
The Rhyolite Hills in Iceland are formed of rhyolite, a silica-rich rock produced as a result of volcanic activity. Rhyolite is made up of crystals of high-silica minerals.

ELECTRICAL CHARGE AND COMPOUNDS

A mineral compound is based on an electrical balance between a positively charged metal and a negatively charged part. In many minerals, negative charge is carried by a "radical": a combination of atoms acting as a single unit. For example, carbon and oxygen combine in a 1:3 ratio to give the CO_3 radical, which acts as a single, negatively charged unit.

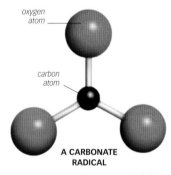

oxygen atom

carbon atom

A CARBONATE RADICAL

Simple and complex compounds
In carbonates, a simple carbon and oxygen group known as a radical combines with one or more metals.

COMMON MINERALS

There are more than 500 known minerals, but only about 100 of these are common. Silicon and oxygen make up about three-quarters of the crust by weight, and silicate minerals such as quartz, feldspar, and olivine are by far the most common minerals in rocks, making up 90 percent of the rocks at Earth's surface. The carbonates calcite and dolomite form sedimentary rocks, such as limestone.

Silicates
Silica tetrahedra link to form quartz. They can act as a radical to combine with one or more metals or semimetals to form other silicate minerals.

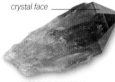

crystal face

QUARTZ CRYSTAL

each silicon atom is bonded to four oxygen atoms that form a tetrahedral shape

silica tetrahedra join at the corners to form a helix

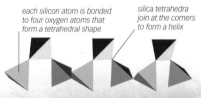

STRUCTURE OF QUARTZ

MINERAL GROUPS AND ASSOCIATIONS

Some minerals belong to chemical groups or series called solid solutions. In some circumstances, minerals are found together in groupings known as associations or assemblages. These patterns of occurrence can provide clues as to the minerals' origin.

SOLID SOLUTIONS

Some minerals do not have specific chemical compositions. Instead, they are homogenous mixtures of two minerals. These homogenous mixtures are known as solid solutions. For example, the olivine group of silicates includes forsterite and fayalite. Forsterite is a magnesium silicate, while fayalite is an iron silicate. Most olivine specimens are homogenous mixtures of the two, with the relative content of magnesium and iron varying in specimens. These minerals are described as part of a solid-solution series, in which forsterite and fayalite are the end-members.

tabular crystal

FAYALITE

light color from magnesium

FORSTERITE

Fayalite and forsterite
The olivine minerals fayalite and forsterite form a solid-solution series, with magnesium-rich forsterite as one end-member and iron-rich fayalite as the other.

PRIMARY AND SECONDARY MINERALS

Primary minerals crystallize directly from magma and remain unaltered. They include essential minerals used to assign a classification name to a rock and accessory minerals that are present in lesser abundance and do not affect the classification of a rock. Secondary minerals are produced by the alteration of a primary mineral after its formation. For example, when copper-bearing primary minerals come into contact with carbonated water, they alter into secondary azurite or malachite.

crystalline copper

massive copper

Primary copper mineral
Primary minerals, such as native copper, form directly in igneous rocks and remain unaltered. Their eventual alteration products are secondary minerals.

chrysocolla

botryoidal malachite

rock matrix

Secondary copper mineral
Chrysocolla and malachite are secondary minerals derived from the chemical weathering of primary copper minerals, such as native copper and bornite.

MINERAL ASSOCIATIONS

Some minerals are consistently found together over large areas because they are found in the same rock type. Other associations occur in encrustations, veins, cavities, or thin layers. The fact that certain minerals are likely to be found together can help in the discovery and identification of minerals. Lead and zinc ore minerals are often associated with calcite and barite, while gold is frequently found in association with quartz.

Associated minerals that form almost simultaneously and are usually present in a specific rock type make up an assemblage. Orthoclase, albite, biotite, and quartz form an assemblage for granite, and plagioclase, augite, magnetite, and olivine for gabbro. Assemblages are key indicators of the environments in which minerals form.

garnet

mica gives silvery sheen

apophyllite

stilbite

Metamorphic mix
The assemblage of garnet, quartz, and mica in this specimen indicates that this rock formed at moderate pressure and low temperatures (up to 400°F/200°C).

Zeolite association
Minerals belonging to the zeolite group of silicates, such as these crystals of apophyllite and stilbite, are often found in association with one another.

Layered rocks in the San Juan River
Erosion at this canyon in Utah, USA, has exposed layers of shale. Differences in the assemblage of minerals in various shale layers can reveal much about the geological history of the region.

CLASSIFYING MINERALS

Classification of minerals is an ongoing study among mineralogists—geologists who specifically study minerals. The ability to delve deep into the structure and chemistry of minerals has increased dramatically with advances in instruments and techniques.

MINERAL OR NOT?

The term "mineral" is commonly applied to certain organic substances, such as coal, oil, and natural gas, when referring to a nation's wealth in resources. However, these materials are more accurately referred to as hydrocarbons. Gases and liquids are not, in the strict sense, minerals. Although ice—the solid state of water—is a mineral, liquid water is not; nor is liquid mercury, which can be found in mercury ore deposits. Synthetic equivalents of minerals, for example emeralds and diamonds produced in the laboratory, are not minerals because they do not occur naturally. The "minerals" referred to in foods are also not strictly minerals—they refer to elements, such as iron, calcium, or zinc.

Synthetic ruby boule
Rubies and other gems grown synthetically are not classified as minerals. Some gems, such as yttrium-aluminum garnet, do not even occur in nature.

CHEMICAL FORMULAE

A chemical formula identifies the atoms present in a mineral and their proportions. In some minerals, the atoms and their proportions are fixed. Pyrite, for example, is always FeS_2, denoting iron (Fe) and sulfur (S) in a 1:2 ratio. In solid solutions, the components may be variable. For olivine, where complete substitution is possible between iron and magnesium (Mg), the formula is $(Fe,Mg)_2SiO_4$, indicating that iron and magnesium are found in varying amounts.

CHEMICAL ELEMENTS

Symbol	Name	Symbol	Name	Symbol	Name	Symbol	Name
Ac	Actinium	Er	Erbium	Mo	Molybdenum	Sb	Antimony
Ag	Silver	Es	Einsteinium	N	Nitrogen	Sc	Scandium
Al	Aluminum	F	Fluorine	Na	Sodium	Se	Selenium
Am	Americium	Fe	Iron	Nb	Niobium	Si	Silicon
Ar	Argon	Fm	Fermium	Nd	Neodymium	Sm	Samarium
As	Arsenic	Fr	Francium	Ne	Neon	Sn	Tin
At	Astatine	Ga	Gallium	Ni	Nickle	Sr	Strontium
Au	Gold	Gd	Gadolinium	No	Nobelium	Ta	Tantalum
B	Boron	Ge	Germanium	Np	Neptunium	Tb	Terbium
Ba	Barium	H	Hydrogen	O	Oxygen	Tc	Technetium
Be	Beryllium	He	Helium	Os	Osmium	Te	Tellurium
Bi	Bismuth	Hf	Hafnium	P	Phosphorus	Th	Thorium
Bk	Berkelium	Hg	Mercury	Pa	Protactinium	Ti	Titanium
Br	Bromine	Ho	Holmium	Pb	Lead	Tl	Thallium
C	Carbon	I	Iodine	Pd	Palladium	Tm	Thulium
Ca	Calcium	In	Indium	Pm	Promethium	U	Uranium
Cd	Cadmium	Ir	Iridium	Po	Polonium	V	Vanadium
Ce	Cerium	K	Potassium	Pt	Platinum	W	Tungsten
Cf	Californium	Kr	Krypton	Pr	Praseodymium	Xe	Xenon
Cl	Chlorine	La	Lanthanum	Pu	Plutonium	Y	Yttrium
Cm	Curium	Li	Lithium	Ra	Radium	Yb	Ytterbium
Co	Cobalt	Lu	Lutetium	Rb	Rubidium	Zn	Zinc
Cr	Chromium	Lw	Lawrencium	Re	Rhenium	Zr	Zirconium
Cs	Cesium	Md	Mendelevium	Rh	Rhodium		
Cu	Copper	Mg	Magnesium	Rn	Radon		
Dy	Dysprosium	Mn	Manganese	S	Sulfur		

CLASSIFYING MINERALS

Minerals are primarily classified according to their chemical composition. Shown below are the major chemical groups, with an example of each. Minerals are further classified into subgroups, with each subgroup taking its name from its most typical mineral. A radical is a group of atoms that acts as a single unit.

CHALCOCITE

Sulfides
The sulfides are formed when a metal or semimetal combines with sulfur. In chalcocite, the metallic element is copper.

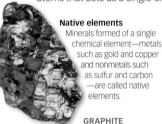

Native elements
Minerals formed of a single chemical element—metals such as gold and copper and nonmetals such as sulfur and carbon —are called native elements.

GRAPHITE

RUBY

Oxides
When oxygen alone combines with a metal or semimetal, an oxide is formed. Corundum is aluminum oxide, with a red variety called ruby.

BRUCITE

Halides
A halogen element (chlorine, bromine, iodine, or fluorine) combined with a metal or semimetal makes a halide. Sylvite is a compound of chlorine and potassium.

SYLVITE

Hydroxides
Hydroxide minerals contain a hydroxyl (hydrogen and oxygen) radical combined with a metallic element. In brucite, the metallic element is magnesium.

coating of blue smithsonite

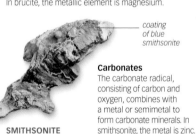

Carbonates
The carbonate radical, consisting of carbon and oxygen, combines with a metal or semimetal to form carbonate minerals. In smithsonite, the metal is zinc.

SMITHSONITE

APATITE

Arsenates, phosphates, and vanadates
In these minerals, a radical of oxygen and either arsenic, phosphorus, or vanadium combines with a semimetal or metal. Apatite is a phosphate.

COLEMANITE

Borates and nitrates
Borates contain radicals of boron and oxygen, and nitrates, radicals of nitrogen and oxygen. In colemanite boron and oxygen combine with calcium and water.

Sulfates, chromates, tungstates, and molybdates
Sulfur, molybdenum, chromium, or tungsten form a radical with oxygen that combines with a metal or semimetal. Celestine is a sulfate.

CELESTINE

Silicates
In this group, silicon and oxygen form a silica radical that combines with metals or semimetals. Silica occurs alone as quartz, as in this amethyst specimen.

AMETHYST

AMBER

Organic minerals
This group includes some naturally occurring substances, such as shell and coral, that are generated by organic means. Amber is a fossil resin.

IDENTIFYING MINERALS

There are certain physical properties determined by the crystalline structure and chemical composition of a mineral. These can commonly help to identify minerals without the use of expensive equipment. Even a beginner can readily use these pointers.

COLOR

Some minerals have characteristic colors—the bright blue of azurite, the yellow of sulfur, and the green of malachite allow for easy identification. This is not true of all minerals—fluorite occurs in virtually all colors, so it is best identified by other properties.

In minerals, color is caused by the absorption or refraction of light of particular wavelengths. This can happen for several reasons. One is the presence of trace elements—"foreign" atoms that are not part of the basic chemical makeup of the mineral in the crystal structure. As few as three atoms per million can absorb enough of certain parts of the visible-light spectrum to give color to some minerals. Color can

also result from the absence of an atom or ionic radical from a place that it would normally occupy in a crystal. The structure of the mineral itself, without any defect or foreign element, may also cause color: opal is composed of minute spheres of silica that diffract light; and the thin interlayering of two feldspars in moonstone gives it color and sheen.

botryoidal habit

Azurite
Some minerals can be identified by their characteristic color. The copper carbonate azurite is always azure blue.

GREEN FLUORITE

YELLOW FLUORITE

PURPLE FLUORITE

Color range
These specimens show only a few of the many colors that can occur in fluorite. Different coloration depends on a number of factors.

vitreous luster   *color play*

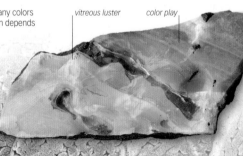

Color variation in opal
The play of colors or fire in opal is due to the arrangement of microscopic silica spheres. A microscope image shows opal's fractured surface.

LUSTER

A mineral's luster is the appearance of its surface in reflected light. There are two broad types of luster: metallic and nonmetallic. Metallic luster is that of an untarnished metal surface, such as gold, silver, or copper. These minerals tend to be opaque. Minerals with nonmetallic luster commonly show transparency or translucency. Vitreous describes the luster of a piece of broken glass; adamantine, the brilliant luster of diamond; resinous, the luster of a piece of resin; and pearly, the luster of mother-of-pearl or pearl. Greasy luster refers to the appearance of being covered with a thin layer of oil, and silky, the appearance of the surface of silk or satin. Dull luster implies little or no reflection, and earthy luster the nonlustrous look of raw earth.

glasslike luster

satinlike sheen

Dull
nonreflective luster
A dull luster is seen in this specimen of hematite. It is nonreflective but not as granular in appearance as earthy luster.

Vitreous
Many silicate minerals, such as this quartz crystal, have a vitreous luster. This luster appears similar to the surface of glass.

Silky
The borate ulexite exhibits a silky luster, with the surface sheen resembling a bolt of satin or silk.

translucent crystal

Resinous
Native sulfur crystals are transparent or translucent, with a resinous luster that resembles the surface of tree resin.

bright sheen

Metallic
The sulfide galena has a metallic luster and a distinctive cleavage. Metallic luster looks like the reflection from new metal.

greasy luster

transparent octahedron

dry, soil-like look

Greasy
Orpiment can appear greasy—resembling an oily surface—or resinous. The difference between the two lusters is subjective.

Adamantine
Adamantine is the brightest of lusters, with an appearance similar to the surface of this diamond. It is brighter than vitreous luster.

Earthy
Minerals with an earthy luster, such as this fine-grained calcite, have the look of freshly broken, dry soil.

STREAK

The color of the powder produced when a specimen is drawn across a surface such as unglazed porcelain is known as streak. A mineral's streak is consistent and is a more useful diagnostic indicator than its color, which can vary. Streak can help distinguish between minerals that are easy to confuse. For example, the iron oxide hematite has a red streak, while magnetite, another iron oxide, gives a black streak.

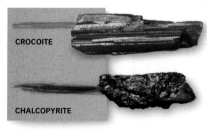
CROCOITE

CHALCOPYRITE

Consistent streak
The streak of a mineral is consistent from specimen to specimen, as long as an unweathered surface is tested. It is the same as the color of the powdered mineral.

CLEAVAGE

The ability of a mineral to break along flat, planar surfaces is called cleavage. It occurs in the crystal structure where the forces that bond atoms are the weakest. Cleavage surfaces are generally smooth and reflect light evenly. Cleavage is described by its direction relative to the orientation of the crystal and by the ease with which it is produced. If cleavage easily produces smooth, lustrous surfaces, it is called perfect. Distinct, imperfect, and difficult indicate less easy kinds of cleavage. Minerals may have different quality cleavages in different directions. Some have no cleavage at all.

cleavage plane

Perfect cleavage
This topaz crystal exhibits perfect cleavage. It breaks cleanly parallel to its base, and is thus said to have perfect basal cleavage.

cleavage planes cross each other

Clear breaks
The cleavage planes of this baryte crystal are clearly visible. Baryte has perfect cleavage in different directions, as seen in this specimen.

FRACTURE

Some minerals can break in directions other than along cleavage planes. These breaks, known as fractures, help in identifying minerals. For example, hackly fractures (with jagged edges), are often found in metals, while shell-like conchoidal fractures are typical of quartz. Other terms for fractures include even (rough but more or less flat), uneven (rough and completely irregular), and splintery (with partially separated fibers).

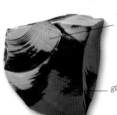

conchoidal fracture

hackly fracture surface

glassy texture

irregular surface

Conchoidal
This obsidian nodule shows conchoidal fracture, with fractures shaped like a bivalve seashell. It is commonly seen in silicates.

Hackly
This gold nugget shows hackly fracture, with sharp edges and jagged points. It is characteristic of most metals.

Uneven
This specimen of chalcopyrite shows uneven fracture. Its broken surface is rough and irregular, with no pattern evident.

TENACITY

The term tenacity describes the physical properties of a mineral based on the cohesive force between atoms in the structure. Gold, silver, and copper are malleable and can be flattened without crumbling. Sectile minerals can be cut smoothly with a knife; flexible minerals bend easily and stay bent after pressure is removed; ductile minerals can be drawn into a wire; brittle minerals are prone to breakage; and elastic minerals return to the original form after they are bent.

Ductile copper
Like many other native metals, copper is ductile. This means that it can be drawn into a wire without breaking.

Malleable gold
The malleability of gold allows it to be wrought into elaborate shapes. It can also be hammered into sheets thinner than paper.

HARDNESS

The hardness of a mineral is the relative ease or difficulty with which it can be scratched. A harder mineral will scratch a softer one, but not vice versa. Minerals are assigned a number between 1 to 10 on the Mohs scale, which measures hardness relative to ten minerals of increasing hardness. Hardness differs from toughness or strength; very hard minerals can be quite brittle. Most hydrous minerals—those that contain water molecules—are soft, as are phosphates, carbonates, sulfates, halides, and most sulfides. Anhydrous oxides—those without water molecules—and silicates are relatively hard.

Fingernail test
The fingernail is about 2½ on the Mohs scale and can scratch talc and gypsum. The hardness of other common items is also noted on the scale.

THE MOHS SCALE OF HARDNESS

Hardness	Mineral	Other materials for hardness testing
1	Talc	Very easily scratched by a fingernail
2	Gypsum	Can be scratched by a fingernail
3	Calcite	Just scratched with a copper coin
4	Flourite	Very easily scratched with a knife but not as easily as calcite
5	Apatite	Scratched with a knife with difficulty
6	Orthoclase	Cannot be scratched with a knife but scratches glass with difficulty
7	Quartz	Scratches glass easily
8	Topaz	Scratches glass very easily
9	Corundum	Cuts glass
10	Diamond	Cuts glass

REFRACTIVE INDEX

Light changes velocity and direction as it passes through a transparent or translucent mineral. The extent of this change is measured by the refractive index: the ratio of light's velocity in air to its velocity in the crystal. A high index causes dispersion of light into its component colors. Refractive indices can be found using specialized liquids or inexpensive equipment.

Double refraction
A calcite rhomb is said to be double refractive. It refracts light at two different angles, thus creating a double image.

FLUORESCENCE

Some minerals exhibit fluorescence—that is, they emit visible light of various colors when subjected to ultraviolet radiation. Ultraviolet lights for testing fluorescence can be obtained from dealers selling collectors' equipment. Fluorescence is an imperfect indicator of a mineral's identity because not all specimens of a mineral show fluorescence, even if they look identical and come from the same location.

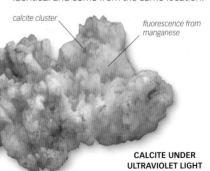

calcite cluster

fluorescence from manganese

Manganoan calcite
This yellowish specimen of manganese-rich calcite fluoresces rose pink when lit by ultraviolet light. Its fluorescence varies with manganese concentration.

CALCITE UNDER NATURAL LIGHT

CALCITE UNDER ULTRAVIOLET LIGHT

WHAT ARE CRYSTALS?

Virtually all minerals are crystalline—solids in which the component atoms are arranged in a particular, repeating, three-dimensional pattern. All crystals of a mineral are built with the same pattern. Some are 10 feet long; others can only be seen with a microscope.

ATOMIC STRUCTURE

A crystal is built up of individual, identical, structural units of atoms or molecules called unit cells. A crystal can consist of only a few unit cells or billions of them. The unit cell is repeatedly repeated in three dimensions, forming the larger internal structure of the crystal. The shape of the unit cell and the symmetry of the structure determine the positions and shapes of the crystal's faces.

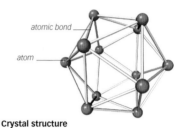

atomic bond

atom

Crystal structure
Stick-and-ball diagrams, such as this one, show how each atom in the structure of a crystal is bonded to others.

Crystals of many different minerals have unit cells that are similar in shape but are made of different chemical elements. The final development of the faces of a crystal is determined by the symmetry of the atomic structure and by the geological conditions at the time of its formation. Certain faces may be emphasized, while others disappear altogether. The final form taken by a crystal is known as its habit (pp.20–21).

atom

Crystal structure
Unit cells are repeated in three dimensions to build the crystal structure.

unit cells combine to form the crystal structure

MARCASITE CRYSTALS

metallic lustre

rosette-shaped aggregate

Structure of marcasite
Crystals of marcasite are created from repeating arrangements of atoms of iron and sulfur.

CRYSTAL SYMMETRY

All crystals exhibit symmetry because each crystal is built up of repeating geometric patterns. These patterns of crystal symmetry are divided into six main groups, or crystal systems (pp.22–23). The first of these symmetrical patterns is the cubic system, in which all crystals exhibit cubic symmetry. The characteristics of cubic symmetry may be explained as follows: if opposite face centers of a cube-shaped cubic crystal, such as halite, are held between the thumb and forefinger and the crystal is rotated through 360 degrees, the pattern of faces will appear identical four times as the different faces and edges come into view.

All cubic crystals have three axes of fourfold symmetry. They have other axes of symmetry, but these differ among classes within the cubic system. For example, cube-shaped crystals of halite have three axes of fourfold symmetry, in addition to its four axes of threefold symmetry.

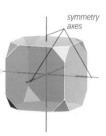

symmetry axes

Cubic symmetry
All cubic crystals, such as those of halite (right), have three axes of fourfold symmetry.

cubic crystal

rock matrix

HALITE

chlorine atom

sodium atom

Halite atomic structure
This diagram shows the cubic arrangement of sodium and chlorine atoms in the halite structure.

TWIN CRYSTALS

When two or more crystals of the same species (a group of minerals that are chemically similar), such as gypsum or fluorite, form a symmetrical intergrowth, they are referred to as twinned crystals. Twins can be described as interpenetrating or contact. Penetration twinning may occur with individual crystals at an angle to one another—for example, forming a cross. It can also occur with individual crystals parallel to one another, as in Carlsbad twinning. If a twin involves three or more individual crystals, it is referred to as a multiple twin or a repeated twin. Albite often forms multiple twins. Many other minerals form twins, but they are particularly characteristic of some, such as the "fishtail" contact twins of gypsum or the penetration twins of fluorite.

parallel twins

area of intergrowth

CONTACT TWIN

CARLSBAD PENETRATION TWIN

Contact and penetration twins
Parallel twinning is a kind of contact twinning in which two or more crystals share a common face or faces. Penetration twinning results from crystals growing into each other.

center of twinning

Cyclic twin
Cyclic twins occur when more than two crystals are twinned at a common center. This specimen of cerussite shows the cyclic twinning of three crystals all at 60° angles to each other.

CRYSTAL HABITS

Habit refers to the external shape of a crystal or an assemblage of intergrown crystals. It includes names of crystal's faces, such as prismatic and pyramidal, names of forms, such as cubic and octahedral, and descriptive terms, such as bladed and dendritic.

CRYSTAL FACES

The three types of crystal face—prism, pyramid, and pinacoid—are determined by a relationship to a crystallographic axis (p.22). Prism faces are parallel to the axis; pyramid faces cut through the axis at an angle; and pinacoid faces are at right angles to the axis. A crystal may have numerous sets of pyramid faces, each at a different angle to the c axis. Crystals may also have major and minor prism faces with edges parallel to each other. In most crystals, some faces are more developed than others.

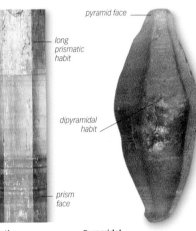

pinacoid face
pyramid faces
prism face

c axis

Naming crystal faces
The names of crystal faces and their relationship to the c axis are shown here. The predominant crystal face gives the crystal its habit name.

Prismatic topaz
Although this topaz crystal exhibits prismatic, pryamidal, and pinacoidal faces, the bulk of the crystal is defined by its prism faces and it is therefore called prismatic.

pinacoid face
prism face
pyramid face

long prismatic habit

prism face

pyramid face

dipyramidal habit

Prismatic
Prism faces clearly predominate in this long specimen of beryl. Its habit is therefore described as long prismatic.

Pyramidal
If pyramid faces dominate in one direction, the habit is pyramidal. If pyramid faces dominate in both directions, as in this specimen of sapphire, the habit is dipyramidal.

CRYSTAL FORMS

Habits can be named after crystal forms: "cubic" implies crystallizing in the form of cubes; "dodecahedral," in the form of dodecahedrons; and "rhombohedral," in the form of rhombohedrons. When crystals of one system crystallize in forms that appear to be the crystals of another system, the habit name is preceded by the word "pseudo." When terminations take different forms in the same crystal, the habit is known as hemimorphic.

Octahedral
This magnetite specimen has crystallized as an octahedron and is said to have an octahedral habit.

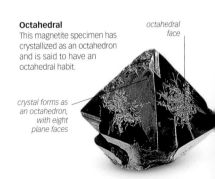

octahedral face

crystal forms as an octahedron, with eight plane faces

AGGREGATES

Aggregates are groups of intimately associated crystals. In general, aggregates are intergrowths of imperfectly developed crystals. In some aggregates, the crystals may be microscopic. The type of aggregation is often typical of a particular mineral species. Terms used to describe aggregates include granular, fibrous, radiating, botryoidal, stalactitic, geodic, and massive.

massive habit

Massive
The massive habit occurs when there is a mass of crystals that cannot be seen individually, as in this specimen of dumortierite.

fibrous strands

Fibrous
The fibrous habit is an aggregate, consisting of slender, parallel, or radiating fibers. This tremolite specimen is a good example.

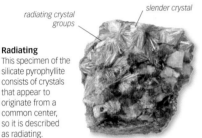

radiating crystal groups

slender crystal

Radiating
This specimen of the silicate pyrophyllite consists of crystals that appear to originate from a common center, so it is described as radiating.

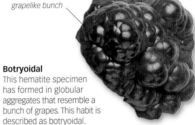

grapelike bunch

Botryoidal
This hematite specimen has formed in globular aggregates that resemble a bunch of grapes. This habit is described as botryoidal.

CRYSTAL APPEARANCE

Some habits are descriptions of the general appearance of a crystal. The term "tabular" describes a crystal with large, flat, parallel faces; "bladed" describes elongated crystals that are flattened like a knife blade; "stalactitic" describes crystal aggregates shaped like stalactites; and "blocky" or "equant" describes crystals with faces that are roughly the same size in all directions.

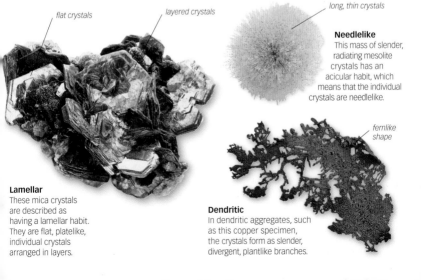

flat crystals

layered crystals

long, thin crystals

Needlelike
This mass of slender, radiating mesolite crystals has an acicular habit, which means that the individual crystals are needlelike.

fernlike shape

Lamellar
These mica crystals are described as having a lamellar habit. They are flat, platelike, individual crystals arranged in layers.

Dendritic
In dendritic aggregates, such as this copper specimen, the crystals form as slender, divergent, plantlike branches.

CRYSTAL SYSTEMS

Crystals are classified into six different systems according to the maximum symmetry of their faces. Each crystal system is defined by the relative lengths and orientation of its three crystallographic axes—imaginary lines that pass through the centre of an ideal crystal.

CUBIC

Cubic crystals have three crystallographic axes (a_1, a_2, and a_3) at right angles and of equal length, and four threefold axes of symmetry. The main forms within this system are cube, octahedron, and rhombic dodecahedron. Halite, copper, gold, silver, platinum, iron, fluorite, and magnetite crystallize in the cubic system, which is also known as the isometric system.

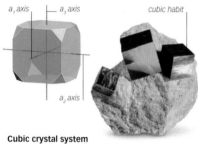

a_1 axis *a_3 axis* *cubic habit*

a_2 axis

Cubic crystal system
Pyrite crystals commonly form as cubes, but they can also occur as pentagonal dodecahedra and octahedra, or combinations of all three forms.

TETRAGONAL

Tetragonal crystals have three crystallographic axes at right angles—two equal in length (a_1 and a_2), and the third (c) longer or shorter. These crystals have one principal, fourfold axis of symmetry. Crystals look like square or octahedral prisms in shape. Rutile, zircon, cassiterite, and calomel are minerals that crystallize in the tetragonal system.

c axis *pyramid face*

a_2 axis *a_1 axis*

Vesuvianite
This vesuvianite crystal—with prismatic, pyramidal, and pinnacoid faces—shows a classic tetragonal form.

HEXAGONAL AND TRIGONAL

Some crystallographers consider hexagonal and trigonal crystals to comprise a single system, whereas others regard them as forming separate systems. Both crystalline forms have three crystallographic axes (a_1, a_2, and a_3) of equal length. These are at 120 degrees to one another and to a fourth axis (c), which is perpendicular to the plane of the other three axes. Trigonal crystals have only threefold symmetry, whereas hexagonal crystals have sixfold symmetry. Minerals that crystallize in the hexagonal system include beryl (emerald and aquamarine) and apatite. Some of the minerals that crystallize in the trigonal system are calcite, quartz, and tourmaline.

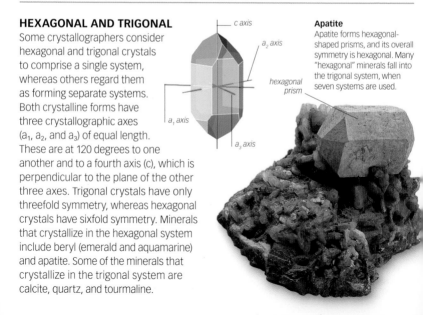

c axis

a_2 axis

hexagonal prism

a_1 axis

a_3 axis

Apatite
Apatite forms hexagonal-shaped prisms, and its overall symmetry is hexagonal. Many "hexagonal" minerals fall into the trigonal system, when seven systems are used.

MONOCLINIC

The term "monoclinic" means "one incline." Monoclinic crystals have three crystallographic axes of unequal length. One (c) is at right angles to the other two (a and b). These two axes are not perpendicular to each other, although they are in the same plane. The crystals have one twofold axis of symmetry. More minerals crystallize in the monoclinic system than in any other crystal system. Examples are gypsum, orthoclase, malachite, and jadeite.

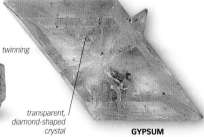

c axis

a axis   *b axis*

Gypsum
The parallelogram shape of this crystal of gypsum demonstrates the two unequal crystallographic axes and the third axis at right angles of the monoclinic system. Orthoclase, which belongs to the same system, often forms twinned crystals.

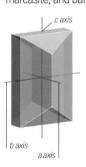

crystal with unequal sides

twinning

transparent, diamond-shaped crystal

ORTHOCLASE

GYPSUM

ORTHORHOMBIC

Orthorhombic means "perpendicular parallelogram". Crystals in this system have three crystallographic axes (a, b, and c) at right angles, all of which are unequal in length. They have three twofold axes of symmetry. Minerals that crystallize in this system include olivine, aragonite, topaz, marcasite, and barite.

c axis

pyramidal face

b axis
a axis

Topaz
The mineral topaz often forms beautiful, orthorhombic prismatic crystals that are usually terminated by pyramids or other prisms. The mineral barite also forms orthorhombic prisms.

TRICLINIC

Triclinic crystals have the least symmetrical shape, with three crystallographic axes of unequal length (a, b, and c) inclined at angles other than 90 degrees to each other. The orientation of a triclinic crystal is arbitrary. Minerals that crystallize in this system include albite, anorthite, kaolin, and kyanite.

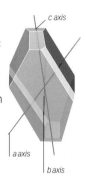

c axis

a axis

b axis

triclinic axinite crystal

Axinite
The silicate axinite is a classic triclinic mineral. Several feldspars, including albite and microcline, are also triclinic.

GEMS

A gem is any mineral that is highly prized for its beauty, durability, and rarity. It is enhanced in some manner by altering its shape, usually by cutting and polishing. Most gems begin as crystals of minerals or as aggregates of crystals.

HISTORY OF GEMS

The use of gemstones in human history goes back to the Upper Paleolithic Period (25,000–12,000 BCE). People were initially drawn by the bright colors and beautiful patterns of gems. When the shaping of stones for adornment first began, opaque and soft specimens were used. As shaping techniques improved, harder stones began to be cut into gems. Beads of the quartz varieties hard carnelian and rock crystal were fashioned in Mesopotamia (now Iraq) in the 7th millennium BCE. Records of the time suggest that people thought that stones had a mystic value—a belief that persists to the present.

wings embedded with gems

Ancient masterpiece
This ancient Egyptian chest ornament is inlaid with gold, finely cut lapis lazuli, carnelian, and other gems. It is from the tomb of Tutankhamun (*c.*1361–1352 BCE).

lapis lazuli

Iraqi carnelian necklace
This necklace was made in Mesopotamia (modern day Iraq) from lapis lazuli, carnelian, and etched carnelian. It dates from about 2500 BCE.

etched carnelian

GEM MINING

Gemstone deposits form in different geological environments. Perhaps the best known are the "pipes" of kimberlite, from which most diamonds are recovered by the hard-rock methods of drilling and blasting. Other gems also recovered from the rock in which they form are quartz varieties, opal, tourmaline, topaz, emerald, aquamarine, some sapphires and rubies, turquoise, lapis lazuli, and chrysoberyl. Hard and dense gemstones that are impervious to chemical weathering are carried by water to placer deposits such as river beds, beaches, and the ocean floor. Placer mining techniques mimic the creation of the placer by separating denser minerals in running water. The simplest methods are panning and sieving, or passing gravel through a trough of flowing water with baffles at the bottom. The lighter material washes away but denser gemstones remain.

Gem panning
Many gemstone minerals, such as sapphire and ruby, are heavier than normal stream gravels. These can be recovered using the slow but thorough panning method.

Diamond mine in Siberia
Russia has become a major supplier of diamonds. In this mine, diamonds are being recovered from a diamond pipe.

FACETING

Gemstones can be shaped in several ways. Opaque or translucent semiprecious stones, such as agate and jasper, are tumble-polished, carved, engraved, or cut with a rounded upper surface and a flat underside. Grinding and polishing of flat faces on the stone is called faceting. Facets are placed in specific geometric positions at specific angles according to the bending of light within a particular stone. Transparent stones, such as amethyst, diamond, and sapphire, are faceted to maximize their brilliance and "fire" or enhance color. Although much material is ground away while cutting, the final value is much enhanced.

Cutting a brilliant
While faceting gemstones, care must be taken to preserve the maximum material and produce the best brilliance and color.

Rough choice
The faceter selects his rough based on color, clarity, and shape, which determine the cut for the final gem.

Sawn in two
The rough is sawn to roughly the final shape of the gem. Accurate sawing saves time in the grinding process.

Faceting begins
The major facets are first ground onto the gem. The accuracy of these determines the final brilliance.

Further facets
Smaller facets are cut after the major facets. Based on the cut, there may be only a few or dozens of these.

Finished off
After the first side of the stone is cut, it is reversed and facets are placed on the second side in the same order.

GEM CUTS

There are three basic types of facet cut: step (with rectangular facets), brilliant (with triangular facets), and mixed (a combination of the two). The first faceting probably involved diamond cutting in Italy prior to the 15th century. First, only the natural faces of octahedral diamond crystals were polished. The rose cut was developed in the 17th century. By about 1700, the brilliant cut (today's favorite for diamonds and other colorless gems) was created. The emerald cut was soon developed to save valuable material, as its rectangular cut conforms to the shape of emerald crystals. Today there are hundreds of possible gem cuts.

Gemstone shapes
A principal criterion for the cutter in choosing a gemstone shape is the shape of the rough gemstone. This ensures that a minimum of valuable material is lost.

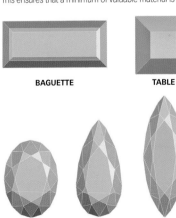

BAGUETTE

TABLE

OVAL

PENDELOQUE

MARQUISE

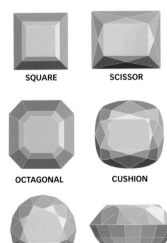

SQUARE

SCISSOR

OCTAGONAL

CUSHION

ROUND

MIXED

WHAT IS A ROCK?

A rock is a naturally occurring and coherent aggregate of one or more minerals. There are three major classes of rock—igneous, sedimentary, and metamorphic. Each of these three classes is further subdivided into groups and types.

TYPES OF ROCK

Igneous rocks form from melted rock called magma. When magmas solidify underground, intrusive rocks such as granite are created. Intrusive rocks are also known as plutonic rocks. If the magma flows onto the surface of the land or ocean bed, extrusive rocks such as basalt, are formed.

Sedimentary rocks are usually made of deposits laid down on Earth's surface by water, wind, or ice. They almost always occur in layers or strata. Stratification survives compaction and cementation and is a distinguishing feature of sedimentary rocks. Some sedimentary rocks are of chemical origin,

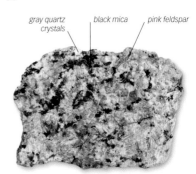
gray quartz crystals   black mica   pink feldspar

Pink granite
In this specimen of igneous pink granite, the three essential components of all granites can be seen: quartz, alkali feldspar, and mica.

having been deposited in solid form from a solution. Others are of biochemical origin and are composed predominantly of the compound calcium carbonate.

When existing rocks are subjected to extreme temperatures or pressures, or both, their composition, texture, and internal structure may be altered to form metamorphic rocks. The original rocks may be igneous, sedimentary, or metamorphic.

Pegmatite dike
Light-colored bands of igneous hydrothermal pegmatite, composed principally of quartz, can be seen here cutting across darker bands of metamorphic gneiss.

Volcanic growth
The eruption of extrusive magmas can create volumes of igneous rock measured in cubic miles on the surface of Earth.

Marble quarry
This dazzling white marble being quarried at Carrara, Italy, is metamorphosed from a very pure limestone.

Meteorites are not considered igneous, sedimentary, or metamorphic but are a group of their own. Many are remnants of asteroids, which are themselves remnants of the formation of the Solar System. Some meteorites are remains of the nickel-iron cores of asteroids; some contain nickel-iron and minerals such as olivine from the mantles of asteroids; and others are made up principally of silicate minerals.

Sedimentary layers
The Colorado River cuts through layers of sedimentary rock in the Grand Canyon, USA. The highest layers are the youngest, while the deepest are the oldest.

THE ROCK CYCLE

The series of processes by which rocks are created, broken down, and reconstituted as new rocks is known as the rock cycle. These processes depend on pressure, temperature, time, and changes in environmental conditions in Earth's crust and surface. At various stages in the rock cycle, old rocks are broken down, new minerals form, and new rocks originate from the components of the old. Thus a rock that began at the surface as an igneous rock may be reworked into a sedimentary rock, metamorphic rock, or new igneous rock to continue the cycle again.

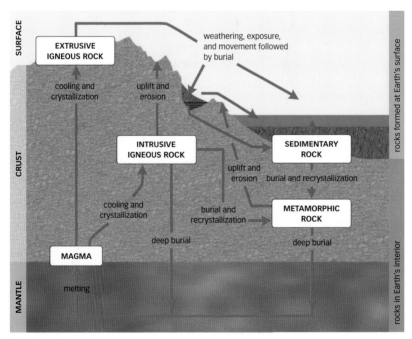

The rock cycle
This diagram summarizes the various elements of the rock cycle, from the creation of fresh igneous rock through erosion, deposition, and its reconstitution into new rock.

COLLECTING ROCKS AND MINERALS

The world of rocks, minerals, gems, and fossils offers endless possibilities for the hobbyist. Only a small amount of specialized knowledge is required to open a whole world of enjoyment of some of nature's finest creations.

WHERE TO LOOK

Most collectors begin by just accumulating rocks, minerals, and fossils. As their collection grows, they start being more selective, keeping only specimens with better color and crystallization and more interesting crystal forms. A wide range of specimens can be purchased from dealers, but it is often more enjoyable to find your own. In many countries, there are guidebooks that give precise directions to collecting localities for rocks, minerals, and fossils.

Sample collection is not without its constraints: working mines and quarries have legal restrictions on people permitted on their premises; old mines are dangerous; old mine dumps have been gone over for decades by other collectors; and public access to land is often restricted. However, traditional collecting sites, such as road cuttings and eroded cliffs on shorelines, continue to provide excellent opportunities for collectors.

Field experience
Rock collecting can be a hobby for a lifetime, as the collector develops knowledge and skills to enhance the activity.

Road cutting
The bank of a road cut through this pegmatite rock reveals giant feldspar crystals. Many fine rock and mineral specimens are derived from road cuttings.

Looking for gold
The gold pan is an essential piece of kit for a collector. Many gemstones, such as garnet and sapphire, can be found by panning.

There is also an increasing number of collecting localities that are open to the public on the payment of a fee. Some clubs for collecting enthusiasts have their own collecting sites, and they also arrange trips to sites that are otherwise inaccessible to the public. Collectors should bear in mind that permission must always be sought to collect samples on private property.

Old working
While mine dumps are good sources of specimens, hidden workings and old machinery can pose a hazard to unwary collectors.

Tempting tunnels
Old mine shafts can be tempting, but are often highly dangerous places. In most cases better specimens are usually found in the mine dumps outside.

SAFETY AND THE COLLECTING CODE

While mineral collecting is generally a safe hobby, there are a few definite hazards that a collector needs to be aware of. The most dangerous collecting localities are around old mines and workings. Tunnels should never be entered—shoring timbers rot quickly, and cave-ins and rock falls are almost guaranteed to happen. Collectors must also pay attention to what is underfoot—old shafts are sometimes covered over. In any case, there is often remarkably poor collecting inside old mines because most material of value has usually already been removed by miners. Mine dumps, by contrast, can be a good source of specimens. However, caution should be exercized because mine dumps are often loosely piled and can be unstable.

When collecting in beach cliffs, road cuttings, and rock falls, pay attention not only to loose material underfoot but also to anything that may fall or roll from above. It is best to avoid a collecting locality if you are not sure that is safe.

TAKING NOTES

When they start out, new collectors often ignore the need to write down information about their finds. But experience soon shows that investing in a notebook and devoting the minimal amount of time it takes to keep at least basic notes is essential. It is especially important to make notes about exactly where specimens were found. A considerable time may go by before you revisit the locality, and by then, in the absence of notes, you will probably be unable to find the spot again. It is useful to make a sketch of important landmarks or outcrops, because these can help relocate a specific spot.

Drawing locations
It is useful to make drawings in notebooks of locations and the specimens they have yielded.

Map and compass
Tools such as a compass and a map or a GPS receiver are essential for identifying localities and relocating them at a later date.

Correcting fluid
Number each specimen with a note about their find-spot. A dab of correction fluid makes a good label and can be removed if necessary.

EQUIPMENT

Mineral collecting is a safe hobby, but some simple pieces of equipment increase the safety factor dramatically. Just a few basics, such as the right hammer and chisel, a hard hat, goggles, gloves, and things you already have, will get you started.

FIELD EQUIPMENT

In addition to the basic collecting tools described here, safety equipment should be considered essential. Access to some collecting localities requires safety clothing such as a hard hat and fluorescent vest. Carry a cell phone with a fully charged battery with you even if you are only going a short distance from the car. A fall into a ravine or another low

HARD HAT

LEATHER GLOVES

SAFETY GOGGLES

Head and hand protection

Flying rock splinters and falling rocks cause injuries to collectors every year. Hands, eyes, and heads are particularly vulnerable areas. Goggles are recommended when breaking or splitting stone.

straight head for splitting hard rock

lump hammer head

sharp end to break rock with precision

flat end

sharp point

rubber or leather grip

wooden handle

GEOLOGISTS' HAMMER

TRIMMING HAMMER

CLUB HAMMER

SAFETY CHISELS

Hammers

Every year rock collectors are injured—sometimes blinded—by using the wrong hammers. Geologists' hammers are made of special steels. Their striking ends are beveled to prevent steel splinters from flying off.

Chisels

Like rock hammers, the chisels used by geologists are made from special steels that resist splintering. Not all are essential but having two or three of different sizes will make cutting rock safer.

trowel

brush for
light cleaning

flat brush

sieve

Extra tools
The experienced collector has a range of equipment for all collecting possibilities, from sieves and pans to various brushes and trowels. Most of these can be bought a few at a time as new collecting localities are visited.

protection from snake bites, cactus spines, sharp stones, jagged metal, and rolling stones, and ensure much better traction.

MAGNIFICATION
There is an entire area of mineral collecting devoted to tiny crystals known as micromounts. Small crystals often develop superb forms and groupings that are obscured as the process of crystallization progresses. Micromount collectors need effective microscopes, or at the least large magnifiers, to examine and enjoy these minute specimens. For collectors not wishing to incur the expense of a microscope, a simple hand lens will reveal much of the beauty of the tiny micromounts.

spot may take you out of sight of potential help and add hours to the time it takes to find you. In desert country, an adequate supply of water is essential, and if you are in snake country take an appropriate snake-bite kit. Clothing suitable to the weather and terrain is, of course, vital. Leave your low-cut shoes and sneakers at home. Leather boots offer better

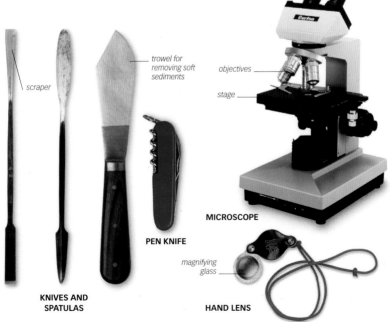

scraper

trowel for
removing soft
sediments

eyepiece

objectives

stage

MICROSCOPE

PEN KNIFE

magnifying
glass

**KNIVES AND
SPATULAS**

HAND LENS

Cleaning tools
There are two types of cleaning tool: those for field use and those for cleaning specimens at home. Tools for field use are more robust and are used for separating specimens from adhering rock.

A closer look
Most collectors of small crystals have a microscope to examine their specimens. The field equipment of every geologist and collector should include a hand lens with a magnification of about 10 times.

ORGANIZATION, STORAGE, AND CLEANING

Finding mineral specimens is only the first stage of collecting. The number of specimens damaged in the course of the journey home or while cleaning can be large. Care must therefore be taken from the moment a specimen is collected.

TRANSPORTING SPECIMENS

Wrapping of some sort is essential when transporting newly collected specimens, whether they are being carried in a backpack or a car. Delicate specimens should be wrapped first in tissue and then in newspaper. If your wrapping material is used up, try leaves, grass, or pine needles as a natural alternative. Unwrap wet specimens and let them dry as soon as you get home. Cotton balls and cellulose wadding should be kept entirely away from specimens, because the fibers are almost impossible to remove.

In the bag
Rock samples can be carried in a cloth specimen bag. More sensitive specimens require elaborate wrapping so that they can be transported safely.

CLEANING SPECIMENS

As a general rule, clean specimens as little as possible, starting with the gentlest methods first. Begin by using a soft brush to remove loose soil and debris. Hard rock specimens, such as gneiss or granite, are unlikely to be damaged by vigorous cleaning. With delicate minerals, such as calcite crystals, it is essential to use a fine, soft brush. Never use hot water to wash a specimen, because the heat

may cause some minerals to crack or shatter. Toothbrushes that use a pulsing water jet are useful cleaning tools. Soaps should be avoided, but if you must use them, choose liquid dishwashing soaps over hand or toilet soaps, which have additives that can penetrate specimens. The use of ultrasonic cleaners is not recommended—they can shatter delicate specimens even at low intensities. Certain

Muddy rocks
Many specimens will be muddy or dirty when collected. Most dirt is more easily removed when it is dry and can be lightly brushed off.

DISTILLED WATER

HYDROCHLORIC ACID

Cleaning liquids
Distilled (or deionized) water is good as a final wash for minerals. Weak hydrochloric acid is good for cleaning silicates, but always be aware of the risks involved.

BRADAWL

FINE POINTED SCRAPER

acids are suitable for cleaning specific minerals. Silicates are not harmed by weak acids, but carbonates and phosphates can be damaged by them. If you do use acids, seek specific information on their use from specialized books or other collectors.

Cleaning up
Removing rock with fine specialist tools is often necessary when collecting fossils. The mineral collector, by contrast, is more likely to brush or wash off dirt from specimens.

STORAGE AND DISPLAY

Once specimens have been collected and cleaned, they need to be stored or, in the case of the most attractive pieces, displayed. Many collectors like to store specimens in card trays inside shallow drawers. Once collected, some minerals are liable to experience physical and chemical effects that may change or sometimes even destroy them. Fortunately, these problems are well known and preventative measures can be taken in advance.

Every specimen collected should be accompanied by a label with as much information about it as is feasible. For display, use a sturdy, preferably glass-fronted cabinet or shelf. Many guests will wish to handle specimens, but they may not be aware that handling can damage delicate examples.

Mineral preservation
Minerals such as orpiment and realgar are sensitive to light and need special storage methods. Other minerals may require either dry or humid conditions.

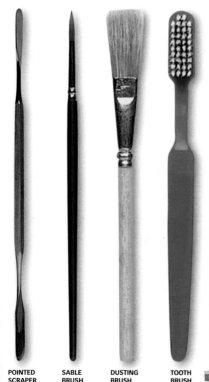

| POINTED SCRAPER | SABLE BRUSH | DUSTING BRUSH | TOOTH BRUSH |

Cleaning tools
A variety of tools is useful for cleaning specimens. Each specimen will present a different cleaning problem, so a selection of tools is necessary.

Informative display
People will admire your best specimens and also value information about them. Some collectors choose to provide museum-style information about specimens.

MINERALS

NATIVE ELEMENTS

There are 88 chemical elements known to occur in nature. Of these, less than two dozen are found uncombined with other elements. This group is called the native elements. Only eight of these native elements are found in significant quantities.

COMPOSITION

The native elements are classified into three groups: metals like copper and gold; semimetals like arsenic; and nonmetals like sulfur and carbon. The metals rarely form well-defined crystals; the semimetals typically occur as nodular masses; and the nonmetals form distinct crystals.

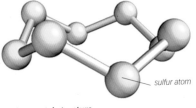

parallel twinned crystals

single crystal

Gold crystals
This crystallized gold specimen is a rarity, because native metals rarely form well-defined crystals. Most occur in wirelike and branching forms or as nuggets.

Sulfur crystal structure
In the orthorhombic crystal structure of sulfur, strongly bonded rings of eight sulfur atoms are weakly bonded to neighboring rings.

sulfur atom

OCCURRENCE AND USES

Native elements are known to form under a wide range of geologic conditions and in a variety of rock types. A native element can occur in several different environments. Some are found in sufficient concentrations to form economically important deposits.

Native gold and silver have been media of exchange for three millennia, and native copper and meteoric iron were among the first metals to be used by humans.

Industrial tools
This tool-maker is producing a diamond-edged industrial cutting tool. Although partly replaced by synthetic diamond, natural diamond continues to be used as an industrial abrasive.

Sulfur crust
Native sulfur builds up around fumaroles, where sulfur-rich gas is vented around volcanoes. These fumaroles often produce magnificently crystallized specimens.

PROFILE

Cubic

▽ 2½–3

● 8.9

◪ None

◩ Hackly, ductile

◪ Rose

◿ Metallic

Native copper
This specimen of native
copper is accompanied
by accessory quartz.

crystalline copper

*massive
copper*

*accessory
quartz*

VARIANT

Dendritic copper A specimen
of crystalline copper in the
branching form

⚛ Cu

COPPER

In its free-occurring metallic state, copper
was probably the first metal to be used by humans.
Neolithic people are believed to have used copper as
a substitute for stone by 8000 BCE. Around 4000 BCE,
Egyptians cast copper in molds. By 3500 BCE, copper
began to be alloyed with tin to produce bronze.

Copper is opaque, bright, and metallic salmon pink on
freshly broken surfaces but soon turns dull brown. Copper
crystals are uncommon, but when formed are either cubic
or dodecahedral, often arranged in branching aggregates.
Most copper is found as irregular, flattened, or branching
masses. It is one of the few metals
that occur in the "native" form
without being bonded to other
elements. Native copper seems
to be a secondary mineral,
a result of interaction between
copper-bearing solutions and
iron-bearing minerals.

Plumbing joint
Because it is easy to shape
and roll the metal, copper
is widely used to make
household pipes.

PROFILE

Cubic

4–4 ½

14.0–19.0

None

Hackly

Whitish steel-gray

Metallic

Platinum nugget
Although most of the platinum mined from placer deposits occurs as small grains, sizeable nuggets are sometimes found.

rounded surface

VARIANTS

Granular habit Most platinum is recovered as small grains

cube-shaped crystal

Platinum crystals Isolated cubic crystals of platinum

 Pt

PLATINUM

The first documented discovery of platinum was by the Spaniards in the 1500s, in the alluvial gold mines of the Río Pinto, Colombia. They called it *platina del Pinto*, from *platina*, which means "little silver," thinking that it was an impure ore of silver. It was not recognized as a distinct metal until 1735. It is opaque, silvery gray, and markedly dense.

Platinum usually occurs as disseminated grains in iron- and magnesium-rich igneous rocks and in quartz veins associated with hematite (p.91), chlorite, and pyrolusite (p.80). When rocks weather, the heavy platinum accumulates as grains and nuggets in the resulting placer deposits. Crystals are rare, but when found they are cubic. Most platinum for commercial use is recovered from primary deposits. Native platinum typically contains iron and metals such as palladium, iridium, and rhodium.

Platinum ring
A 2.5-carat, brilliant-cut diamond has been set in a platinum mounting in this ring.

Iron meteorite
Most native iron is in Earth's core, but iron from meteorites, such as this one, was used from about 3000 BCE. Native iron is usually alloyed with nickel.

intermixture of kamacite and taenite crystals

metallic appearance

crust formed as surface melts and then solidifies on entry to Earth's atmosphere

PROFILE

Cubic

 4

7.3–7.9

 Basal

Hackly

Steel-gray

 Metallic

Fe,Ni

IRON

Five percent of Earth's crust is made up of iron. Native iron is rare in the crust and is invariably alloyed with nickel. Low-nickel iron (up to 7.5 percent nickel) is called kamacite, and high-nickel iron (up to 50 percent nickel) is called taenite. Both crystallize in the cubic system. A third form of iron-nickel, mainly found in meteorites and crystallizing in the tetragonal system, is called tetrataenite. All three forms are generally found either as disseminated grains or as rounded masses.

Kamacite is the major component of most iron meteorites (p.335). It is found in most chondritic meteorites (p.337), and occurs as microscopic grains in some lunar rocks. Taenite and tetrataenite are mainly found in meteorites, often intergrown with kamacite. Iron is also plentiful in the Sun and other stars.

Viking axe head
This iron Viking axe head from Frykat, Denmark, has a shape commonly used in weapons.

PROFILE

Hexagonal

▽ 2–2 ½

♨ 9.7–9.8

▨ Perfect basal

◩ Uneven

◪ Silver-white

↗ Metallic

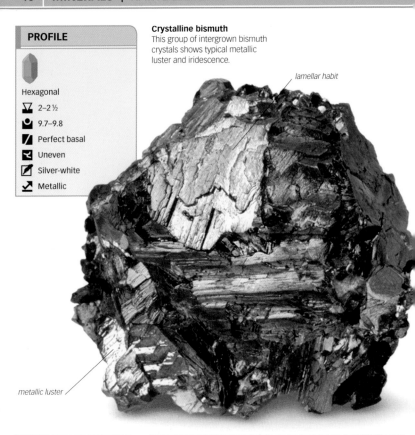

Crystalline bismuth
This group of intergrown bismuth crystals shows typical metallic luster and iridescence.

lamellar habit

metallic luster

VARIANT

Native bismuth Partly crystalline bismuth on rock

⚛ Bi

BISMUTH

As a native metal, bismuth has been known since the Middle Ages. A German monk named Basil Valentine first described it in 1450. Bismuth is often found uncombined with other elements, forming indistinct crystals, often in parallel groupings. It is hard, brittle, and lustrous. It is also found in grains and as foliated masses. Silver-white, it usually has a reddish tinge that distinguishes it. Specimens may have an iridescent tarnish.

Bismuth is found in hydrothermal veins and in pegmatites (p.260) and is often associated with ores of tin, lead, or copper (p.37), from which it is separated as a by-product. Bismuth expands slightly when it solidifies, making its alloys useful in the manufacture of metal castings with sharp detailing. Bismuth salts are often used as soothing agents for digestive disorders.

Hopper-shaped crystals
Laboratory-grown bismuth crystals with cavernous faces like these exhibit an array of colors.

Massive antimony
This specimen of massive antimony has a pale silvery gray color and the occasional small crystal.

massive habit

small crystalline mass

⚛ Sb

ANTIMONY

Although recognized as a metal since the 8th century or earlier, antimony was only identified as an element in 1748. Crystals are rare but when found are either psuedocubic or thick and tabular. Antimony usually occurs in massive, foliated, or granular form. It is lustrous, silvery, bluish white in color, and has a flaky texture that makes it brittle. It almost always contains some arsenic and is found in veins with silver (p.43), arsenic (p.45), and other antimony minerals.

Antimony is extremely important in alloys. Even in minor quantities, it imparts strength and hardness to other metals, particularly lead, whose alloys are used in the plates of automobile storage batteries, in bullets, and in coverings for cables. Combined with tin and lead, antimony forms antifriction alloys called babbitt metals, which are used as components of machine bearings. Like bismuth (p.40), antimony expands slightly on solidifying, making it a useful alloying metal for detailed castings.

PROFILE

Cubic

2½–3

19.3

None

Hackly

Golden yellow

Metallic

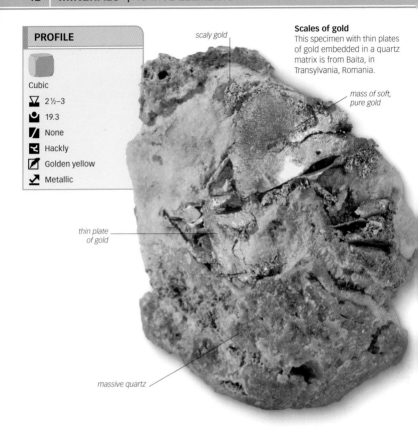

scaly gold

Scales of gold
This specimen with thin plates
of gold embedded in a quartz
matrix is from Baita, in
Transylvania, Romania.

*mass of soft,
pure gold*

*thin plate
of gold*

massive quartz

VARIANTS

Gold nugget An irregularly
shaped gold nugget

quartz

Gold crystals Crystalline gold
in a dull quartz matrix

Au

GOLD

Throughout human history, gold has been the most
prized metal. It is opaque, has a highly attractive metallic
golden yellow color, is extremely malleable, and is usually
found in a relatively pure form. It is remarkably inert, so it
resists tarnish. These qualities have made it exceptionally
valuable. Gold usually occurs as treelike growths, grains,
and scaly masses. It rarely occurs as well-formed crystals,
but when found these are octahedral or dodecahedral.

Gold is mostly found in hydrothermal veins
with quartz (p.168) and sulfides.
Virtually all granitic igneous rocks—
in which it occurs as invisible,
disseminated grains—contain
low concentrations of gold.
Almost all of the gold recovered
since antiquity has come from
placer deposits—weathered gold
particles concentrated in river
and stream gravel.

Garnet in gold
This gold ring has an
unusual demantoid
(yellow-green) garnet
set in it.

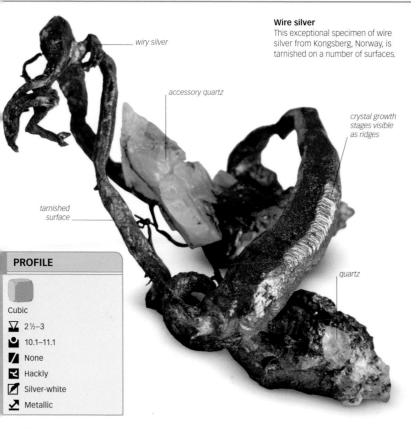

Wire silver
This exceptional specimen of wire silver from Kongsberg, Norway, is tarnished on a number of surfaces.

wiry silver

accessory quartz

crystal growth stages visible as ridges

tarnished surface

quartz

PROFILE

Cubic

2½–3

10.1–11.1

None

Hackly

Silver-white

Metallic

VARIANTS

Tarnished silver A tarnished specimen of wiry silver

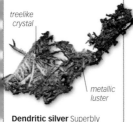

treelike crystal

metallic luster

Dendritic silver Superbly crystalline, dendritic silver

Ag

SILVER

The earliest silver ornaments and decorations were found in tombs that date as far back as 4000 BCE. Silver coinage began to appear around 550 BCE. Opaque and bright silvery white with a slightly pink tint, silver readily tarnishes to either gray or black. Natural crystals of silver are uncommon, but when found they are cubic, octahedral, or dodecahedral. Silver is usually found in granular habit and as wiry, branching, lamellar, or scaly masses.

Widely distributed in nature, silver is a primary hydrothermal mineral. It also forms by alteration of other silver-bearing minerals. Much of the world's silver production is a by-product of refining lead, copper (p.37), and zinc. Silver is the second most malleable and ductile metal, and it is important in the photographic and electronic industries.

Silver inkwell
This Guild of Handicraft textured silver inkwell of square, tapering form has a blue enamel cabochon.

PROFILE

Orthorhombic

▽ 1½–2½

■ 2.1

▨ Indistinct

▨ Conchoidal to uneven, brittle

▨ White

↗ Resinous to greasy

Sulfur crystals
Yellow orthorhombic crystals of sulfur are set in a rock matrix in this specimen from Conil, Andalucía, Spain.

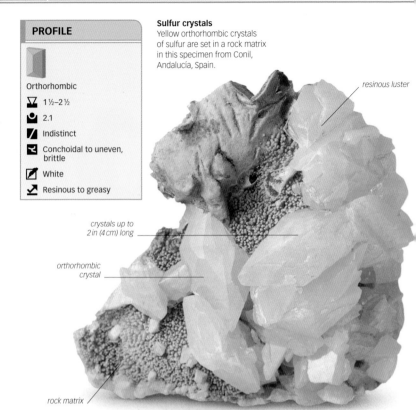

resinous luster

crystals up to 2 in (4 cm) long

orthorhombic crystal

rock matrix

VARIANTS

Fumarole crystals A crust of very small sulfur crystals from a fumarole in Java, Indonesia

needlelike crystal

Acicular sulfur Elongated sulfur crystals on rock

⚛ S

SULFUR

The ninth most abundant element in the Universe, after oxygen and silicon, sulfur is the most abundant constituent of minerals. It occurs in the form of sulfides (pp.49–64), sulfates (pp.132–41), and elemental sulfur. The bright yellow or orangish color of sulfur makes the mineral easy to identify. Sulfur forms pyramidal or tabular crystals, encrustations, powdery coatings, and granular or massive aggregates. Crystalline sulfur may exhibit as many as 56 different habits.

Most sulfur forms in volcanic fumaroles, but it can also result from the breakdown of sulfide ore deposits. Massive sulfur is found in thick beds in sedimentary rocks, particularly those associated with salt domes. Sulfur is a poor conductor of heat, which means that specimens are warm to the touch.

Powdered sulfur
Sulfur is used in a number of industrial and medicinal applications, including in the production of sulfuric acid.

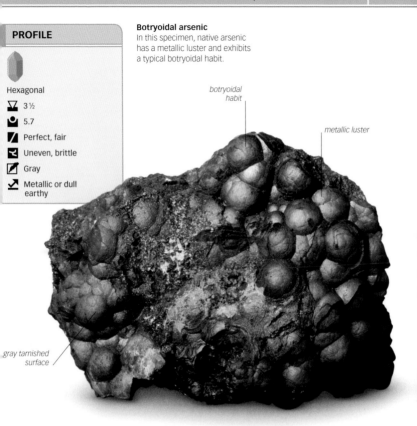

Botryoidal arsenic
In this specimen, native arsenic has a metallic luster and exhibits a typical botryoidal habit.

botryoidal habit

metallic luster

gray tarnished surface

PROFILE

Hexagonal

3 ½

5.7

Perfect, fair

Uneven, brittle

Gray

Metallic or dull earthy

VARIANT

Massive arsenic A darkly tarnished, massive specimen of native arsenic

As

ARSENIC

Known since antiquity, arsenic is widely distributed in nature, although it is unusual in native form. It is classified as a semimetal, because it possesses some properties of metals and some of nonmetals. Crystals are rare, but when found they are rhombohedral. Arsenic usually occurs in massive, botryoidal to reniform, or stalactitic habits, often with concentric layers. On fresh surfaces, arsenic is tin-white, but it quickly tarnishes to dark gray.

Native arsenic is found in hydrothermal veins, often associated with antimony (p.41), silver (p.43), cobalt, and nickel-bearing minerals. It is highly poisonous, although it is used in some medicines to treat infections. Arsenic-based compounds can be used in alloys to increase high-temperature strength and as a herbicide and pesticide.

Arsenic paint
Ancient Egyptian artists used orange-red colors made from powdered arsenic sulfide.

Massive graphite
As seen in this massive specimen, graphite has a soapy or greasy feeling when touched.

perfect cleavage

massive habit

metallic luster

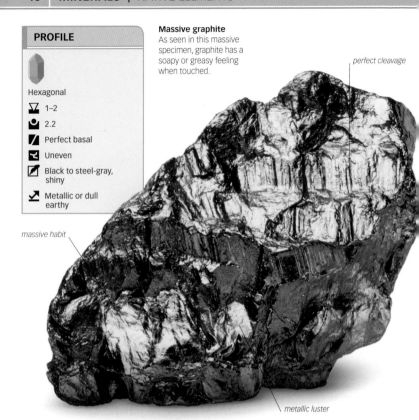

VARIANTS

Black graphite A lump of compact, black graphite

Crystalline graphite A graphite crystal exhibiting metallic luster

 C

GRAPHITE

Like diamond, graphite is a form of native carbon. It takes its name from the Greek term *graphein*, which means "to write"—a reference to the black mark it leaves on paper. Graphite is opaque and dark gray to black. It occurs as hexagonal crystals, flexible sheets, scales, or large masses. It may be earthy, granular, or compact.

Graphite forms from the metamorphism of carbonaceous sediments and the reaction of carbon compounds with hydrothermal solutions. Graphite looks dramatically different from diamond and is at the other end of the hardness scale. Graphite's softness is due to the way carbon atoms are bonded to each other—rings of six carbon atoms are arranged in widely spaced horizontal sheets. The atoms are strongly bonded within the rings but very weakly bonded between the sheets.

Graphite pencil
The familiar pencil "lead" contains graphite. The first use of graphite pencils was described in 1575.

Diamond in a matrix
An octahedral diamond crystal rests in the kimberlite matrix in which it was found.

yellowish octahedral crystal

rock matrix

adamantine luster

Carbonado A form of black industrial diamond

Bort diamond A crystal of black bort diamond

Pink diamond A rare pink diamond crystal

 C

DIAMOND

The hardest known mineral, diamond is pure carbon. Its crystals typically occur as octahedrons and cubes with rounded edges and slightly convex faces. Crystals may be transparent, translucent, or opaque. They range from colorless to black, with brown and yellow being the most common colors. Other forms include bort or boart (irregular or granular black diamond) and carbonado (microcrystalline masses). Colorless gemstones are most often used in jewelry.

Most diamonds come from two rare volcanic rocks—lamproite and kimberlite (p.269). The diamonds crystallize in Earth's mantle, generally more than 95 miles (150 km) deep, and are formed up to Earth's surface through volcanism. Diamonds are also found in sediment deposited by rivers or melting glaciers.

Hope Diamond
Blue in color, the 45.5-carat Hope diamond is probably the world's most famous diamond.

SULFIDES

Sulfides are minerals in which sulfur (a nonmetal) is combined either with a metal or a semimetal. Some sulfides are brilliantly colored, and most of them have low hardness and high specific gravity. Sulfides are common and are found widely in nature.

Red River deposit
Sulfide deposits in the Rio Tinto area of southwestern Spain have been mined for silver, zinc, and copper since 800 BCE.

COMPOSITION

Most sulfides have simple atomic structures, in which sulfur atoms are stacked alternately with metal or semimetal atoms and arranged as cubes, octahedra, or tetrahedra. This yields highly symmetrical crystal forms. Except in a few sulfides, such as orpiment and realgar, the symmetrical form also gives rise to many of the properties also found in metals, including metallic luster and electrical conductivity.

OCCURRENCE AND USES

Sulfides tend to form primarily in hydrothermal veins, from fluids circulating within fractures in Earth's crust. Sulfides such as pyrite and marcasite can form in sedimentary environments; others may form in magmas. It is common to find several sulfide minerals together.

Sulfides are the major ore minerals of many metals, including lead, zinc, iron, antimony, bismuth, molybdenum, nickel, silver, and copper—all of which have industrial uses. Gold is commonly found in sulfide deposits.

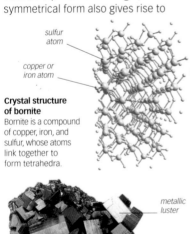

sulfur atom

copper or iron atom

Crystal structure of bornite
Bornite is a compound of copper, iron, and sulfur, whose atoms link together to form tetrahedra.

metallic luster

cubic habit

Crystalline pyrite
The iron sulfide pyrite, also called fool's gold, is one of the most common sulfides. The cubic crystals of pyrite reflect its simple atomic structure.

Die production
Sphalerite—a zinc sulfide—is the principal ore of zinc, which is used for die-cast components to galvanize, or coat, iron and steel.

PROFILE

Monoclinic

2–2½

7.2–7.4

Indistinct

Subconchoidal, sectile

Black

Metallic

uneven fracture

metallic luster

luster less brilliant on exposed surfaces

darkened, weathered surface

Blocky, prismatic crystals
In this pseudomorph specimen, argentite has replaced acanthite, while retaining the outward form of acanthite's cubic symmetry.

VARIANT

Thorny acanthite Dark, spiky acanthite crystals

Ag_2S

ACANTHITE

A silver sulfide, acanthite is the most important ore of silver. It takes its name from the Greek *akantha*, which means "thorn" and refers to the spiky appearance of some of its crystals. It also occurs in massive form and has an opaque, grayish black color. Above 350°F (177°C), silver sulfide crystallizes in the cubic system, and it used to be assumed that cubic silver sulfide—known as argentite— was a separate mineral from acanthite. It is now known that they are the same mineral, with acanthite crystallizing in the monoclinic system at temperatures below 350°F (177°C).

Acanthite forms in hydrothermal veins with other minerals, such as silver (p.43), galena (p.54), pyrargyrite (p.70), and proustite (p.72). It also forms as a secondary alteration product of primary silver sulfides. When heated, acanthite fuses readily and releases sulfurous fumes. The most famous locality of acanthite, the Comstock Lode in Nevada, USA, was so rich in silver that a branch of the US mint was established at nearby Carson City to coin its output.

PROFILE

Orthorhombic

⊠ 3

⬗ 5.1

▧ Poor

⬧ Uneven to conchoidal, brittle

▨ Pale grayish black

⬈ Metallic

massive habit

uneven fracture

iridescent surface

purple oxidation

Massive bornite
This specimen of tarnished bornite shows the oxidation colors that give it the names "purple copper ore" and "peacock ore."

VARIANT

brownish red on fresh surface

Bornite crystals Well-developed bornite crystals with curved faces

♣ Cu₅FeS₄

BORNITE

One of nature's most colorful minerals, bornite is a copper iron sulfide named after the Austrian mineralogist Ignaz von Born (1742–91). A major ore of copper, its natural color can be coppery red, coppery brown, or bronze. It can also show iridescent purple, blue, and red splashes of color on broken, tarnished faces, which explains its common name, "peacock ore." Bornite is also known as "purple copper ore" and "variegated copper ore."

Bornite crystals are uncommon. Although they exhibit orthorhombic symmetry, crystals, when found, are cubic, octahedral, or dodecahedral, often with curved or rough faces. Bornite is frequently compact, granular, or massive and alters readily to chalcocite (p.51) and other copper minerals upon weathering. It forms mainly in hydrothermal copper ore deposits with minerals such as chalcopyrite (p.57), pyrite (p.62), marcasite (p.63), and quartz (p.168). It also forms in some silica-poor, intrusive igneous rocks and in pegmatite veins and contact metamorphic zones.

PROFILE

Monoclinic

- 2½–3
- 5.5–5.8
- Indistinct
- Conchoidal
- Blackish lead gray
- Metallic

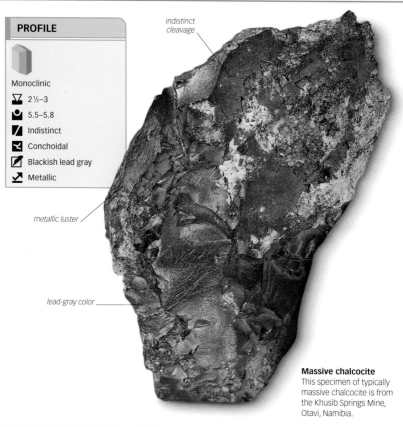

indistinct cleavage

metallic luster

lead-gray color

Massive chalcocite
This specimen of typically massive chalcocite is from the Khusib Springs Mine, Otavi, Namibia.

VARIANT

Prismatic crystals Short, prismatic chalcocite crystals on dolomite

Cu_2S

CHALCOCITE

The name chalcocite is derived from the Greek word for copper, *chalcos*. Chalcocite is one of the most important ores of copper. It is usually massive but, on rare occasions, occurs in short, striated prismatic or tabular crystals or as pseudohexagonal prisms formed by twinning. It is opaque, dark metallic gray, and becomes dull on exposure to light. Chalcocite was formerly known as chalcosine, copper glace, and redruthite, but these names are now obsolete.

Chalcocite forms at relatively low temperatures (up to 400°F/200C°), often as alteration products of other copper minerals such as bornite (p.50). It is found in hydrothermal veins and porphyry copper deposits with other minerals—bornite, covellite (p.52), sphalerite (p.53), galena (p.54), chalcopyrite (p.57), calcite (p.114), and quartz (p.168). Deposits in Cornwall, England, have been worked since the Bronze Age. Concentrated in secondary alteration zones, chalcocite can yield more copper than the element's primary deposits.

PROFILE

Hexagonal

- 1½–2
- 4.6–4.7
- Perfect basal
- Uneven
- Lead gray to black, shiny
- Submetallic to resinous

iridescence

foliated habit

metallic blue color

oxidized material

Iridescent covellite
This spectacular, massive covellite specimen showing classic purple iridescence is from the Leonard Mine at Butte, Montana, USA.

VARIANT

tabular crystal

Tabular covellite Rare covellite crystals in their tabular habit

♣ CuS

COVELLITE

Named in 1832 after the Italian minerologist Niccolo Covelli, who first described it, covellite is a copper sulfide. A minor ore of copper (p.37), covellite is opaque, with a bright metallic blue or indigo color. It is easy to recognize because of its brassy yellow, deep red, or purple iridescence. Covellite is generally massive and foliated in habit, although sometimes spheroidal. In crystalline form, it occurs as thin, tabular, and hexagonal plates, which are flexible when thin enough. Plates formed from its perfect basal cleavage are likewise flexible. It fuses very easily when heated, emitting a blue flame.

Covellite is a primary mineral in some places, but it typically occurs as an alteration product of other copper sulfide minerals such as bornite (p.50), chalcocite (p.51), and chalcopyrite (p.57). It sometimes forms as a coating on other copper sulfides. It rarely occurs as a volcanic sublimate, as on Mt. Vesuvius, where Niccolo Covelli first collected it. Covellite is abundant in the massive copper mines in Arizona, USA.

PROFILE

Cubic

🔽 3½–4

⚖ 3.9–4.1

▰ Perfect in six directions

▱ Conchoidal

▱ Brownish to light yellow

▱ Resinous to adamantine, metallic

Sphalerite crystals
These superbly formed sphalerite crystals occur with well-crystallized pyrite and quartz. They are from Casapalca, Lima, Peru.

complex sphalerite crystal

quartz

pyrite

resinous luster

VARIANT

Massive sphalerite The most common habit of sphalerite

dark red crystal

Ruby blende Brilliant red crystals of ruby blende sphalerite

🜨 ZnS

SPHALERITE

Sphalerite is the principal ore of zinc. Pure sphalerite is colorless and rare. Normally, iron is present, causing the color to vary from pale greenish yellow to brown and black with increasing iron content. Its complex crystals combine tetrahedral or dodecahedral forms with other faces. Sphalerite gets its name from the Greek *sphaleros*, meaning "deceitful," because its lustrous dark crystals can be mistaken for other minerals. It is often coarsely crystalline or massive, or forms banded, botryoidal, or stalactitic aggregates.

Sphalerite is found associated with galena (p.54) in lead-zinc deposits. It occurs in hydrothermal vein deposits, contact metamorphic zones, and replacement deposits formed at high temperature (1,065°F/575°C or above). It is also found in meteorites and lunar rocks.

Oval cut
This oval cut shows off the golden brown color of sphalerite. Such stones are cut for collectors.

PROFILE

Cubic

2½

7.6

Perfect

Subconchoidal

Lead-gray

Metallic

Galena crystals
Galena is usually found in
cube-shaped crystals, but the
crystal shape can also incorporate
the faces of octahedra, as here.

*octahedral face cuts
across cubic crystal*

metallic luster

accessory dolomite

VARIANT

Perfect cleavage Cubic
galena crystals with perfect
cleavage in three directions

PbS

GALENA

There are more than 60 known minerals that contain
lead, but by far the most important lead ore is galena,
or lead sulfide. It is possible that galena was the first ore
to be smelted to release its metal—lead beads found in
Turkey have been dated to around 6500 BCE. Galena is
opaque and bright metallic gray when fresh, but it dulls
on exposure to the atmosphere. Its crystals are cubic,
octahedral, dodecahedral, or combinations of these forms.
Irregular, coarse, or fine crystalline masses are common.

Galena is common in hydrothermal lead, zinc, and
copper (p.37) ore deposits worldwide and is often
associated with sphalerite (p.53), chalcopyrite (p.57), and
pyrite (p.62). It is also found in contact metamorphic rocks.
Galena weathers easily to form secondary lead minerals,
such as cerussite (p.119), anglesite (p.132), and pyromorphite
(p.151). Galena is both the principal ore of lead and the main
source of silver (p.43)—it often contains a considerable
amount of silver in the form of acanthite as an impurity. It
can also be a source of other metals.

Massive pentlandite
This typical massive specimen of pentlandite also contains pyrrhotite.

granular habit

pyrrhotite

uneven fracture

PROFILE

Cubic

 3½–4

 4.6–5.0

None

Conchoidal

Bronze-brown

Metallic

$(Fe,Ni)_9S_8$

PENTLANDITE

Named in 1856 after the Irish scientist Joseph Pentland, its discoverer, pentlandite is a nickel and iron sulfide. Nickel is usually a smaller component than iron, but both may be present in equal parts. Pentlandite mainly has a massive or granular habit, and its crystals cannot be seen by the naked eye. It is opaque, metallic yellow in color, and has a bronzelike tarnish.

Pentlandite occurs in silica-poor, intrusive igneous rocks. It is almost always accompanied by pyrrhotite, with other sulfides such as chalcopyrite (p.57) and pyrite (p.62), and with some arsenides. The chief ore of nickel, pentlandite is relatively widespread, but commercial deposits are scarce. In Ontario, Canada, nickel from an ancient meteorite is thought to have enriched the ore. Pentlandite is also found as an accessory mineral in some meteorites. Silver (p.43) can be present in the pentlandite structure, yielding the mineral argentopentlandite; when cobalt replaces the iron and nickel, the mineral becomes cobaltpentlandite.

PROFILE

Hexagonal

2–2½

8.0

Perfect

Subconchoidal to uneven

Scarlet

Adamantine to dull

Crystalline cinnabar
This massive specimen from
Monte Amiata, Tuscany,
Italy, also contains
cinnabar crystals.

calcite

cystalline
cinnabar

rock matrix

VARIANT

adamantine
luster

Massive cinnabar A specimen
of massive cinnabar with a
nonmetallic, adamantine luster

HgS

CINNABAR

A mercury sulfide, cinnabar takes its name from
the Persian *zinjirfrah* and Arabic *zinjafr*, which mean
"dragon's blood." It is bright scarlet to deep grayish red
in color. It is the major source of mercury. Crystals are
uncommon but when found they are rhombohedral,
tabular, or prismatic. It usually occurs as massive or
granular aggregates, but sometimes powdery coatings.

Cinnabar is often found with other minerals—such as
stibnite (p.61), pyrite (p.62), and marcasite (p.63)—in veins
near recent volcanic rocks.
It is also found around hot
springs. Cinnabar is believed
to have been mined and
used in Egypt in the early
2nd millennium BCE. It has
also been mined for at least
2,000 years at Almadén,
Spain. This site still yields
excellent crystals.

Powdered cinnabar
Since ancient times, artists
have used bright red
powdered cinnabar for
the pigment vermillion.

PROFILE

Tetragonal
⊿ 3½–4
▣ 4.2
◪ Distinct
◩ Uneven, brittle
◪ Green-black
⬈ Metallic

quartz crystal

twinned chalcopyrite crystals

metallic luster

brassy yellow coloration

Chalcopyrite crystals
Crystallized specimens of chalcopyrite can sometimes contain both twinned crystals and quartz crystals.

VARIANTS

metallic luster

Massive chalcopyrite A specimen with an iridescent tarnish to it

tetrahedral habit

Brassy yellow chalcopyrite A specimen with an uneven fracture and tetrahedral habit

♣ CuFeS$_2$

CHALCOPYRITE

One of the minerals worked at Rio Tinto, Spain, since Roman times, chalcopyrite is a copper and iron sulfide. It is opaque and brassy yellow when freshly mined, but it commonly develops an iridescent tarnish on exposure to the atmosphere. This tetragonal mineral forms tetrahedral crystals, which can be up to 4 in (10 cm) long on a face. It commonly occurs as massive aggregates and less frequently as botryoidal masses or as scattered grains in igneous rocks.

Chalcopyrite forms under a variety of conditions. It is mostly found in hydrothermal sulfide veins as a primary mineral deposited at medium and high temperatures (400°F/200°C or above), and as replacements, often with large concentrations of pyrite (p.62). It is also found as grains in igneous rocks and is an important ore mineral in porphyry copper deposits. Rarely, it occurs in metamorphic rocks. Chalcopyrite is an important ore of copper owing to its widespread occurrence. In some cases, selenium can replace a portion of the sulfur.

Realgar crystals
These bright red, prismatic realgar crystals are in a rock matrix and accompanied by gray quartz.

rare prismatic
realgar crystal

rock
matrix

light gray
quartz

PROFILE

Monoclinic

 1½–2

 3.6

 Good

 Conchoidal

Scarlet to orange-yellow

Resinous to greasy

 AsS

REALGAR

An important ore of arsenic, realgar is bright red or orange in color. Crystals are not often found, but when they occur they are short, prismatic, and striated. Realgar mostly occurs as coarse to fine granular masses and as encrustations. Realgar disintegrates on prolonged exposure to light, forming an opaque yellow powder, which is principally pararealgar. Therefore, specimens are kept in darkened containers.

Realgar is typically found in hydrothermal deposits at low temperature (up to 400°F/200°C) often with orpiment (p.59) and other arsenic minerals. It also forms as a sublimate around volcanoes, hot springs, and geyser deposits and as a weathering product of other arsenic-bearing minerals. Realgar is often found with stibnite (p.61) and calcite (p.114).

Powdered realgar
Scarlet to orange-yellow in color, powdered realgar was once used as a pigment and in fireworks.

uneven fracture

Foliated orpiment
Made up of thin layers, this specimen shows classic orpiment foliation. It has a resinous luster and uneven fracture.

foliated appearance

sinous luster

PROFILE

Monoclinic

 1½–2

3.5

 Perfect

Uneven, sectile

Pale yellow

 Resinous

VARIANT

Crystalline orpiment Rare, stubby, prismatic crystals

As_2S_3

ORPIMENT

An arsenic sulfide, orpiment is a soft yellow or orange mineral. Widely distributed, it is typically powdery or massive, but it is also found as cleavable, columnar, or foliated masses. Distinct crystals are uncommon, but when found they are short prisms. Orpiment occurs in hydrothermal veins at low temperature (up to 400°F/ 200°C), hot spring deposits, and volcanic fumaroles, and it may occur with stibnite (p.61) and realgar (p.58). It also results from the alteration of other arsenic-bearing minerals.

When heated, orpiment gives off the garlic odor typical of arsenic minerals. The luster is resinous on freshly broken surfaces but pearly on cleavage surfaces. It was used as a pigment, mainly in ancient times in the Middle East. It was also used later in the West but soon replaced due to its toxicity.

Yellow pigment
Powdered orpiment was used as a yellow pigment, especially to make gold-colored paint.

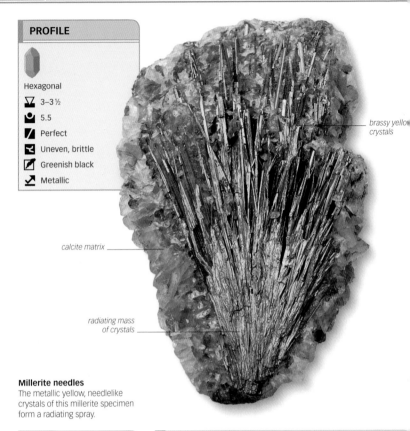

brassy yellow crystals

calcite matrix

radiating mass of crystals

Millerite needles
The metallic yellow, needlelike crystals of this millerite specimen form a radiating spray.

VARIANT

hairlike crystal

geode

Millerite geode Thin, radiating crystals of millerite have formed in this hollow space

 NiS

MILLERITE

A nickel sulfide, millerite commonly occurs as delicate, needlelike, opaque golden crystals. It can form free-standing, single crystals or occur as tufts, matted groups, or radiating sprays. It is also massive and frequently found with an iridescent tarnish. Nickel is more abundant in Earth's crust than copper (p.37), but it is generally more dispersed. Millerite is an ore of the element nickel, which is used in corrosion-resistant metal alloys, especially in the copper-nickel coinage that has replaced silver. It was named in 1845 after the English mineralogist W.H. Miller, who was the first person to study it.

Millerite normally forms at low temperatures (up to 400°F/200°C). It is often found in cavities in limestone (p.319) or dolomite (p.320), in carbonate veins and other associated rocks, within coal (p.253) deposits, and in serpentinite (p.298). It can occur as a later-formed mineral in nickel sulfide deposits and as an alteration product of other nickel minerals. Millerite is also found in meteorites and as a sublimate on Mount Vesuvius, Italy.

PROFILE

Orthorhombic

⊻ 2

◔ 4.6

🖊 Perfect

◩ Subconchoidal

🔲 Lead-gray to steel-gray

⤢ Metallic

Stibnite crystals
This group of long, prismatic, striated stibnite crystals is on a quartz and barite matrix.

prismatic crystal

striations on prism face

quartz and barite

VARIANTS

Stibnite sheets Thin layers of stibnite with sheetlike cleavage

Acicular stibnite A mass of radiating, needlelike crystals

🜋 Sb_2S_3

STIBNITE

The principal ore of antimony, stibnite is antimony sulfide. Its name comes from the Latin *stibium*. Lead-gray to silvery gray in color, it often develops a black, iridescent tarnish on exposure to light. It normally occurs as elongated, prismatic crystals that may be bent or twisted. These crystals are often marked by striations parallel to the prism faces. Stibnite typically forms coarse, irregular masses or radiating sprays of needlelike crystals, but it can also be granular or massive.

A widespread mineral, stibnite occurs in hydrothermal veins, hot-spring deposits, and replacement deposits that form at low temperatures (up to 400°F/200°C). It is often associated with galena (p.54), cinnabar (p.56), realgar (p.58), orpiment (p.59), pyrite (p.62), and quartz (p.168). It is found in massive aggregates in granite (pp.258–59) and gneiss (p.288) rocks. Stibnite is used to manufacture matches, fireworks, and percussion caps for firearms. Powdered stibnite was used in the ancient world as a cosmetic for eyes to make them look larger.

PROFILE

Cubic

6–6½

5.0

None

Conchoidal

Greenish black to brownish black

Metallic

Cubic pyrite
These three perfectly formed pyrite crystals—up to 1½in (3.5cm) wide—from Navajún, La Rioja, Spain, are in a marl matrix.

brassy yellow color

cubic habit

metallic luster

marl matrix

conchoidal fracture

VARIANTS

Octahedral pyrite A group of octahedral crystals with quartz

brownish coating

Pyrite nodule A ball-shaped, nodular group of pyrite crystals

Pyritohedral pyrite A classic pyrite pyritohedral crystal

FeS_2

PYRITE

Known since antiquity, pyrite is commonly referred to as "fool's gold." Although much lighter than gold, its brassy color and relatively high density misled many novice prospectors. Its name is derived from the Greek word *pyr*, meaning "fire," because it emits sparks when struck by iron. It is opaque and pale silvery yellow when fresh, turning darker and tarnishing with exposure to oxygen. Pyrite crystals may be cubic, octahedral, or twelve-sided "pyritohedra," and are often striated. Pyrite can also be massive or granular, or form either flattened disks or nodules of radiating, elongate crystals.

Pyrite occurs in hydrothermal veins, by segregation from magmas, in contact metamorphic rocks, and in sedimentary rocks, such as shale (p.313) and coal (p.253), where it can either fill or replace fossils.

Pyrite beads
With care, brittle pyrite can be ground into beads, such as those strung together in this necklace.

PROFILE

Orthorhombic

⊻ 6–6½

◖ 4.9

▰ Distinct

▰ Uneven or irregular

▱ Gray to black

↗ Metallic

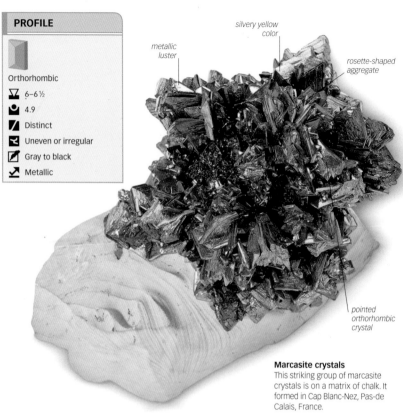

metallic luster

silvery yellow color

rosette-shaped aggregate

pointed orthorhombic crystal

Marcasite crystals
This striking group of marcasite crystals is on a matrix of chalk. It formed in Cap Blanc-Nez, Pas-de Calais, France.

VARIANT

spear-shaped crystal

limestone matrix

Spear-shaped marcasite
Several groups of spear-shaped, twinned crystals

⚛ FeS_2

MARCASITE

An iron sulfide, marcasite is chemically identical to pyrite (p.62), but unlike pyrite it has an orthorhombic crystal structure. Marcasite is opaque and pale silvery yellow when fresh but darkens and tarnishes on exposure. It has a predominantly pyramidal or tabular crystal form. It is also found in characteristic twinned, curved, sheaflike shapes that resemble a cockscomb. Nodules with radially arranged fibers are common. Marcasite can also be massive, stalactitic, or reniform.

Marcasite is found near Earth's surface. It forms from acidic solutions percolating downward through beds of shale (p.313), clay, limestone (p.319), or chalk (p.321), where it often fills or replaces fossils. Marcasite also occurs as nodules in coal (p.253).

Art Deco jewelry
Marcasite was a popular choice for Victorian and Art Deco jewelry, although most of the material used was actually pyrite.

Layered masses
The crystallized molybdenite masses in this specimen show a typical layered structure.

granite matrix

metallic luster

hexagonal, foliated mass

PROFILE

Hexagonal or trigonal

 1–1½

 4.7

 Perfect basal

 Uneven

 Greenish or bluish gray

 Metallic

MoS_2

MOLYBDENITE

A molybdenum sulfide, molybdenite is the most important source of molybdenum, which is an important element in high-strength steels. Molybdenite was originally thought to be lead, and its name is derived from the Greek word for lead, *molybdos*. It was recognized as a distinct mineral by the Swedish chemist Carl Scheele in 1778.

Molybdenite is soft, opaque, and bluish gray. It forms tabular hexagonal crystals, foliated masses, scales, and disseminated grains. It can also be massive or scaly. The platy, flexible, greasy-feeling hexagonal crystals of molybdenite can be confused with graphite (p.46), although molybdenite has a much higher specific gravity, a more metallic luster, and a slightly bluer tinge. Molybdenite occurs in granite (pp.258–59), pegmatite (p.260), and hydrothermal veins at high temperature (1,065°F/575°C or above) with other minerals—fluorite (p.109), ferberite (p.145), scheelite (p.146), and topaz (p.234). It is also found in porphyry ores and in contact metamorphic deposits.

SULFOSALTS

Sulfosalts are a group of mostly rare minerals that contain two or more metals in combination with sulfur (a nonmetal) and semimetals such as arsenic and antimony. Sulfosalt minerals have a high density, a metallic luster, and are usually brittle.

COMPOSITION
Sulfosalts have complex crystal structures. The structures of many sulfosalts appear to be based on fragments of simpler sulfur compounds. Metals commonly found in sulfosalts are lead, silver, thallium, copper, tin, bismuth, and germanium.

OCCURRENCE
Sulfosalts occur in small amounts in hydrothermal veins formed at low temperatures (up to 400°F/200°C). They are generally associated with the more common sulfides. A single Swiss deposit is known to have yielded up to 30 different sulfosalt minerals.

USES
Sulfosalts are typically found in small amounts but in a few deposits are economically important. Sometimes, they can constitute minor ores of silver, mercury, and antimony.

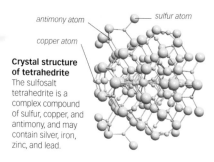

antimony atom — *sulfur atom*

copper atom

Crystal structure of tetrahedrite
The sulfosalt tetrahedrite is a complex compound of sulfur, copper, and antimony, and may contain silver, iron, zinc, and lead.

prismatic crystal

quartz matrix

Bournonite
This specimen shows crystals typical of the sulfosalt bournonite. Twinned crystals growing parallel to each other give the mineral its informal name, cogwheel ore.

Silver coins
Pyragyrite, a sulfosalt mineral, yields the metal silver, which was used to produce the ancient coins seen here.

Sulfosalt deposit
Many sulfosalt minerals are found in Cornwall, England. These stone buildings once housed steam engines to pump water from mine shafts.

PROFILE

Cubic

4

4.6–4.7

None

Subconchoidal to uneven, brittle

Black

Metallic

Crystalline tennantite
This mass of tetrahedral tennantite crystals is set in a rock matrix and has an iridescent tarnish.

iridescence

tetrahedral crystal

VARIANT

steel-gray coloring

Massive tennantite A specimen of massive tennantite from Cornwall, England

$(Cu,Fe)_{12}As_4S_3$

TENNANTITE

Named in 1819 after the English chemist Smithson Tennant, tennantite is a copper iron arsenic sulfide. Iron, zinc, mercury, bismuth, and silver may substitute for up to 15 percent of the copper in tennantite. Tennantite is gray-black, steel-gray, iron-gray, or black in color. It forms cubic and tetrahedral crystals. It may also occur in massive, granular, and compact forms. Tennantite is an end member of a solid-solution series with the similar mineral tetrahedrite (p.73). The two have very similar properties, making it difficult to distinguish between them. Their crystal habits are similar and both exhibit contact and penetration twinning.

Tennantite is found in hydrothermal and contact metamorphic deposits, often associated with sphalerite (p.53), galena (p.54), chalcopyrite (p.57), fluorite (p.109), barite (p.134), and quartz (p.168). Deposits are found in Freiberg, Saxony, Germany; Lengenbach, Switzerland; and Butte, Montana, and Aspen and Central City, Colorado, USA.

Enargite crystals
These superb enargite crystals are striated and show a prismatic habit.

uneven fracture

metallic luster

striation

PROFILE

Orthorhombic

 3

 4.4–4.5

 Perfect

Uneven, brittle

Black

Metallic

 Cu_3AsS_4

ENARGITE

A copper arsenic sulfide, enargite takes its name from the Greek word *enarge*, which means "distinct"— a reference to its perfect cleavage. An important ore of copper, it has a bright metallic luster, is opaque, and has a gray-black to iron-black to violet-black color when fresh. It turns dull black on exposure to light and pollutants. Enargite may occur in massive or granular habits. Crystals are usually small, either tabular or prismatic, sometimes pseudohexagonal or hemimorphic (with different terminations at each end), and have striations along the prism faces. Enargite crystals occasionally form star-shaped multiple twins.

Enargite forms in hydrothermal vein deposits at low to medium temperature (up to 1,065°F/575°C) and in replacement deposits, where it is associated with bornite (p.50), covellite (p.52), sphalerite (p.53), galena (p.54), chalcopyrite (p.57), pyrite (p.62), and other copper sulfides. It also occurs in the cap rocks of salt domes, with minerals such as anhydrite (p.133).

Fibrous habit
This jamesonite specimen, set in a rock matrix, has the fibrous habit typical of the mineral.

metallic luster

rock matrix

fibrous crystals

PROFILE

Monoclinic

 2–3

 5.5–6.0

 Good

 Uneven to conchoidal

 Grayish black

Metallic

 $Pb_4FeSb_6S_{14}$

JAMESONITE

Named in 1825 after the Scottish mineralogist Robert Jameson, jamesonite is a lead iron antimony sulfide. It is opaque lead-gray, but can often develop an iridescent tarnish. Jamesonite is normally found as needlelike or fibrous crystals combined together into columnar, radiating, plumose (featherlike), or feltlike masses.

Jamesonite occurs in hydrothermal veins at low or medium temperature (up to 1,065°F/575°C), where hot, chemical-rich fluids have permeated joints and fault lines, depositing minerals during cooling. In hydrothermal veins, it often occurs with other lead and antimony sulfides and sulfosalt minerals. Jamesonite also occurs in quartz associated with carbonate minerals, such as calcite (p.114), dolomite (p.117), and rhodochrosite (p.121). Jamesonite is a minor ore of antimony, which is used as a strengthening agent in alloys. It is widespread in small amounts, with good specimens coming from Freiburg, Saxony, Germany; Yakutia, Russia; Trepca, Serbia; Dachang, China; Cornwall, England; and Oruro, Bolivia.

short, tabular crystal

pseudohexagonal outline

metallic luster

twinned crystals

Pseudohexagonal crystals
Many short, prismatic crystals in this stephanite specimen show pseudohexagonal twinning.

PROFILE

Orthorhombic

 2–2½

 6.2–6.5

 Imperfect

 Subconchoidal to uneven, brittle

 Iron-black

 Metallic

 Ag_5SbS_4

STEPHANITE

A silver antimony sulfide, stephanite was named in honor of Archduke Victor Stephan, the mining director of Austria, in 1845. It is sometimes called brittle or black silver ore. It is opaque, iron-black to black in color, and has a metallic luster on fresh faces. Stephanite crystals range from short prismatic to tabular and are repeatedly twinned to form pseudohexagonal groups. Stephanite may also occur in massive and granular habits.

Stephanite is generally found in small amounts in late-stage hydrothermal silver veins associated with native silver (p.43), sulfides, and other sulfosalts, such as acanthite (p.49) and tetrahedrite (p.73). It was found in sufficient quantity to be an ore of silver in Comstock Lode, Nevada, USA.

Historic silver processing
This 1550 woodcut from Georgius Agricola's treatise *De Re Metallica* shows silver ore being processed.

prismatic crystal

dark red color darkens further on exposure to light

twinned crystals

adamantine luster

Dark ruby silver
The dark red color of pyrargyrite can be seen in these superb twinned, prismatic crystals.

PROFILE

Hexagonal

2 ½

5.8

Distinct

Conchoidal to uneven, brittle

Purplish red

Adamantine

 Ag_3SbS_3

PYRARGYRITE

An important ore of silver, pyrargyrite takes its name from the Greek words *pyros*, which means "fire," and *argent*, which means "silver"—an allusion to its silver content and its translucent, dark red color. Also known as dark ruby silver, pyrargyrite turns opaque dull gray when exposed to light. Therefore, prized specimens are stored in the dark. Pyrargyrite is typically massive or granular. It can also occur as well-formed prismatic crystals with rhombohedral, scalenohedral, or flat terminations, different at each end and frequently twinned.

Pyrargyrite forms in hydrothermal veins at relatively low temperature (up to 400°F/200°C) with the minerals sphalerite (p.53), galena (p.54), tetrahedrite (p.73), proustite (p.72), and calcite (p.114). It also forms by the alteration of other minerals.

Roman silver
This Roman *denarius* (silver coin) of the first century BCE shows gladiators fighting.

PROFILE

Orthorhombic

▽ 2½–3

◖ 5.8

▨ Indistinct

✂ Subconchoidal to uneven

▨ Steel-gray

↗ Metallic

Cogwheel ore
This specimen of bournonite, accompanied by white baryte, shows the twinned habit that gives the mineral its informal name.

blades of barite

twinned crystals forming coglike shape

VARIANT

prismatic bournonite crystals

quartz matrix

Prismatic bournonite A group of twinned prismatic crystals of bournonite

♣ PbCuSbS₃

BOURNONITE

A lead copper antimony sulfide, bournonite occurs as heavy, dark crystal aggregates and masses, as well as interpenetrating cruciform (crosslike) twins. When repeatedly twinned, bournonite has the appearance of a toothed wheel, giving rise to the informal name cogwheel ore. Untwinned crystals of this opaque mineral are tabular or short prismatic and usually have smooth and bright faces. Bournonite was first mentioned as a mineral in 1797 but was named only in 1805 after the French mineralogist Count J.L. de Bournon.

A widely distributed mineral, bournonite is found in hydrothermal veins at medium temperatures (400–1,065°F/200–575°C) and associated with sphalerite (p.53), galena (p.54), chalcopyrite (p.57), pyrite (p.62), tetrahedrite (p.73), and other sulfide minerals. Particularly prized specimens of bournonite come from the Harz Mountains of Germany, where a few crystals exceed ¾in (2.2cm) in diameter. This mineral has been used as a minor ore of antimony (p.41).

adamantine luster

semitransparent, red coloration

Ruby silver
This stunning specimen of proustite shows the semitransparent red coloration that gives it the name common ruby silver.

VARIANTS

striation

prismatic crystal

Striated proustite A prismatic, semitransparent crystal

Dull proustite A dull, opaque specimen after exposure to light

Ag_3AsS_3

PROUSTITE

As its original name ruby silver ore suggests, proustite is translucent and red and is an important source of silver (p.43). It has also been called light red silver ore. The name proustite comes from the French chemist Joseph Proust, who distinguished it from the related mineral pyrargyrite (p.70) by chemical analysis in 1832. Its striated, often brilliant crystals are typically prismatic with rhombohedral or scalenohedral terminations, often resembling the dogtooth spar form of calcite (p.114) in habit. Proustite also occurs as massive or granular aggregates. The mineral turns from transparent scarlet to dull opaque gray in strong light, so specimens are stored in the dark.

Proustite forms in hydrothermal veins at low temperature (up to 400°F/200°C) with other silver minerals, such as acanthite (p.49), stephanite (p.69), and tetrahedrite (p.73), and with native arsenic (p.45), galena (p.54), and calcite (p.114). It also forms in the secondary zone of silver deposits. Large crystals come from Chañarcillo, Chile, and Freiburg, Saxony, Germany.

Tetrahedral crystals
This group of relatively rare tetrahedrite crystals shows twinning and coats a rock matrix.

triangular crystal face

quartz crystal

twinned, tetrahedral crystals

PROFILE

  $(Cu,Fe)_{12}Sb_4S_{13}$

Cubic

 3–4

 4.6–5.1

 None

 Subconchoidal to uneven

Brown to black to cherry-red

 Metallic

TETRAHEDRITE

The name tetrahedrite comes from this mineral's characteristic tetrahedral crystals, although it also occurs as massive, compact, or granular aggregates. Tetrahedrite is opaque, metallic gray, or nearly black, and it sometimes coats or is coated with brassy yellow chalcopyrite (p.57). It forms a continuous solid-solution series with the similar mineral tennantite (p.66), in which arsenic replaces antimony in the crystal structure. Bismuth also substitutes for antimony and forms bismuthian tetrahedrite or annivite.

Tetrahedrite is an important ore of copper and sometimes silver. It forms in hydrothermal veins at low to medium temperatures (up to 1,065°F/575°C), often with bornite (p.50), galena (p.54), chalcopyrite, pyrite (p.62), barite (p.134), and quartz (p.168). It is also found in contact metamorphic deposits.

Copper ore
This 9th-century brass Arabic astrolabe is believed to have been made of copper extracted from tetrahedrite.

OXIDES

The minerals in this group have crystal structures in which metals or semimetals occupy spaces between oxygen atoms. The properties of oxides vary: the metallic ores and gemstone varieties tend to be hard and have a high specific gravity.

COMPOSITION

Oxides can be either simple or multiple. Simple oxides, such as cuprite (Cu_2O), contain only one metal or semimetal and oxygen. Multiple oxides have two different metal sites, both of which may be occupied by several different metals or semimetals. The minerals in the spinel ($MgAl_2O_4$) group are examples of multiple oxides.

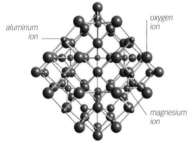

aluminum ion

oxygen ion

magnesium ion

Spinel crystal structure
In spinel, magnesium and aluminum combine with oxygen. Other metals can replace magnesium and aluminum to form the spinel series of minerals.

black crystals

adamantine shine

Cassiterite crystals
The simple tin oxide cassiterite, seen here as a group of twinned prismatic crystals, is the world's primary source of tin.

Queensland
The Queensland region of eastern Australia is a treasure trove of minerals. Several deposits of alluvial sapphire (aluminum oxide) are found here.

OCCURRENCE AND USES

Oxides occur as accessory minerals in many igneous rocks, especially as early crystallizing minerals in ultrabasic rocks, in pegmatites, and as decomposition products of sulfide minerals. Many resist weathering and are found concentrated in placers.

Many oxide minerals are important ores of chromium, uranium, tantalum, zinc, tin, cerium, tungsten, manganese, copper, and titanium. Other oxides, such as quartz and corundum, are important gemstone minerals.

Chrome bumper
The large, chrome-plated front bumper of this classic American 1956 Chevrolet is a dramatic example of chromium derived from the oxide chromite.

PROFILE

Hexagonal

⬙ Varies

⬙ 1.0

⬙ Perfect, difficult

⬙ Conchoidal, brittle

⬙ White

⬙ Vitreous

Iceberg
This small, beached iceberg
still shows some of its original
depositional layering.

*broken edge
of glacier*

layering

VARIANTS

Frost Crystalline ice in
a frostlike form

Hailstone A huge (2 in x 3½ in
/ 5 cm x 9 cm) hailstone

⬙ H_2O

ICE

Although largely absent at lower latitudes, ice
is probably the most abundant mineral exposed on
Earth's surface. Liquid water is not classified as a mineral
because it has no crystalline form. As snow, ice forms
crystals that seldom exceed ¼ in (7 mm) in length, although
as massive aggregates in glaciers, individual crystals may
be up to 17½ in (45 cm) long. Other forms of ice include
branching, treelike frost, skeletal, hopper-shaped,
prismlike frost, and hailstones and icicles made up of
many randomly oriented crystals.

Ice crystals are generally colorless, but the common
white color of ice is due to gaseous inclusions of air that
reflect light. There are at least nine polymorphs—different
crystalline forms—of ice, each forming under different
pressure and temperature conditions, but only one form
exists at Earth's surface. The hardness of ice varies with its
crystal structure, purity, and temperature. At temperatures
found in the Arctic and high-alpine zones, ice is so hard it
can erode stone when windblown.

PROFILE

Tetragonal

5½–6

3.9

Perfect

Subconchoidal

White to pale yellow

Adamantine to metallic

albite matrix

bipyramidal anatase crystal

opaque crystal

Bipyramidal anatase
This specimen shows two bipyramidal anatase crystals perched on a matrix of albite crystals.

VARIANTS

rock matrix

Black anatase Schist speckled with tiny black anatase crystals

Octahedral crystal A perfectly formed, modified bipyramidal anatase crystal

TiO_2

ANATASE

Formerly known as octahedrite, anatase is a polymorph of titanium dioxide. Its name comes from the Greek word *anatasis,* which means "extension"—a reference to the elongate octahedral crystals that are the most common habit of anatase. Anatase crystals can also be tabular and, rarely, prismatic. Hard and brilliant, the crystals can be brown, yellow, indigo-blue, green, gray, lilac, or black in color.

Anatase forms in veins and crevices in metamorphic rocks, such as schists (pp.291–92) and gneisses (p.288), and is derived from the leaching of surrounding rocks by hydrothermal solutions. Anatase also forms in pegmatites (p.260), often in association with the minerals brookite (p.77), ilmenite (p.90), fluorite (p.109), and aegirine (p.209). It is found in sediments and is sometimes concentrated in placer deposits. Much anatase is formed by the weathering of titanite (p.234). Weathered anatase becomes rutile (p.78). Although rutile replaces anatase, it retains the anatase crystal shape.

PROFILE

Orthorhombic

- 5½–6
- 4.1
- Indistinct
- Subconchoidal to uneven
- White, grayish, yellowish
- Metallic to adamantine

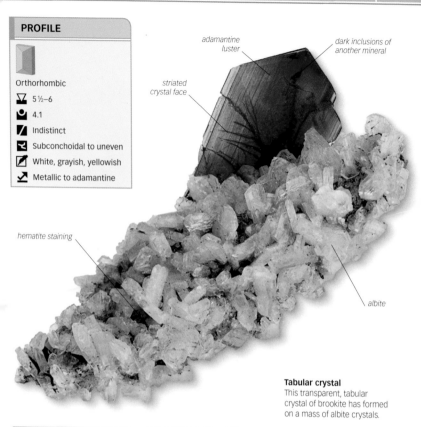

adamantine luster

dark inclusions of another mineral

striated crystal face

hematite staining

albite

Tabular crystal
This transparent, tabular crystal of brookite has formed on a mass of albite crystals.

Dipyramidal crystal A black brookite specimen with metallic luster

TiO$_2$

BROOKITE

Named in 1825 after British crystallographer H.J. Brooke, brookite, like anatase (p.76) and rutile (p.78), is composed of titanium dioxide. However, unlike anatase and rutile, brookite exhibits orthorhombic symmetry. Usually brown and metallic, brookite may also be red, yellow-brown, or black. Crystals can be tabular or, less commonly, pyramidal or pseudohexagonal. They may be thin or thick and up to 2 in (5 cm) long. Iron is almost always present in this mineral's structure to a small degree, and brookite containing niobium is also known.

Brookite occurs in hydrothermal veins, in some contact metamorphic rocks, and as a detrital mineral in sedimentary deposits. Being relatively dense, it is common in areas with natural concentrations of heavy minerals, such as the diamond placer deposits of Brazil. It generally occurs with other minerals, including rutile, anatase, and albite (p.177). Brookite is widespread in mineral veins in the Alps. In the Fronolen locality in northern Wales, UK, it forms crystals on crevice walls in diabase rock.

PROFILE

Tetragonal

⊻ 6–6½

⬤ 4.2

▰ Good

⬕ Conchoidal to uneven

▱ Pale brown to yellowish

⬈ Adamantine to submetallic

Single crystal
This large, semitransparent, and striated single crystal of rutile originates from Val di Vizze, Trentino-Alto Adige, Italy.

uneven fracture

adamantine sheen

vertical striations along length of crystal

typical prismatic crystal shape

VARIANTS

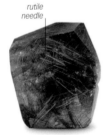

rutile needle

Rutilated quartz Pale-golden rutile crystals in polished quartz

uneven fracture

Massive rutile Dark-hued crystals in rock matrix

⚛ TiO_2

RUTILE

A form of titanium oxide, rutile takes its name from the Latin *rutilis*, which means "red" or "glowing." It often appears as pale golden, needlelike crystals inside quartz (p.168). When not enclosed in quartz, it is usually yellowish or reddish brown, dark brown, or black. Crystals are generally prismatic but can also be slender and needlelike. Multiple twinning is common and is either knee-shaped, net- or latticelike, or radiating, forming wheel-like twins. Rutile may also radiate in starlike sprays from hematite crystals.

Rutile often occurs as a minor constituent of granites (pp.258–59), gneisses (p.288), and schists (p.291), and also in hydrothermal veins and in some clastic sediments. It commonly forms microscopic, oriented inclusions in other minerals, producing an asterism effect.

Quartz rutile cabochon
Slender rutile crystals are clearly visible inside this polished, convex-cut, colorless quartz.

black crystals

twinned crystals

PROFILE

Tetragonal

6–7

7.0

Indistinct

Subconchoidal to uneven

White, grayish, brownish

Adamantine to metallic

crystals form as short prisms

rock matrix

Prismatic crystals
These twinned cassiterite crystals are short, dark-colored, and prismatic, occurring on a rocky matrix.

VARIANT

varlamoffite crystals

Varlamoffite cassiterite A specimen displaying the yellow variety of tin oxide

SnO_2

CASSITERITE

The tin oxide cassiterite takes its name from the Greek word for tin, *kassiteros*. Also called tinstone, it is the only important ore of tin. Colorless when pure, it commonly appears brown or black due to iron impurities. Rarely, it is gray or white. Its crystals are usually heavily striated prisms and pyramids. Twinned crystals are quite common. It can also be massive, occurring as a botryoidal, fibrous variety (wood tin) or as water-worn pebbles (stream tin).

Cassiterite forms in association with igneous rocks in hydrothermal veins at high temperature (1,065°F/575°C or above), with tungsten minerals such as ferberite (p.145), and with topaz (p.234), molybdenite (p.64), and tourmaline (p.224). Durable and relatively dense, it becomes concentrated in placer deposits after erosion from its primary rocks.

Brilliant gemstone
This faceted, golden orange cassiterite gem is transparent with a resinous luster.

dull luster

uneven fracture

Massive pyrolusite
This dark gray specimen of
massive pyrolusite has an
even fracture.

PROFILE

Tetragonal

 6–6½

4.4–5.1

 Perfect

 Uneven, brittle, splintery

 Black or bluish black

 Metallic to earthy

MnO_2

PYROLUSITE

Pyrolusite is the primary ore of the element
manganese. Specimens are typically light gray to
black in color. Pyrolusite usually occurs as massive
aggregates. It also forms metallic coatings, crusts, fibers,
nodules, botryoidal masses, concretions, and coatings
that may be powdery or branching. Crystals are rare;
when found, they are opaque and prismatic.

Pyrolusite forms under highly oxidizing conditions
as an alteration product of manganese minerals, such as
rhodochrosite (p.121). It has been found in bogs, lakes, and
shallow marine environments and as a deposit laid down
by circulating waters. Excellent crystals are found at Horni
Blatna, Czech Republic, and at Bathurst, New Brunswick,
Canada. The mineral is mined extensively in Russia, India,
Georgia, and Ghana. Pyrolusite is used as a decolorizing
agent in glass, as a coloring agent in bricks, and in dry cell
batteries. It is also used in the manufacture of steel and
saltwater-resistant manganese-bronze, which is used to
make ships' propellers.

PROFILE

Orthorhombic

⊻ 8½

🗓 3.7

▨ Distinct

⬚ Uneven to conchoidal

▧ Colorless

⬈ Vitreous

striation on crystal face

Cyclic twin
The cyclic twinning of chrysoberyl exhibited by this specimen is common in the mineral.

greenish yellow twinned crystal

transparent with vitreous luster

pseudohexagonal twinned crystal

VARIANTS

Siberian alexandrite A group of twinned alexandrite crystals with mica from Russia

Yellow gemstone Cat's eye chrysoberyl in the most desirable honey-yellow color

⚛ BeAl$_2$O$_4$

CHRYSOBERYL

A beryllium aluminum oxide, chrysoberyl is hard and durable. It is inferior in hardness only to corundum (p.95) and diamond (p.47). Chrysoberyl is typically yellow, green, or brown in color. It forms tabular or short prismatic crystals and heart-shaped or pseudohexagonal twinned crystals. Alexandrite, one of its gemstone varieties, is one of the rarest and most expensive gems. Another variety, cat's eye, is also prized as a gemstone. It contains parallel fibrous crystals of other minerals that reflect light across the surface of a polished gemstone— an effect known as chatoyancy.

Chrysoberyl occurs in some granite pegmatites (p.260), gneisses (p.288), mica schists, and marbles (p.301). Crystals that weather out of the parent rock are often found in streams and gravel beds.

Color change
Alexandrite exhibits color change—from brilliant green in daylight to cherry-red under tungsten light.

Orthorhombic

6–6½

5.2–8.0

Distinct

Subconchoidal or uneven

Red, brown, or black

Submetallic to resinous

Ferrocolumbite
This opaque, tabular crystal
of ferrocolumbite exhibits a
submetallic to resinous luster.

metallic
luster

uneven fracture

Yttrotantalite Dark crystals
of the coltan series mineral
yttrotantalite (yttrium-rich
tantalite) in a light matrix

$(Fe,Mn)(Nb,Ta)_2O_6$–$(Fe,Mn)(Ta,Nb)_2O_6$

COLUMBITE–TANTALITE

Columbite forms the coltan series—a nearly complete
solid-solution series—with the mineral tantalite. Minerals
at the columbite end of this series are niobium-rich, and
those at the tantalite end are tantalum-rich. Tantalite
and columbite have similar crystal structures, but
tantalite is denser, and tantalum atoms replace niobium
atoms in the columbite crystal structure. The name
of the mineral is prefixed with "ferro-" or "mangano-"
depending on the content of iron or manganese.
Ferrocolumbite is the most common mineral of the
coltan group. Scandium and tungsten may also be
present as minor constituents.

Coltan minerals are brown or black in color and are
often iridescent. They are either massive or form tabular
or short, prismatic crystals. They are the most abundant
and widespread of the niobates and tantalates, and
are the most important ores of niobium and tantalum.
Coltan minerals mainly occur in granite pegmatite
rocks (p.260) and in detrital deposits.

Botryoidal uraninite
This uraninite specimen demonstrates the botryoidal habit common in this mineral.

botryoidal habit

yellow uranium oxide

dull to submetallic luster

PROFILE

Cubic

 5–6

6.5–11.0

None

Uneven to subconchoidal

Brownish black

Submetallic, pitchy, dull

UO_2

URANINITE

Discovered by the German chemist M.H. Klaproth in 1789, uraninite is a major ore of uranium. The pioneering work on radioactivity by Pierre and Marie Curie was based on uranium extracted from uraninite ores. It is black to brownish black, dark gray, or greenish. It commonly occurs in massive or botryoidal forms, or in banded or granular habits, and less commonly as opaque octahedral or cubic crystals.

Uraninite crystals occur in granitic pegmatites (p.260). Uraninite forms with cassiterite (p.79) and arsenopyrite in hydrothermal sulfide veins at high temperatures (1,065°F/575°C or above). It also forms at medium temperatures (400–1,065°F/200–575°C) as pitchblende. It also occurs as small grains in sandstones and conglomerates, where it may have weathered into secondary uranium minerals.

Uranium pellets
These ceramic pellets of enriched uranium are ready for use in nuclear reactors.

indistinct cleavage

iridescence

conchoidal fracture

Massive samarskite
This specimen of massive samarskite exhibits an iridescent sheen on some surfaces.

PROFILE

Orthorhombic

 5–6

 5.7

 Indistinct

 Conchoidal, brittle

Dark reddish brown to black

Vitreous to resinous

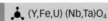 $(Y,Fe,U)(Nb,Ta)O_4$

SAMARSKITE

Named in 1847 after Vasili Yefrafovich von Samarski-Bykhovets of Russia, samarskite is a complex oxide of yttrium, iron, tantalum, niobium, and uranium. Two types of samarskite are recognized—samarskite-(Y) or yttrium samarskite; and samarskite-(Yb) or ytterbium samarskite. The mineral is usually black and opaque but translucent in thin fragments. Crystals are stubby, opaque, and prismatic with a rectangular cross section—although samarskite is commonly found in the massive form. It is often brown or yellowish brown due to surface alteration. Specimens with high uranium content have a yellow-brown, earthy rind. Samarskite samples are usually radioactive.

Samarskite is usually found in rare, earth-bearing granitic pegmatites (p.260). It forms in similar conditions as columbite (p.82), so the minerals are closely associated. Samarskite is also associated with monazite (p.150), garnet, and other minerals. Yttrium from samarskite has been used in cathode-ray televisions, optical glass, and special ceramics.

modified octahedra

uneven fracture

Octahedral pyrochlore
In this specimen of pyrochlore, modified octahedra display multiple twinning.

Cubic

5–5 ½

4.5

Distinct

Subconchoidal to uneven

Light brown, yellowish brown

Vitreous to resinous

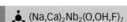 $(Na,Ca)_2Nb_2(O,OH,F)_7$

PYROCHLORE

A major source of the element niobium, pyrochlore is a complex niobium sodium calcium oxide. Its name comes from the Greek *pyr* and *chloros*, which mean "fire" and "green" respectively—a reference to some specimens that turn green after heating. Pyrochlore is orange, brownish red, brown, or black in color. Crystals are typically well-formed octahedra with modified faces. They are frequently twinned or occur as either granular or massive aggregates. Pyrochlore often contains traces of uranium and thorium, and it may be radioactive. In such cases, its internal structure may be disrupted.

Pyrochlore forms in pegmatite rocks (p.260) and in igneous rocks dominated by carbonate minerals. It is an accessory mineral in silica-poor rocks, often occurring with magnetite (p.92), apatite (p.148), and zircon (p.233). It also accumulates in some detrital deposits. Niobium is a major alloying element in nickel-based superalloys. It has been used either alone or together with zirconium in claddings for nuclear-reactor cores.

Microlite crystals
This specimen of crystalline microlite contains tantalum in place of the niobium typically found in pyrochlore.

vitreous luster

uneven fracture on surfaces

twinned octahedra

PROFILE

Cubic

 5–5½

6.4

Distinct to difficult

Subconchoidal to uneven

Yellowish to brownish

Resinous to vitreous

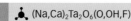 $(Na,Ca)_2Ta_2O_6(O,OH,F)$

MICROLITE

Named in 1835, microlite takes it name from the Greek word *micros,* which means "small"—a reference to the small size of the crystals found in the locality where the mineral was first discovered. Microlite can, in fact, form excellent octahedral crystals, which can be up to ⅜ in (1 cm) on an edge. It also occurs as irregular grains. Specimens can be yellow, brown, black, green, or reddish. Microlite is related to pyrochlore (p.85), and both minerals are dominated by rare-earth elements: microlite by tantalum and pyrochlore by niobium.

Microlite is found in pegmatites (p.260), especially those rich in lepidolite (p.198) or other lithium-bearing minerals, and in albite (p.177). It is a major ore of tantalum, which is especially useful in high-capacitance electronic devices, particularly those used in miniaturized circuitry. Microlite is also used in corrosion-resistant chemical equipment. Excellent crystals are found at Dixon, New Mexico, USA; Shingus, Gilgit, Pakistan; Mattawa, Ontario, Canada; and at numerous localities in Brazil.

twinned crystal

adamantine luster on crystal faces

translucent red

Red cuprite
Cuprite crystals are octahedral, cubic, or rarely dodecahedral. They come from Bisbee and other regions in Arizona, USA.

PROFILE

Cubic

 3½–4

6.1

Distinct

Conchoidal, brittle

Brownish red, shining

Adamantine, submetallic

Cu_2O

CUPRITE

A relatively soft, heavy copper oxide, cuprite is an important ore of copper. Its crystals are either cubic or octahedral in shape and commonly striated. Massive or granular aggregates with the appearance of sugar are common. Cuprite is translucent and bright red when freshly broken but turns to a dull metallic gray color on exposure to light and pollutants. Cuprite is sometimes known as ruby copper due to its distinctive red color.

In the variety called chalcotrichite or plush copper ore, the crystals are a rich carmine color, fibrous, capillary, and are silky in appearance. They are found in loosely matted aggregates. Cuprite of the tile ore variety is soft, earthy, brick-red to brownish red in color, and often contains intermixed hematite (p.91) or goethite (p.102).

VARIANT

Chalcotrichite Bright red, hairlike crystals of the chalcotrichite variety

Step cut
Rare transparent cuprite is sometimes cut for collectors, as in this rectangular step cut.

Crystalline zincite
This specimen of coarsely crystalline zincite in a white calcite matrix is from Sterling Hill, New Jersey, USA.

deep red zincite

white calcite matrix

coarsely crystalline texture

PROFILE

Hexagonal

4–5

5.7

Perfect

Conchoidal

Orange-yellow

Resinous, submetallic

VARIANT

Granular habit Granular zincite with black franklinite

🔬 ZnO

ZINCITE

Red oxide of zinc is another name for zincite, which is a minor ore of zinc. Zincite occurs mostly as cleavable or granular masses. Natural crystals are rare, but when they occur they are pyramidal, pointed at one end and flat at the other. These crystals can be orange, red, yellow, or green.

Zincite is found mainly as an accessory mineral in zinc-ore deposits and is commonly associated with black franklinite and white calcite. It may also be a rare constituent of volcanic ash. Crystals are found only in secondary veins or fractures, where zincite forms by the chemical alteration or metamorphism of zinc deposits. Some so-called natural zincite crystals in the collectors' market are, in fact, large crystals that have formed in the chimneys of smelters. Natural crystals are rarely fluorescent; artificial crystals may range from fluorescent green to fluorescent yellow. The classic locality for fine zincite crystals is Franklin, New Jersey, USA. It is also found at Varmland and Nordmark, Sweden.

psuedocubic
perovskite crystal

striations
on crystal

plagioclase matrix

Perovskite crystals
In this specimen, two striated,
pseudocubic perovskite
crystals are set in a matrix
of plagioclase feldspar.

PROFILE

Orthorhombic

 5½

 4.0

 Imperfect

 Subconchoidal to uneven

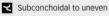 Gray to colorless

 Adamantine or metallic

 $CaTiO_3$

PEROVSKITE

A calcium titanium oxide, perovskite was named after
the Russian mineralogist Count Lev Alekseevich Perovski
in 1839. The composition of perovskite varies considerably:
niobium can substitute for up to 44.9 percent titanium
by weight, and cerium and sodium can substitute for
calcium. When specimens are black, they have a metallic
luster; when brown or yellow, they appear adamantine.
Although perovskite is an orthorhombic mineral, its
crystals are usually pseudocubic. Perovskite crystals
can be pseudooctahedral in varieties where niobium
or cerium has replaced a large amount of titanium.
The crystals tend to be deeply striated and are
frequently twinned.

Perovskite occurs in igneous rocks that are rich
in iron and magnesium. It also occurs in contact
metamorphic rocks associated with magnesium- and
iron-rich intrusive igneous rocks and in some chlorite
and talc schists. It is also found in carbonaceous
chondrite meteorites (p.337).

PROFILE

Hexagonal

- 5–6
- 4.7
- None
- Conchoidal
- Black to reddish brown
- Metallic to submetallic

metallic luster

lamellar ilmenite

twinned ilmenite crystals

oligoclase feldspar matrix

Ilmenite crystals
This specimen exhibits opaque, black, lamellar, and twinned crystals of ilmenite.

VARIANT

ilmenite crystal

quartz

Tabular crystals Thin, gray, tabular ilmenite crystals with actinolite and quartz

 $FeTiO_3$

ILMENITE

Named after the Il'menski Mountains near Miass, Russia, where it was discovered, ilmenite is a major source of titanium. Usually thick and tabular, its crystals sometimes occur as thin lamellae (fine plates) or rhombohedra. Ilmenite can also be massive, or occur as scattered grains. Intergrowths with hematite (p.91) or magnetite (p.92) are common, and ilmenite can be mistaken for these minerals because of its opaque, metallic, gray-black color. Unlike magnetite, however, ilmenite is nonmagnetic or very weakly magnetic; and it can be distinguished from hematite by its black streak. It may weather to a dull brown color.

Ilmenite is widely distributed as an accessory mineral in igneous rocks, such as diorite (p.264) and gabbro (p.265). It is a frequent accessory in kimberlite rocks (p.269), associated with diamond (p.47). It is also found in veins, pegmatite rocks (p.260), and black beach sands associated with magnetite, rutile (p.78), zircon (p.233), and other heavy minerals.

Rhombohedral hematite
These superb hematite crystals from Elba, Italy, demonstrate hexagonal or rhombohedral form and metallic luster.

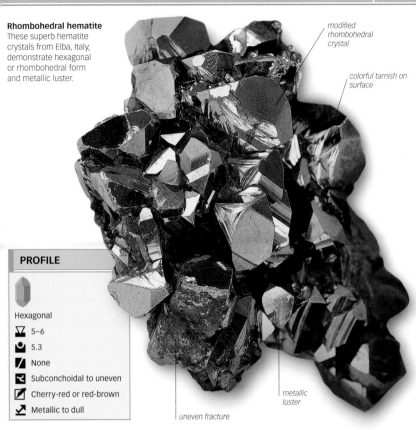

modified rhombohedral crystal

colorful tarnish on surface

uneven fracture

metallic luster

VARIANTS

Kidney ore A perfect example of hematite's botryoidal habit

Specular hematite
Brilliant platy crystals of specular hematite

Iridescent hematite
An iridescent crystal on rock

Fe_2O_3

HEMATITE

Dense and hard, hematite is the most important ore of iron (p.39) because of its high iron content and its abundance. The mineral occurs in various habits: steel-gray crystals and coarse-grained varieties with a brilliant metallic luster are known as specular hematite; thin, scaly forms make up micaceous hematite; and crystals in petal-like arrangements are called iron roses. Hematite also occurs as short, black, rhombohedral crystals and may have an iridescent tarnish. The soft, fine-grained, and earthy form of hematite is used as a pigment.

Important hematite deposits occur in sedimentary beds or in metamorphosed sediments. A compact variety known as kidney ore has a kidney-shaped surface. A form of ground hematite called rouge is used to polish plate glass and jewelry.

Oval cabochon
This oval cabochon of black hematite is faceted on top. Hematite cabochons have been sold as "marcasites."

PROFILE

Cubic

⬙ 5½–6

⬥ 5.2

◩ None

⬀ Conchoidal to uneven

◪ Black

⬈ Metallic to semimetallic

magnetic field

iron fillings attracted by magnetic surface

Magnetic magnetite
Magnetic specimens of magnetite, such as this one covered with iron filings, are known as lodestones.

VARIANTS

Octahedral crystal A magnetite crystal showing classic octahedral form

Magnetite crystals A cluster of black magnetite crystals

 Fe_2O_4

MAGNETITE

An iron oxide, magnetite is named after the Greek shepherd boy Magnes, who noticed that the iron ferrule of his staff and the nails of his shoes clung to a magnetite-bearing rock. All magnetite can be picked up with a magnet, but some magnetite is itself naturally magnetic and attracts iron filings and deflects compass needles. Magnetite usually forms octahedral crystals, although it sometimes occurs as highly modified dodecahedrons. Specimens can also be massive or granular, occurring as disseminated grains and as concentrations in black sand. Magnetite is similar in appearance to hematite (p.91), but hematite is nonmagnetic and has a red streak.

Magnetite occurs in a range of geological environments. It forms at high temperatures (1,065°F/575°C or above) as an accessory mineral in metamorphic and igneous rocks and in sulfide veins. A major ore of iron (p.39), magnetite forms large ore bodies. Economically important deposits occur in silica-poor intrusions of igneous rocks and in banded ironstones (p.329).

Swedish fergusonite
In this specimen from Ytterby, Sweden, fergusonite crystals rest on a matrix of feldspar.

feldspar

fergusonite crystal

PROFILE

Tetragonal

 5½–6½

4.2–5.7

Poor

Subconchoidal, brittle

Brown, yellow-brown, greenish gray

Vitreous to submetallic

 (Ce,Y,La,Nd)NbO$_4$

FERGUSONITE

Named after the Scottish mineralogist Robert Ferguson (1767–1840), the fergusonite group contains several minerals. All fergusonites may be considered as sources of the rare metals they contain. The most common is fergusonite-(Y), which is rich in yttrium. Its crystals are prismatic to pyramidal in shape and black to brownish black. Fergusonite-(Ce) is cerium-rich, dark red to black in color, and forms prismatic dipyramidal crystals—although these are rare. Fergusonite-(Nd), a neodymium-bearing fergusonite, is usually granular. Another member of the fergusonites, formanite-(Y), is found as tabular crystals and anhedral pebbles. Yet other fergusonites, most of which appear in minor quantities, bear the prefix "beta."

Fergusonites can also have varying amounts of erbium, lanthanum, niobium, dysprosium, uranium, thorium, zirconium, and tungsten. They can be found in granitic pegmatites (p.260) associated with other rare-earth minerals and in placer deposits.

Massive romanèchite
This specimen of massive romanèchite demonstrates its dull luster.

massive habit

dull luster

PROFILE

Orthorhombic

5–6

4.7

None

Uneven

Brownish black, shiny

Submetallic to dull

VARIANT

Botryoidal romanèchite
Dense, submetallic, botryoidal romanèchite

$(Ba, H_2O) (Mn_4 + Mn_3 +)_5 O_{10}$

ROMANÈCHITE

A hard, black, barium manganese oxide, romanèchite is named for its occurrence at Romanèche-Thorins, France. It is one of the manganese oxides that were formerly grouped together under the name psilomelane, which has been applied to several distinct minerals. Although the name psilomelane is no longer used to refer to a particular mineral, it continues to be used as a term of convenience for a group of barium-bearing manganese oxides. Romanèchite specimens are usually fine-grained or fibrous. Crystals are rare; when found, they are prismatic.

Romanèchite forms as an alteration product of other manganese minerals and is an ore of manganese. The mineral also forms in bogs, lakes, and shallow seas. Although romanèchite is named after a French locality, it was first identified at Schneeberg, Saxony, Germany. Other important deposits of romanèchite are at Tekrasni, India; Pilbara, Australia; Cornwall, England; and Hidalgo County, New Mexico, USA.

PROFILE

Hexagonal

⊻ 9

● 4–4.1

▮ None

◪ Conchoidal to uneven

▨ Colorless

⤡ Adamantine to vitreous

Sapphire crystal
This water-worn crystal has a pyramidal form and exhibits the color zoning that is common in sapphire.

color zoning

blue coloring due to traces of titanium

VARIANTS

vitreous luster

Ruby in matrix
Prismatic Kashmir rubies embedded in a rock matrix

Common corundum
An opaque, dipyramidal crystal of common corundum

⚛ Al_2O_3

CORUNDUM

After diamond, corundum is the hardest mineral on Earth. The name corundum comes from the Sanskrit *kuruvinda*, meaning "ruby"—the name given to red corundum. Ruby and sapphire are gem varieties of corundum. An aluminum oxide, corundum is commonly white, gray, or brown, but gem colors include red ruby and blue, green, yellow, orange, violet, and pink sapphire. Colorless forms also occur. Ruby forms a continuous color succession with pink sapphire; only stones of the darker hues are considered to be ruby.

Corundum crystals are generally hexagonal, either tabular, tapering barrel-shaped, or dipyramidal. Corundum can also be massive or granular. It forms in syenites (p.262), certain pegmatites (p.260), and in high-grade metamorphic rocks. It is concentrated in placer deposits.

Antique ruby ring
In this ring, a square-cut ruby has been set at right angles to its square setting.

PROFILE

Cubic

 7 ½–8

3.6–4.1

None

Conchoidal to uneven

White

Vitreous

Spinel octahedrons
In this specimen, octahedral crystals of pleonaste, or black spinel, are set in a quartz matrix.

octahedral spinel crystal

quartz matrix

VARIANTS

Spinel aggregate Numerous ruby spinel crystals

Black spinel A modified octahedron of black spinel on a rock matrix

$MgAl_2O_4$

SPINEL

Spinel is the name of both an individual mineral and of a group of metal-oxide minerals that share the same crystal structure. Minerals in this group include gahnite (p.97), franklinite, and chromite (p.99). Spinel is found as glassy, hard octahedra, or as grains or masses. Although familiar as a blue, purple, red, or pink gemstone, spinel also occurs in other colors. Red spinel is called ruby spinel; its blood-red color is due to the presence of chromium.

A minor constituent of peridotites (p.266), kimberlites (p.269), basalts (p.273), and other igneous rocks, spinel also forms in aluminum-rich schists (pp.291–92) and metamorphosed limestones. Water-worn crystals come from stream deposits. The earliest known spinel dates back to 100 BCE and was discovered near Kabul, Afghanistan.

Spinel gemstone
This superb faceted spinel shows excellent red-lavender color and good clarity.

octahedral crystal

rock matrix

Octahedral gahnite
This blue octahedron of gahnite is
from Franklin, New Jersey, USA.
Other gahnite localities are
Colorado and Maine, USA.

PROFILE

Cubic

 7½–8

4.6

Indistinct

Conchoidal, irregular

Grayish

Vitreous

$ZnAl_2O_4$

GAHNITE

A zinc aluminum oxide, gahnite is a member of the
spinel group and frequently forms the simple octahedral
crystals typical of the group. Crystals usually show
good external form. They may be striated on faces and
cleavage surfaces. Usually dark green or blue to black
in color, they can reach up to 4½ in (12 cm) on an edge.
Crystals can sometimes be gray, yellow, or brown in
color. Gahnite also occurs as irregular grains and
masses, and in some lithium pegmatites (p.260) as
gem-clear nodules.

Gahnite was named in 1807 after the Swedish chemist
and mineralogist John Gottlieb Gahn. It is found in
crystalline schists (pp.291–92) and gneisses (p.288),
in granites (pp.258–59) and granitic pegmatites, and in
contact metamorphosed limestones. It sometimes forms
from the low-grade metamorphism of bauxite (p.101) and
is also found in placer deposits. Superb crystals occur at
Salida and Cotopaxi, Colorado, USA; at Falun, Sweden;
and at Minas Gerais, Brazil.

uneven fracture

submetallic luster

crystal appears octahedral

massive habit

Hausmannite crystals
In this hausmannite specimen, pseudooctahedral crystals rest on a base of massive hausmannite.

PROFILE

Tetragonal

 5½

 4.8

 Perfect

 Uneven

 Reddish brown

 Submetallic

 $Mn^{2+}Mn_2^{3+}O_4$

HAUSMANNITE

Named in 1827 after Johann Friedrich Ludwig Hausmann, a German professor of mineralogy, hausmannite is dark brown or black and is usually granular or massive. Well-formed crystals are uncommon yet distinctive. They are pseudooctahedral in shape but often have additional faces. Small amounts of iron and zinc may substitute for manganese in the hausmannite structure. Hausmannite forms in hydrothermal veins, and it also occurs where manganese-rich rocks have been metamorphosed. It is often found associated with other manganese oxides, such as pyrolusite (p.80), romanéchite (p.94), and the manganese–iron mineral bixbyite. Superb crystals, up to 1½in (4 cm) long, come from Brazil, South Africa, and Germany.

Hausmannite is an ore of manganese, which is added to aluminum and magnesium alloys to improve corrosion resistance. Manganese oxides are important in the manufacture of steel, where they absorb the sulfur in iron ores and impart strength.

PROFILE

Cubic

▽ 5 ½

◓ 4.7

▧ None

◪ Uneven

▧ Brown

⬈ Metallic

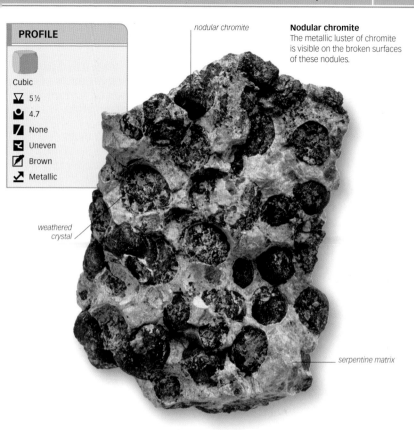

nodular chromite

Nodular chromite
The metallic luster of chromite is visible on the broken surfaces of these nodules.

weathered crystal

serpentine matrix

VARIANT

Massive chromite A glossy black specimen of chromite

 $FeCr_2O_4$

CHROMITE

A member of the spinel mineral group, chromite is an iron chromium oxide and the most important ore of chromium. Crystals are uncommon, but when found they are octahedral. Chromite is usually massive or in the form of lenses and tabular bodies, or it may be disseminated as granules. It is sometimes found as a crystalline inclusion in diamond. Chromite is dark brown to black in color and can contain some magnesium and aluminum.

Chromite is most commonly found as an accessory mineral in iron- and magnesium-rich igneous rocks or concentrated in sediments derived from them. It occurs as layers in a few igneous rocks that are especially rich in iron and magnesium. Almost pure chromite is found in similar layers in sedimentary rocks. The layers are preserved when the sedimentary rocks metamorphose to form serpentinite (p.298). Referred to as chromitites, these rocks are the most important ores of chromium. The weathering of chromite ore bodies can also lead to its concentration in placer deposits.

HYDROXIDES

Hydroxides form when metallic elements combine with a hydroxyl radical. They are found predominantly as weathering products of other minerals. Hydroxide minerals are usually less dense and softer than oxide minerals. Many hydroxides are important ore minerals.

COMPOSITION

Nearly all hydroxides form at low temperatures (up to 400°F/200°C), when water reacts with an oxide. They contain the hydroxyl radical, which is a single chemical unit made up of one atom of hydrogen and one atom of oxygen.

hydrogen ion

octahedron

Crystal structure of diaspore
In the aluminum hydroxide diaspore, aluminum ions are in octahedral coordination with hydroxyl groups, forming strips of octahedra.

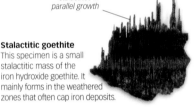

stalactites in parallel growth

Stalactitic goethite
This specimen is a small stalactitic mass of the iron hydroxide goethite. It mainly forms in the weathered zones that often cap iron deposits.

OCCURRENCE AND USES

Hydroxide minerals are found in most places where water has altered primary oxides. Some hydroxides are also precipitated directly. They are often important ore minerals. The aluminum hydroxides diaspore, bohemite, and gibbsite constitute bauxite, the ore of aluminum. Goethite, an iron hydroxide, is an ore of iron.

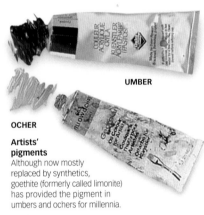

UMBER

OCHER

Artists' pigments
Although now mostly replaced by synthetics, goethite (formerly called limonite) has provided the pigment in umbers and ochers for millennia.

Les-Baux-De-Provence
The mixture of aluminum hydroxide minerals called bauxite is named after the village of Les-Baux-de-Provence in southeastern France, where it was first recognized in 1821.

Pisolitic bauxite
This bauxite specimen shows a classic pisolithic habit, meaning that it is made up of numerous pisoliths—grains up to the size of a pea.

pisolitic structure

pisolith

aluminum oxide matrix

dull to earthy luster

PROFILE

Crystal system None

1–3

2.3–2.7

None

Uneven

Usually white

Earthy

VARIANT

Bauxite as an ore Primary ore of the metal aluminum

Mixture of hydrous aluminum oxides

BAUXITE

Although bauxite is not a mineral, it is one of the most important ores because it is the sole source of aluminum. The product of weathering of aluminum-rich rocks, it contains several constituent minerals. Bauxite is variably creamy yellow, orange, pink, or red because of the presence of quartz (p.168), clays, and hematite (p.91) and other iron oxides in addition to several hydrated aluminum oxides.

Bauxite forms as extensive, shallow deposits in humid tropical environments. It may be nodular, pisolitic, or earthy. Deposits are soft, easily crushed, and textureless or hard, dense, and pealike. Bauxite may also be porous but strong and stratified, or it may retain the form of its parent rock.

Versatile aluminum
A key metal of the modern age, aluminum is used to make products ranging from takeout trays to spacecraft.

PROFILE

Orthorhombic

⊽ 5–5½

◖ 4.3

▧ Perfect

▨ Uneven

▧ Brownish yellow to ocher-red

▧ Adamantine to metallic

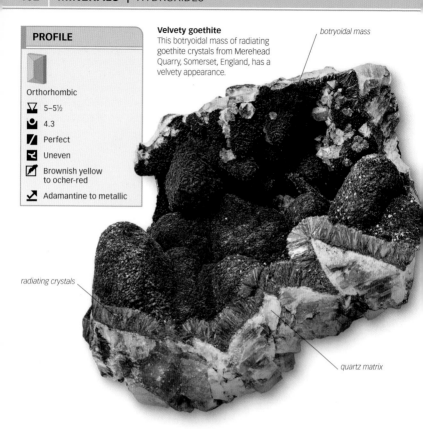

Velvety goethite
This botryoidal mass of radiating goethite crystals from Merehead Quarry, Somerset, England, has a velvety appearance.

botryoidal mass

radiating crystals

quartz matrix

VARIANTS

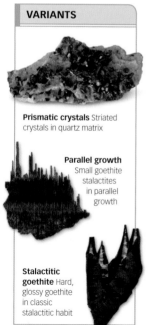

Prismatic crystals Striated crystals in quartz matrix

Parallel growth Small goethite stalactites in parallel growth

Stalactitic goethite Hard, glossy goethite in classic stalactitic habit

♣ FeO(OH)

GOETHITE

Named after the German mineralogist Johann Wolfgang von Goethe in 1806, goethite is a common mineral. It can be brownish yellow, reddish brown, or dark brown in color, depending on the size of the crystal in the specimen—small crystals appear lighter, and larger ones darker. It can occur as opaque black, prismatic and vertically striated crystals; velvety, radiating fibrous aggregates; flattened tablets or scales; and reniform or botryoidal masses. Goethite can also occur in stalactitic or massive forms and in tufts and drusy coatings.

Goethite is an iron oxide hydroxide, although manganese can substitute for up to 5 percent of the iron. It forms as a weathering product in the oxidation zones of veins of iron minerals, such as pyrite (p.62), magnetite (p.92), and siderite (p.123). Goethite may occur with these minerals in the gossan, or iron hat, which is the weathered capping of an iron ore deposit. It also occurs in a form called bog iron ore, which can be produced by living organisms.

PROFILE

Monoclinic

⬙ 4

⬤ 4.3

▨ Perfect, good

◩ Uneven

▧ Reddish brown to black

⬈ Submetallic

Prismatic manganite
This specimen is a mass of pseudoorthorhombic prisms showing typical deep striations on the crystal faces.

flat termination

submetallic luster

striation

uneven fracture

VARIANT

bundles of manganite crystals

Crystal bundles Manganite crystals grouped in bundles

♣ MnO(OH)

MANGANITE

A widespread and important ore of manganese, manganite is hydrated manganese oxide. The mineral had been described by a number of different names since 1772, but was finally given its current name, which it owes to its manganese component, in 1827. Opaque and metallic dark gray or black, crystals of manganite are mostly pseudoorthorhombic prisms, typically with flat or blunt terminations, and are often grouped in bundles and striated lengthwise. Multiple twinning is common. Manganite can also be massive or granular; it is then hard to distinguish by eye from other manganese oxides, such as pyrolusite (p.80).

An important ore of manganese, manganite occurs in hydrothermal deposits formed at low temperature (up to 400°F/200°C) with calcite (p.114), siderite (p.123), and barite (p.134), and in replacement deposits with goethite (p.102). Manganite also occurs in hot-spring manganese deposits. It alters to pyrolusite and may form by the alteration of other manganese minerals.

Dark red diaspore
In this specimen, a mass of dark red, thin, platy diaspore crystals rests in a matrix of corundum.

trace chromium gives lilac color

platy crystal

corundum matrix

Orthorhombic

 6½–7

 3.4

 Perfect, imperfect

 Conchoidal, brittle

White

Vitreous

 AlO(OH)

DIASPORE

Diaspore takes its name from the Greek word *diaspora*, which means "scattering"—a reference to the way diaspore crackles and depreciates under high heat. Its crystals are thin and platy, elongated, tabular, prismatic, or needlelike and are often twinned. Diaspore can be massive or can occur as disseminated grains. It may be colorless, white, grayish white, greenish gray, light brown, yellowish, lilac, or pink in color. The same specimen can appear to have different colors when viewed from different directions.

Diaspore forms in metamorphic rocks, such as schists (p.292) and marbles (p.301), where it is often associated with corundum (p.95), spinel (p.96), and manganite (p.103). It is widespread in bauxite (p.101), laterite (p.326), and aluminous clays.

Faceted gem
Zultanite, which is a rare, transparent type of diaspore crystal from Turkey, is a collector's gem.

PROFILE

Hexagonal

▽ 2½

◘ 2.4

▰ Perfect

▱ Uneven, sectile

▱ White

⤴ Waxy to vitreous/pearly

Fibrous brucite
This fibrous mass of brucite with a vitreous luster is from Timmins, Ontario, Canada.

vitreous luster

fibrous habit

VARIANTS

brucite crystal

Tabular crystals Tabular brucite in a rock matrix

Nemalite A fibrous variety of brucite

▲ $Mg(OH)_2$

BRUCITE

Named after the American mineralogist Archibald Bruce in 1824, brucite is magnesium hydroxide. Usually white, it can be pale green, gray, or blue. Manganese may substitute to some degree for magnesium, producing yellow to red coloration. Its crystals can be tabular or form aggregates of plates. They tend to be soft, and range from waxy to glassy in appearance. Fine large crystals have been collected from nemalite, a variety of brucite that occurs in fibres and laths. Brucite may also occur in massive, foliated, fibrous, or, more rarely, granular habits.

Brucite is found in metamorphic rocks, such as schist (p.292), and in low-temperature hydrothermal veins (up to 400°F/200°C) in marbles (p.301) and chlorite schists. It is used as a primary source of medical magnesia and as a fire retardant.

Kiln lining
Because of its high melting point, brucite is used to line kilns, such as the potter's kiln being used here.

HALIDES

Minerals in this group consist of metals combined with one of the four common halogen elements: fluorine, chlorine, iodine, or bromine. Halides tend to be soft and many crystallize in the cubic system.

COMPOSITION

Compositionally and structurally, there are three broad categories of halide mineral: simple halides, halide complexes, and oxyhydroxy-halides. Simple halides form when a metal combines with a halogen. Halite and fluorite are examples of simple halides. In halide complexes, the halide is usually bound to aluminum, creating a molecule that behaves as a single unit, which is in turn bound to a metal. For example, in cryolite, fluorine and aluminum are bound to sodium. Oxyhydroxy-halides are very rare. Atacamite is an example of these halides.

cubic crystal

Fluorite crystals
Fluorite is an example of a simple halide. It forms octahedral or cubic crystals, and usually forms in hydrothermal veins.

OCCURRENCE

Many halides occur in evaporite deposits. Others occur in hydrothermal veins or form when halide-bearing waters act upon the oxidation products of other minerals.

USES

Halides are important industrial minerals. Halite, or table salt, is the classic example. Other halides are used as fertilizers, in glass making and metal refining, and as minor ores.

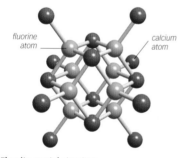

fluorine atom

calcium atom

Fluorite crystal structure
In the crystal structure of fluorite, every calcium atom is coordinated with eight fluorine atoms at the corners of a cube. This yields cubic crystals.

Fertilizing crops
The halides sylvite and carnallite are important sources of potash for fertilizers. Potash reduces many diseases, rot, and mildew of food plants.

Salt Lake
Thick, white crusts of the halide mineral halite encrust rocks along the edge of the Great Salt Lake, Utah, USA.

Granular carnallite
This granular mass of carnallite has a red color due to inclusions of hematite.

granular surface

color due to impurities

PROFILE

Orthorhombic

⛏ 2½

💧 1.6

▨ None

▨ Conchoidal

▨ White

▨ Greasy

$KMgCl_3 \cdot 6H_2O$

CARNALLITE

First discovered in Germany, carnallite was named after Rudolph von Carnall, a Prussian mining engineer, in 1856. It is usually white or colorless but may appear reddish or yellowish depending on the presence of hematite (p.91) or goethite (p.102) impurities. Hydrated potassium and magnesium chloride, carnallite is generally massive to granular in habit. Crystals are rare because they absorb water from the air and dissolve. When found, crystals are thick and tabular, pseudohexagonal, or pyramidal.

Carnallite forms in the upper layers of marine evaporite salt deposits, where it occurs with other potassium and magnesium evaporite minerals. The mineral is Russia's most important source of magnesium. Caustic potash, a potassium hydroxide, is produced from carnallite.

Potash fertilizer
Carnallite is an important source of potash, which is used in fertilizers, and caustic potash.

Cryolite crystals
This mass of translucent cryolite crystals on rock has patches of siderite on it.

greasy luster

nearly cubic crystal

brown siderite

PROFILE

Monoclinic

- 2½
- 3.0
- None
- Uneven
- White
- Vitreous to greasy

VARIANT

pseudocubic outline

greasy luster

Massive cryolite specimen
A close-up of a massive cryolite fragment

Na_3AlF_6

CRYOLITE

Few people have heard of cryolite, but it is one of the most important minerals of our age. Aircraft could not fly without it, and modern engineering of all kinds would be stunted in its absence. Synthetic cryolite is an essential ingredient in aluminum production. The mineral takes its name from the Greek terms *kryos* and *lithos*, which mean "ice" and "stone"—an allusion to its translucent, icelike appearance. Cryolite is usually colorless or white. Rarely it can be brown, yellow, reddish brown, or black. It occurs commonly as coarse, granular, or massive aggregates and rarely, as pseudocubic crystals.

Cryolite forms mainly in certain granites (pp.258–59) and granitic pegmatites (p.260). The largest deposit of cryolite, at Ivigtut, Greenland, is now exhausted. Lesser amounts are found in Spain, Russia, and the USA.

Cryolite in aviation
Synthetic cryolite is used to separate aluminum— an indispensable metal in aviation—from its ores.

Cubic

4

3.0–3.3

Perfect octahedral

Flat conchoidal

White

Vitreous

Twinned crystals
This group of fine, green cubic fluorite crystals exhibits the classic penetration twins, which are typical of this mineral.

zones of purple and green

twinned crystals

cubic habit

iron-stained coating

VARIANTS

Pink octahedron An octahedral crystal of rare pink fluorite

Yellow fluorite A group of bright yellow fluorite cubes

Near-white fluorite
A group of unusually colorless cubes

CaF_2

FLUORITE

An important industrial mineral, fluorite used to be known as fluorspar. The name fluorite comes from the Latin word *fluere*, which means "to flow"—a reference to its use in iron smelting to improve the fluidity of slags and the refining of metals. Fluorite commonly occurs as vibrant, well-formed crystals. A single crystal may have zones of different colors that follow the contour of the crystal faces. Fluorite crystals are widely found in cubes, while fluorite octahedra—which are often twinned—are much less common. The mineral can also be massive, granular, or compact.

Fluorite occurs in hydrothermal deposits and as an accessory mineral in intermediate intrusive and silica-rich rocks. It is used in the manufacture of high-octane fuels and steel and in the production of hydrofluoric acid.

Blue John
Veins of banded purple, white, and yellow fluorite, known as Blue John, are visible in this vessel.

PROFILE

Cubic

⚊ 2½

⚊ 2.1–2.6

⚊ Perfect cubic

⚊ Conchoidal

⚊ White

⚊ Vitreous

cubic crystal

vitreous luster

rock matrix

Halite crystals
In this specimen from Inowroclaw, Poland, cubic crystals of halite cover a rock matrix.

VARIANTS

Cubic halite Twinned, cubic crystals on rock matrix

Massive halite A specimen of massive pink halite

Blue halite
Unusual blue cubic halite on rock

· NaCl

HALITE

Culinary rock salt is actually halite. Its name is derived from the Greek word *hals*, which means "salt." Most halite is colorless, white, gray, orange, or brown, but it can also be bright blue or purple. The orange color comes from inclusions of hematite (p.91), while the blue and purple colors indicate defects in the crystal structure. Halite is commonly found in massive and bedded aggregates as rock salt. It also occurs in coarse, crystalline masses or in granular and compact forms.

Halite crystals are usually cubic. Sometimes, halite may form "hopper" crystals—in which the outer edges of the cube faces have grown more rapidly than their centers, leaving cavernous faces. It is widespread in saline evaporite deposits.

Table salt
Mined since ancient times and also used as a currency, common table salt is the mineral halite.

interlocking
cubic crystal

transparent at
crystal margin

vitreous luster

PROFILE

Cubic

2½

2.0

Perfect cubic

Uneven

White

Vitreous

Sylvite crystals
The pinkish, interlocking, cubic
crystals in this specimen are
typical of sylvite.

VARIANT

Sylvite in potash A specimen
of massive potash containing
the mineral sylvite

KCl

SYLVITE

Millions of tons of sylvite are mined annually for the
manufacture of potassium compounds, such as potash
fertilizers. Sylvite is also used to manufacture metallic
potassium. The mineral was first discovered in 1823 on
Mount Vesuvius, Italy, where it occurs as encrustations
on lava. The name sylvite comes from its Latin medicinal
name, *sal digestivus Sylvii*, which means "digestive salt,"
and it is also known as sylvine. Usually colorless to white or
grayish, sylvite can be tinged
blue, yellow, purple, or red. Sylvite
crystals are cubic, octahedral,
or both. It commonly occurs as
crusts and as columnar, granular,
or massive aggregates.

Sylvite is found in thick beds
either mixed or interbedded with
halite (p.110), gypsum (p.136), and
other evaporite minerals, although
it is rarer than halite.

Sylvite fertilizer
Crushed potash, as seen
here, is used as a fertilizer
and comes from the
mineral sylvite.

PROFILE

Tetragonal

1–2

6.5

Distinct

Conchoidal

Pale yellow-white

Adamantine

rock matrix

yellowish crust
of calomel

Calomel encrustations
A thin crust of yellowish calomel
crystals coats a rock matrix
in this specimen.

VARIANT

black
calomel
crystal

Calomel in matrix Crystals
of black calomel in a
rock matrix

A HgCl

CALOMEL

A mercury chloride, calomel takes its name from two
Greek words: *ómorfi*, which means "beautiful," and *méli*,
which means "honey"—an allusion to its sweet taste,
although it is, in fact, toxic. Calomel is also referred to as
horn quicksilver and horn mercury. Specimens are soft,
heavy, and plasticlike, with crystals that are pyramidal,
tabular, or prismatic, often with complex twinning. Calomel
is also found as crusts and can be massive and earthy.
It fluoresces brick red.

Calomel occurs as a secondary mineral in the oxidized
zones of mercury-bearing deposits, together with native
mercury, cinnabar (p.56), goethite (p.102), and calcite (p.114).
It was used as a laxative and a disinfectant as well as in
the treatment of syphilis from the 16th century until the
early 20th century, when the toxic effect of its mercury
component was discovered. Calomel's use as a teething
powder in Britain was suspended only in 1954, following
widespread poisoning. It is still used as an ore of mercury
and in insecticides and fungicides.

CARBONATES

There are approximately 80 known carbonate minerals. Most of them are rare, but the common carbonates calcite and dolomite are major rock-forming minerals. Carbonates form rhombohedral crystals and are soft, soluble in hydrochloric acid, and often vividly colored.

COMPOSITION

All carbonates contain the carbonate group CO_3 as the basic compositional and structural unit. This group has a carbon atom in the center of an equilateral triangle of oxygen atoms, giving rise to the trigonal symmetry of many carbonate minerals. This basic unit is joined by one or more metals or semimetals such as calcium, sodium, aluminum, manganese, barium, zinc, and copper.

OCCURRENCE

Calcite and dolomite are found in sediments such as chalk and limestone. They also occur in seashells and coral reefs, in evaporate deposits, and in metamorphic rocks, such as marble. Other carbonates, such as rhodochrosite, azurite, and malachite, are principally secondary minerals.

USES

The carbonate minerals calcite and dolomite are important in the manufacture of cement and building stone. Other carbonates find uses as ores of metals: witherite of barium; strontianite of strontium; siderite of iron; rhodochrosite of manganese; smithsonite of zinc; and cerussite of lead.

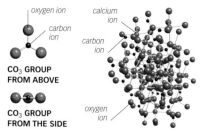

oxygen ion

carbon ion

calcium ion

carbon ion

oxygen ion

CO_3 GROUP FROM ABOVE

CO_3 GROUP FROM THE SIDE

Calcite crystal structure
In calcite, three oxygen ions surround each carbon ion in a CO_3 group. Each calcium ion combines with six oxygen ions to form an octahedron.

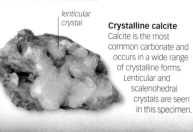

lenticular crystal

Crystalline calcite
Calcite is the most common carbonate and occurs in a wide range of crystalline forms. Lenticular and scalenohedral crystals are seen in this specimen.

intricate growth pattern

Malachite jewel box
The copper carbonate malachite has been a favorite carving stone for three millennia.

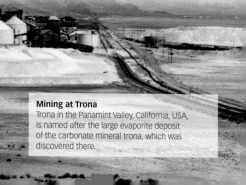

Mining at Trona
Trona in the Panamint Valley, California, USA, is named after the large evaporite deposit of the carbonate mineral trona, which was discovered there.

PROFILE

Hexagonal

3

2.7

Perfect rhombohedral

Subconchoidal, brittle

White

Vitreous

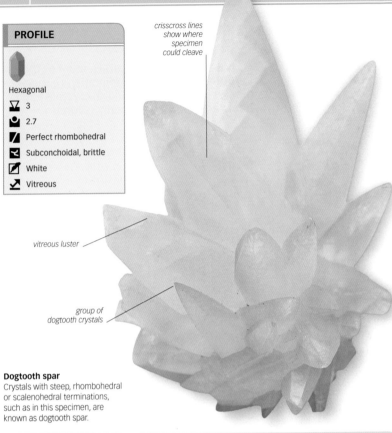

crisscross lines show where specimen could cleave

vitreous luster

group of dogtooth crystals

Dogtooth spar
Crystals with steep, rhombohedral or scalenohedral terminations, such as in this specimen, are known as dogtooth spar.

VARIANTS

Butterfly twin A twinned, pink crystal of calcite

Nailhead spar A rhombohedral calcite crystal on galena

Scalenohedron
A single scalenohedral calcite crystal

 $CaCO_3$

CALCITE

The most common form of calcium carbonate, calcite is known for the variety and beautiful development of its crystals. These occur most often as scalenohedra and are commonly twinned, sometimes forming heart-shaped, butterfly twins. Crystals with rhombohedral terminations are also common; those with shallow rhombohedral terminations are called nailhead spar. Highly transparent calcite is called optical spar.

Although calcite can form spectacular crystals, it is usually massive, occurring either as marble (p.301) or as limestone (p.319). It is also found as fibers, nodules, stalactites, and earthy aggregates. Calcite specimens can occur in metamorphic deposits, igneous rocks, and hydrothermal veins.

Alabaster sphinx
Virtually all ancient Egyptian "alabaster," such as that used to make this small sphinx, was actually calcite.

semitransparent crystal

radiating habit

prismatic crystal

PROFILE

Orthorhombic

3½–4

2.9

Distinct

Subconchoidal, brittle

White

Vitreous inclining to resinous

Pseudohexagonal crystals
This specimen consists of a radiating group of prismatic, semitransparent, pseudohexagonal, twinned aragonite crystals.

VARIANTS

Intergrown crystals A mass of pseudohexagonal crystals of aragonite

Flos ferri
Coral-like aragonite crystals on rock matrix

Cyclic twin
A classic aragonite cyclic twin from Spain

$CaCO_3$

ARAGONITE

Although aragonite has the same chemical composition as calcite (p.114), its crystals are different. They are tabular, prismatic, or needlelike, often with steep pyramidal or chisel-shaped ends, and can form columnar or radiating aggregates. Multiple twinned crystals are common, appearing hexagonal in shape. Although aragonite sometimes looks similar to calcite, it is easily distinguished by the absence of rhombohedral cleavage. Specimens can be white, colorless, gray, yellowish, green, blue, reddish, violet, or brown.

Aragonite is found in the oxidized zones of ore deposits and in evaporites, hot spring deposits, and caves. It is also found in some metamorphic and igneous rocks. Banded stalactitic aragonite can be polished as an ornamental stone.

Mother of pearl
Aragonite is also produced by some living animals. It is seen here forming the inner layer of a marine mollusk shell.

twinned crystals

galena

rock matrix

Witherite crystals
This specimen contains a group of witherite crystals and galena on a rock matrix.

PROFILE	
Orthorhombic	
	3–3½
	4.3
	Distinct, imperfect
	Uneven, brittle
	White
	Vitreous

 $BaCO_3$

WITHERITE

This barium carbonate was named in 1790 after the English mineralogist William Withering. Witherite is white, colorless, or tinged yellow, brown, or green. Its crystals are always twinned, either as prisms which appear hexagonal in shape, or as pyramids, which are frequently paired. They can also be short to long prismatic or tabular and may have striations running across the prism faces. Witherite can also be fibrous, botryoidal, spherular, columnar, granular, or massive.

Most witherite comes from hydrothermal veins formed at low temperatures (up to 400°F/200°C), usually resulting from the alteration of baryte (p.134). Specimens feel relatively heavy for their size due to the presence of the high-density element barium. Witherite is preferred over the commonly found barium mineral barite for the preparation of other barium compounds because it is more soluble in acids. These compounds are used in case-hardening steel, in copper refining, in sugar refining, in vacuum tubes, and in many other applications.

PROFILE

Hexagonal

3½–4

2.8–2.9

Perfect rhombohedral

Subconchoidal

White

Vitreous

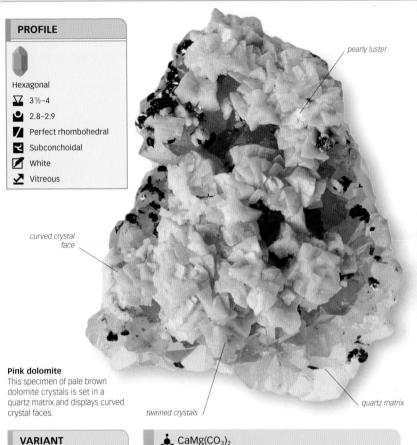

pearly luster

curved crystal face

twinned crystals

quartz matrix

Pink dolomite
This specimen of pale brown dolomite crystals is set in a quartz matrix and displays curved crystal faces.

VARIANT

saddle-shaped crystal

Tabular crystals Pink, saddle-shaped, tabular crystals of dolomite in a crustlike form

$CaMg(CO_3)_2$

DOLOMITE

An important rock-forming mineral, dolomite is named after the French mineralogist Déodat Gratet de Dolomieu. It is a colorless to white, pale brown, grayish, reddish, or pink mineral. Its crystals are commonly rhombohedral or tabular, often have curved faces, and sometimes cluster in saddle-shaped aggregates. Dolomite may be striated horizontally and twinned. Some crystals may be up to 2 in (5 cm) long. It can also be coarse to fine granular, massive, and, rarely, fibrous.

Dolomite is the main constituent in dolomite rocks and dolomitic marbles. It occurs as a replacement deposit in limestone (p.319) affected by magnesium-bearing solutions, in talc schists, and in other magnesium-rich metamorphic rocks. Dolomite is found in hydrothermal veins associated with lead, zinc, and copper ores. It is also found in altered, silica-poor igneous rocks, in some carbonatites (p.272), and in serpentinites (p.298). Crystals of dolomite frequently form in cavities in limestone and marble (p.301).

PROFILE

Hexagonal

⬙ 4

⬙ 3.0

▨ Perfect rhombohedral

◪ Conchoidal, brittle

▨ White

↗ Vitreous

coarse crystalline habit

perfect rhombohedral cleavage

Magnesite crystals
This crystalline mass of magnesite is on a rock matrix.

VARIANT

Rhombohedral magnesite
Rare, rhombohedral crystals of the colorless form of magnesite

⚛ $MgCO_3$

MAGNESITE

This carbonate of magnesium takes its name from its magnesium component. It is generally massive, lamellar, fibrous, chalky, or granular. Distinct crystals are rare, but when found they are either rhombohedral or prismatic. Most commonly white or light gray, magnesite can be yellow or brownish when iron substitutes for some of the magnesium.

Magnesite forms mainly as an alteration product in magnesium-rich rocks, such as peridotites (p.266). It can occur as a primary mineral in limestones (p.319) and talc or chlorite schists, in cavities in volcanic rocks, and in oceanic salt deposits. It is also found in some meteorites (pp.335–37). An important source of magnesium, magnesite is used as a refractory material, as a catalyst and filler in the production of synthetic rubber, and in the manufacture of chemicals and fertilizers. Magnesium derived from magnesite is alloyed with aluminum, zinc, or manganese for use in aircraft, spacecraft, road vehicles, and household appliances.

Tabular crystals
In this specimen, a mass of tabular cerussite crystals covers a rock matrix.

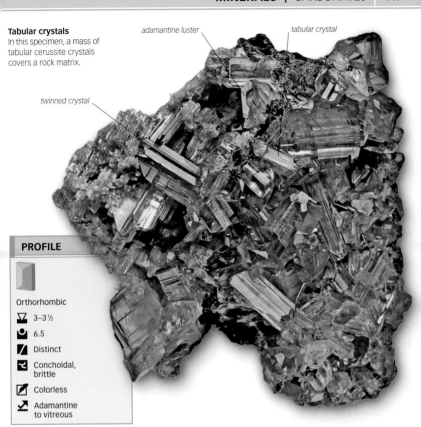

adamantine luster

tabular crystal

twinned crystal

Orthorhombic

3–3½

6.5

Distinct

Conchoidal, brittle

Colorless

Adamantine to vitreous

VARIANTS

Cyclic twin A star-shaped, crystalline specimen of cerussite from Zambia

Jack-straw cerussite Delicate, needlelike crystals of jack-straw cerussite

Prismatic crystal A striated, colorless, prismatic crystal of cerussite

$PbCO_3$

CERUSSITE

Known since antiquity, cerussite is named after the Latin word *cerussa,* which describes a white lead pigment. After galena (p.54), it is the most common ore of lead. Cerussite is generally colorless or white to gray, but may be blue to green due to copper impurities. Its crystal habits are highly varied. Cerussite forms tabular or pyramidal crystals or, sometimes, twins that may be star-shaped or reticulated (netlike) masses. Fragile aggregates of randomly grown prismatic crystals known as jack-straw cerussite are also common. The adamantine luster of cerussite crystals is particularly bright.

A widespread secondary mineral that occurs in the oxidation zones of lead veins, cerussite is formed by the action of carbonated water on other lead minerals, particularly galena and anglesite (p.132).

Collector's gem
Faceted cerussite stones, such as this rare gem, are brilliant but too soft to be worn.

PROFILE

Monoclinic

⬦ 3½–4

● 3.8

◣ Perfect

◪ Conchoidal, brittle

◩ Blue

⬈ Vitreous to dull earthy

Large crystals
In this specimen of azurite, large, well-formed crystals rest on a goethite matrix.

vitreous luster

goethite matrix

blocky, azure-blue crystal

VARIANTS

Bladed crystal A single, bladed azurite crystal

Tabular crystals Thin, parallel azurite crystals on a rock matrix

Radiating crystals
A spherical concretion of azurite

$Cu_3(CO_3)_2(OH)_2$

AZURITE

A deep blue copper carbonate hydroxide, azurite was used as a blue pigment in 15th- to 17th-century European art and probably in the production of blue glaze in ancient Egypt. It takes its name from the Persian word *lazhuward*, which means "blue." Azurite forms either tabular or prismatic crystals with a wide variety of habits. Tabular crystals commonly have wedge-shaped terminations. Azurite forms rosette-shaped crystalline aggregates or occurs in massive, stalactitic, or botryoidal forms. Well-developed crystals are dark azure blue in color, but massive or earthy aggregates may be paler.

Azurite is a secondary mineral formed in the oxidized portions of copper deposits. Massive azurite used for ornamental purposes is sometimes called chessylite, after Chessy, France.

Cabochon gemstone
This cabochon exhibits the vivid blue color of azurite and the green color of malachite.

PROFILE

Hexagonal

3½–4

3.6

Perfect rhombohedral

Uneven

White

Vitreous to pearly

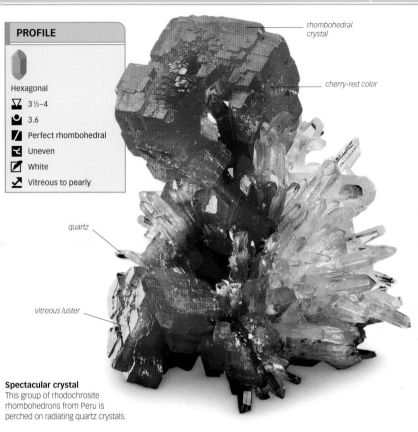

rhombohedral crystal

cherry-red color

quartz

vitreous luster

Spectacular crystal
This group of rhodochrosite rhombohedrons from Peru is perched on radiating quartz crystals.

VARIANTS

Classic crystals
Rhombohedral rhodochrosite in classic rose-pink color

Red rhodochrosite Bright, cherry-red color typical of many manganese minerals

$MnCO_3$

RHODOCHROSITE

A prized collectors' mineral, rhodochrosite is a manganese carbonate. It was given its name—derived from the Greek *rhodokhros*, which means "of rosy color"—in 1800. Rhodochrosite has a classic rose-pink color, but specimens can also be brown or gray. It forms dogtooth or rhombohedral crystals like calcite (p.114), but it may also occur in stalactitic, granular, nodular, botryoidal, and massive habits.

Rhodochrosite is found in hydrothermal ore veins with sphalerite (p.53), galena (p.54), fluorite (p.109), and manganese oxides. It also occurs in metamorphic deposits and as a secondary mineral in sedimentary manganese deposits. Abundant at Butte, Montana, and other localities, rhodochrosite is sometimes mined as an ore of manganese.

Rhodochrosite carvings
These two decorative ducks were carved from banded rhodochrosite and white calcite.

Ankerite rhombohedra
This group of ankerite rhombohedra is set in a rock matrix.

twinned crystals

rock matrix

rhombohedral crystal

perfect cleavage

PROFILE

Hexagonal

 3½–4

 2.9

 Perfect

Subconchoidal

White

Vitreous to pearly

 Ca(Fe,Mg,Mn,)(CO$_3$)$_2$

ANKERITE

Considered a rock-forming mineral, ankerite is calcium carbonate with varying amounts of iron, magnesium, and manganese in its structure. It was named in 1825 after the Austrian mineralogist M.J. Anker. Although usually pale buff in color, ankerite can be colorless, white, gray, or brownish. Much ankerite becomes dark on weathering, and many specimens are fluorescent. Ankerite forms rhombohedral crystals similar to those of dolomite (p.117), often with similarly curved faces forming saddle-shaped groups; it can also form prismatic crystals. However, ankerite is more commonly massive or coarsely granular.

Ankerite forms as a secondary mineral from the action of iron- and magnesium-bearing fluids on limestone (p.319) or dolomite rock (p.320). It is a waste mineral in hydrothermal ore deposits and also occurs in carbonatites (p.272), low-grade metamorphosed ironstones, and banded ironstone formations (p.329). Ankerite is also found in iron ore deposits with siderite (p.123).

PROFILE

Hexagonal

⬚ 3½–4

⬛ 3.9

⬛ Perfect rhombohedral

⬛ Uneven or subconchoidal

⬛ White

⬛ Vitreous to pearly

Rhombohedral crystals
This group of well-formed siderite rhombohedra with many twinned crystals rests on a rock matrix.

rhombohedral crystal

pearly luster

twinned crystals

quartz

VARIANTS

Botryoidal siderite Grapelike siderite bunches on a base of massive siderite

Single crystal A large, rhombohedral, single crystal of siderite

♦ FeCO₃

SIDERITE

An ore of iron, siderite takes its name from the Greek word *sideros*, which means "iron." Formerly known as chalybite, siderite can form rhombohedral crystals, often with curved surfaces. The mineral can also form scalenohedral, tabular, or prismatic crystals. Single crystals up to 6 in (15 cm) long are found in Quebec, Canada. However, siderite is more commonly massive or granular and sometimes botryoidal or globular in habit.

A widespread mineral, siderite occurs in igneous, sedimentary, and metamorphic rocks. In sedimentary rocks, siderite occurs in concretions (p.333) and in thin beds with coal (p.253) seams, shale (p.313), and clay. Well-formed crystals are found in hydrothermal metallic veins and in some granitic and syenitic pegmatites (p.260). An outcrop of siderite originally mined for iron by American colonists is still visible at Roxbury, Connecticut. Rare transparent siderite is sometimes cut as gemstones for collectors.

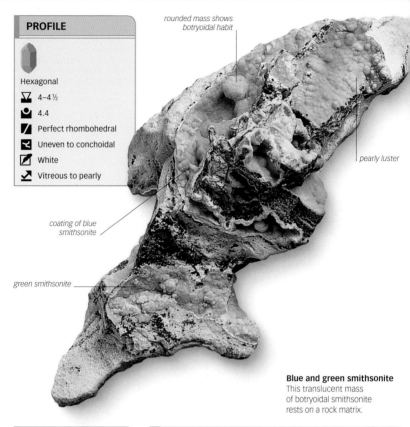

PROFILE

Hexagonal

4–4½

4.4

Perfect rhombohedral

Uneven to conchoidal

White

Vitreous to pearly

rounded mass shows botryoidal habit

pearly luster

coating of blue smithsonite

green smithsonite

Blue and green smithsonite
This translucent mass of botryoidal smithsonite rests on a rock matrix.

VARIANT

White smithsonite A mass of earthy smithsonite on a rock matrix

$ZnCo_3$

SMITHSONITE

An ore of zinc that continues to be frequently mined, smithsonite may have provided the zinc component of brass in ancient metallurgy. Specimens can be of various colors, such as yellow, orange, brown, pink, lilac, white, gray, green, and blue. Although smithsonite rarely forms crystals, when found, they are prismatic, rhombohedral, or scalenohedral and often have curved faces. A zinc carbonate, smithsonite commonly occurs as massive, botryoidal, spherular, or stalactitic masses, or sometimes, as honeycombed aggregates called dry-bone ore.

Smithsonite is a common mineral, found in the oxidation zones of many zinc ore deposits and in adjacent calcareous rocks. It is often found with malachite (p.125), azurite (p.120), pyromorphite (p.151), cerussite (p.119), and hemimorphite (p.227).

Cabochon
Soft smithsonite is occasionally cut into cabochon gemstones for collectors.

Botryoidal malachite
This specimen of malachite on chrysocolla is from Etoile du Congo Mine in Katanga province, Congo.

rock matrix

botryoidal habit

chrysocolla

VARIANTS

Fibrous malachite
A radiating group of fibrous malachite crystals

Stalactitic malachite
A group of radiating, fibrous malachite crystals

Malachite section
A section cut through a malachite stalactite

$Cu_2CO_3(OH)_2$

MALACHITE

Possibly the earliest ore of copper, malachite is believed to have been mined in the Sinai and eastern deserts of ancient Egypt from as early as 3000 BCE. Single crystals are uncommon; when found, they are short to long prisms. Malachite is usually found as botryoidal or encrusting masses, often with a radiating fibrous structure and banded in various shades of green. It also occurs as delicate fibrous aggregates and as concentrically banded stalactites.

Malachite occurs in the altered zones of copper deposits, where it is usually accompanied by lesser amounts of azurite (p.120). It is primarily valued as an ornamental material and gemstone. Single masses that weighed up to 51 tons were found in the Ural Mountains of Russia in the 19th century.

Polished malachite
This specimen of the mineral malachite has been polished to show dark and light color bands.

BORATES

Borate minerals are compounds containing boron and oxygen. Most borate minerals are rare, but a few, such as borax, ulexite, colemanite, and kernite, form large, commercially mined deposits. Borates tend to be soft and either white or colorless.

COMPOSITION

Structurally, boron and oxygen may form a triangle (BO_3) or a tetrahedron (BO_4), each with a boron atom. These structures act as a single chemical unit that bonds to a metal, such as sodium in borax and calcium in colemanite. Borates tend to contain water molecules or a hydroxyl (OH) group, which acts as a chemical unit bonded into their structure. Some borates contain both.

silky luster

crystals have translucent ends

Ulexite
This is a classic evaporite borate. A hydrous sodium calcium borate, ulexite can form parallel, fibrous crystals that act as fiberoptics when viewed from an end.

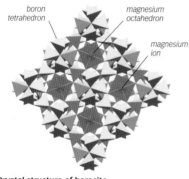

boron tetrahedron

magnesium octahedron

magnesium ion

Crystal structure of boracite
In boracite, densely packed boron tetrahedra combine with the metals magnesium and iron (not shown). The borate radical is in the form of tetrahedra.

OCCURRENCE AND USES

Borates appear in two geologic environments. In the first, borate-bearing solutions that result from volcanic activity flow into a closed basin, where evaporation takes place. Basin deposits usually occur in desert regions, such as the Mojave Desert and Death Valley in California. Borax, ulexite, and colemanite occur in these evaporate deposits. In the second environment, borate minerals are formed as a result of rocks being altered by heat and pressure at relatively high temperatures (1,065°F/575°C or above).

Borates are used as pottery glazes, solvents for metal-oxide slags in metallurgy, welding fluxes, fertilizer additives, soap supplements, and water softeners.

Fireworks
Boron carbide is used to give a green color to fireworks, in place of the toxic barium compounds that were once used.

Borax crust
This crust formed at the edge of Searles Lake in southern California, USA, is principally composed of borax, a borate produced by evaporation.

Borax crystals
This group of prismatic borax crystals coated with an opaque layer of tincalconite is set on a rock matrix.

prismatic crystal

coating of white tincalconite

rock matrix

PROFILE

Monoclinic

 2–2½

 1.7

 Perfect, imperfect

 Conchoidal

White

Vitreous to earthy

$Na_2B_4O_5(OH)_4 \cdot 8H_2O$

BORAX

An important source of boron, borax has been mined since ancient times. A hydrated sodium borate, borax's colorless crystals dehydrate in air to become the chalky mineral tincalconite. Specimens can also be white, gray, pale green, or pale blue. Borax has short prismatic to tabular crystals, although in commercial deposits it is predominantly massive.

Borax is an evaporite formed in dry lake beds with halite (p.110) and other borates and evaporite sulfates and carbonates. It is used in metal-casting and steel-making. Molten borax beads were historically used to test the composition of other minerals—powdered minerals were fused with the beads, and color change in the beads revealed what the minerals contained.

Boron soap
Compounds derived from borax and, to a lesser extent, ulexite, are key components of many soaps.

PROFILE

Monoclinic

⊻ 2½

◓ 2.0

▮ Perfect

◪ Uneven

▧ White

↗ Vitreous to silky

parallel, needlelike crystals

Ulexite slice
This ulexite specimen has a fibrous structure and has been sliced and polished to show its fiberoptic effect.

transparent face

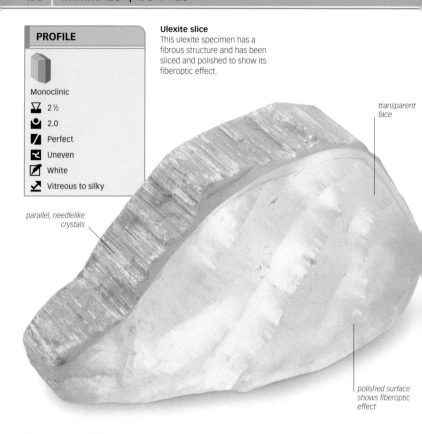

polished surface shows fiberoptic effect

VARIANT

Fibrous crystals Parallel, fibrous ulexite crystals with a silky luster

♣ NaCaB$_5$O$_6$(OH)$_6$·H$_2$O

ULEXITE

An important economic borate mineral, ulexite is named after the German chemist George Ludwig Ulex, who determined its composition in 1850. It is either colorless or white and has a number of habits. It is commonly found in nodular, rounded, or lenslike crystal aggregates, which often resemble balls of cotton. Less commonly, ulexite is found in dense veins of parallel fibers known as television stone because the fibers transmit light from one end of the crystal to the other. Ulexite also occurs in radiating or compact aggregates of crystals.

Ulexite is found in playa lakes and other evaporite basins in deserts, where it is derived from hot, boron-rich fluids. The mineral commonly occurs with colemanite (p.130), anhydrite (p.133), and glauberite (p.141).

Television stone
An unusual property of the form of ulexite shown above is its ability to "transmit" images.

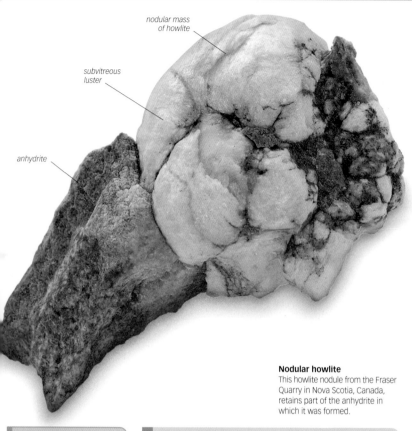

nodular mass of howlite

subvitreous luster

anhydrite

Nodular howlite
This howlite nodule from the Fraser Quarry in Nova Scotia, Canada, retains part of the anhydrite in which it was formed.

PROFILE

Monoclinic

 3½

 2.6

 None

Conchoidal to uneven

White

Subvitreous

$Ca_2B_5SiO_9(OH)_5$

HOWLITE

Named in 1868 after the Canadian chemist, geologist, and mineralogist Henry How, howlite is a calcium borosilicate hydroxide. It generally forms cauliflowerlike nodular masses. The nodules are white, with fine gray or black veins of other minerals running across in an erratic, often weblike pattern. Crystals are rare, but when found they are tabular and seldom exceed ³/₈ in (1 cm) in length. When dyed, howlite specimens resemble and are sometimes sold as turquoise (p.154), although they are easily distinguished by their inferior hardness and lighter color.

Howlite usually occurs associated with other boron minerals, such as kernite and borax (p.127). It is easily fused and is used to make carvings, jewelry components, and other decorative items.

Stained howlite
This tumble-polished and dyed or stained piece of howlite looks similar to turquoise.

vitreous luster

prismatic structure

translucent crystal

Complex crystals
Colemanite commonly occurs as colorless, brilliant, and complex crystals, as in this specimen.

PROFILE

Monoclinic

 4–4½

 2.4

 Perfect, distinct

 Uneven to subconchoidal

 White

Vitreous to adamantine

$CaB_3O_4(OH)_3 \cdot H_2O$

COLEMANITE

An important source of boron, colemanite was named in 1884 after William Coleman, the owner of the mine in California where it was discovered. It is colorless, white, yellowish white, or gray. Colemanite occurs as short prismatic or equant crystals in nodules or as granular or coarse, massive aggregates. It is usually massive in commercial deposits, but individual crystals up to 8 in (20 cm) long have also been found.

Colemanite is found in playas and other evaporite deposits, where it replaces other borate minerals, such as borax (p.127) and ulexite (p.128), which were originally deposited in huge inland lakes. Borosilicates derived from colemanite and other minerals are used to make glass that is resistant to chemicals, electricity, and heat.

Heat-resistant glass
Borosilicate glass is used in car headlights, laboratory glassware, ovenware, and industrial equipment.

SULFATES, MOLYBDATES, CHROMATES, AND TUNGSTATES

Sulphates, molybdates, chromates, and tungstates share similar structures and chemical behavior. Sulfates are soft and lightweight, chromates are rare and brightly colored, and tungstates and molybdates are dense, hard, brittle, and vividly colored.

COMPOSITION

Sulfate minerals have a tetrahedral crystal structure, with four oxygen atoms at each corner and a sulfur atom in the center. The sulfate tetrahedron behaves chemically as a single, negatively charged radical or unit. All sulfates contain an SO_4 group.

The basic structural unit of the chromates, molybdates, and tungstates is also a tetrahedron formed from four oxygen atoms, with a central chromium (Cr), molybdenum (Mo), or tungsten (W) atom, respectively. The chromate minerals all contain a CrO_4 group, the molybdates an MoO_4 group, and the tungstates a WO_4 group.

Barite crystals
This large group of tabular barite crystals is from the Wet Grooves mine, Yorkshire, England. Barite has important industrial and medicinal uses.

vitreous luster

tabular crystal

OCCURRENCE

Sulfates, such as gypsum, occur in evaporite deposits; others, such as barite, mainly occur in hydrothermal veins. Many tungstates are found in hydrothermal veins and pegmatites. Chromates and molybdates are often found as secondary minerals.

USES

The sulfates gypsum and barite are major industrial minerals. Chromates, tungstates, and molybdates are rare but when found concentrated are important ores of the metals they contain.

sulfur atom

oxygen atom

SULFATE

chromium atom

oxygen atom

CHROMATE

molybdenum atom

oxygen atom

MOLYBDATE

tungsten atom

oxygen atom

TUNGSTATE

Crystal structure
Tetrahedra are the structural basis of the sulfates, chromates, tungstates, and molybdates. The central metal atom gives each group its name.

Plaster cast
About 75 percent of the calcium sulfate gypsum that is mined is used to make plaster of Paris. Most is used for wallboards, but some finds medical uses, such as making plaster casts.

Mineral-rich Madagascar
The island of Madagascar is rich in minerals. It is a prime locality for rich, blue crystals of the sulfate celestine, which is mostly mined for collectors.

PROFILE

Orthorhombic

- 2½–3
- 6.4
- Good, distinct
- Conchoidal, brittle
- Colorless
- Adamantine to resinous, vitreous

rock matrix

prismatic crystal

Anglesite crystals
These striated prismatic crystals of anglesite are on a rock matrix with galena.

galena

VARIANTS

Pyramidal crystal A pointed crystal of anglesite with galena

adamantine luster

Single crystal A crystal of anglesite that has an adamantine luster

PbSO$_4$

ANGLESITE

Named in 1832 after the large deposit of this mineral found on the island of Anglesey in Wales, anglesite is colorless to white, grayish, yellow, green, or blue and often fluoresces yellow under ultraviolet light. It commonly occurs in massive, granular, or compact forms. It has a number of crystal habits: thin to thick tabular, prismatic, pseudorhombohedral, and pyramidal with striations along the length. Exceptionally large crystals—up to 31 in (80 cm) long—have been found.

Used since ancient times as an ore of lead, anglesite forms in the oxidation zones of lead deposits. It is an alteration product of galena (p.54), formed when galena comes into contact with sulfate solutions. Anglesite is sometimes found in concentric layers with a core of unaltered galena.

Oval-cut anglesite
Anglesite is soft and easily cleaved. It is one of the stones used to test the skills of master gem cutters.

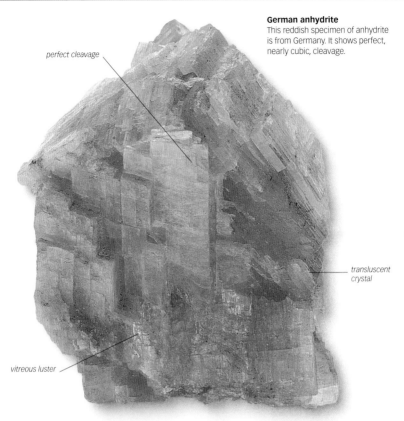

German anhydrite
This reddish specimen of anhydrite is from Germany. It shows perfect, nearly cubic, cleavage.

perfect cleavage

transluscent crystal

vitreous luster

PROFILE

Orthorhombic

 3½

3.0

 Perfect, good

Uneven to splintery

White

Vitreous to pearly

 CaSO$_4$

ANHYDRITE

An important rock-forming mineral, anhydrite is a calcium sulfate. It takes its name from the Greek word *anhydrous*, which means "without water." Anhydrite is usually colorless to white. Specimens can also be brownish, reddish, or grayish or pale shades of pink, blue, or violet. Individual crystals are uncommon, but when found they are blocky or thick tabular. Crystals up to 4 in (10 cm) long come from Swiss deposits. Anhydrite is usually massive, granular, or coarsely crystalline.

Anhydrite is one of the major minerals in evaporite deposits and commonly occurs in salt deposits associated with halite (p.110) and gypsum (p.136). It alters to gypsum in humid conditions. Anhydrite is often a constituent of cap rocks above salt domes that act as reservoirs for natural oil. It also occurs in volcanic fumaroles and in seafloor hydrothermal "chimneys." Anhydrite is used in fertilizers and as a drying agent in plasters, cement, paints, and varnishes.

PROFILE

Orthorhombic

3–3½

4.5

Perfect

Uneven

White

Vitreous, pearly, resinous

Barite crystals
This large group of tabular barite crystals is from the Wet Grooves Mine in Yorkshire, England.

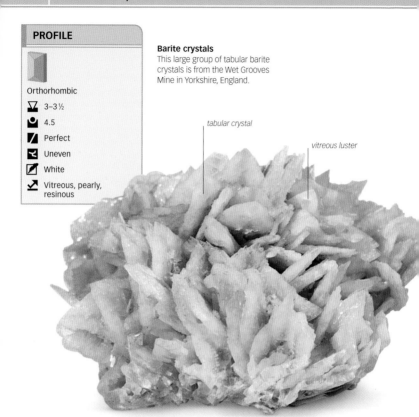

tabular crystal

vitreous luster

VARIANTS

cockscomb

Cockscomb White cockscomb barite resting on sphalerite

Prismatic crystals
A group of yellow prismatic barite crystals

Stalagmite section
Barite in a stalagmitic form

$BaSO_4$

BARITE

The barium sulfate barite takes its name from the Greek word *barys*, which means "heavy"—a reference to its high specific gravity. It has also been called heavy spar. Barite crystals are sometimes tinged yellow, blue, or brown. Golden barite comes from South Dakota. Crystals are well formed, usually either prismatic or tabular. Cockscomb (crested aggregates) and desert roses (rosette aggregates) of crystals are common. Transparent, blue barite crystals may resemble aquamarine but are distinguished by their softness, heaviness, and crystal shape. Barite can also be stalactitic, stalagmitic, fibrous, concretionary, or massive.

Barite is a common accessory mineral in lead and zinc veins. It is also found in sedimentary rocks, clay deposits, marine deposits, and cavities in igneous rocks.

Barite gemstone
Although transparent barite is soft and difficult to cut, it is sometimes faceted for collectors.

Orthorhombic

3–3½

4.0

Perfect

Uneven

White

Vitreous, pearly on cleavage

Celestine crystals
This superbly crystallized specimen of blue celestine crystals is from Madagascar. The largest crystal is more than 1 ½ in (3.5 cm) long.

vitreous luster

large, tabular crystal

blue coloration

small celestine crystals

granular celestine

VARIANTS

Colorless celestine
Prismatic, colorless crystals on a sulfur matrix

Single crystal A light blue prismatic crystal of celestine

$SrSO_4$

CELESTINE

Often light blue in color, celestine takes its name from the Latin word *coelestis*, which means "heavenly"—an allusion to the color of the sky. Specimens can also be colorless, white, light red, green, medium to dark blue, or brown. Celestine crystals are commonly more than 4 in (10 cm) long. Well-formed, transparent, light- to medium-blue, tabular crystals are common, and some have been known to reach more than 30 in (75 cm) in length. Crystals can also be blocky, bladed, or form elongate pyramids. Celestine may also be massive, fibrous, granular, or nodular in habit.

Celestine forms in cavities in sedimentary rocks (pp.306–33). It commonly occurs in evaporite deposits and can also be precipitated directly from seawater. It can occasionally form in hydrothermal deposits. Celestine is an ore of strontium.

Collector's gem
Celestine is too soft to wear. Faceted celestine demonstrates the skills of master cutters.

PROFILE

Monoclinic

- 2
- 2.3
- Perfect
- Splintery
- White
- Subvitreous to pearly

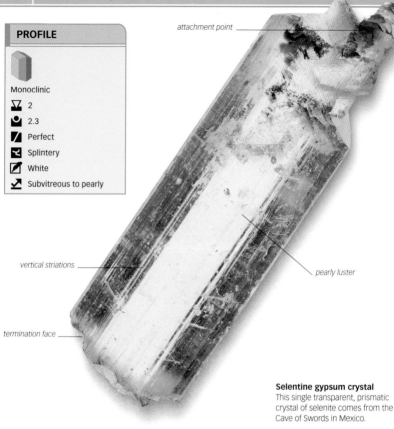

attachment point

vertical striations

pearly luster

termination face

Selentine gypsum crystal
This single transparent, prismatic crystal of selenite comes from the Cave of Swords in Mexico.

VARIANTS

silky sheen

Gypsum satin spar Fibrous gypsum crystals

bladed crystal

Desert rose Spherical clusters of bladed selenite

Fishtail twin Colorless, translucent selenite gypsum with fishtail twinning

$CaSO_4 \cdot 2H_2O$

GYPSUM

A widespread calcium sulfate hydrate, gypsum is found in a number of forms and is of great economic importance. It is colorless or white but can be tinted light brown, gray, yellow, green, or orange due to the presence of impurities. Single, well-developed crystals can be blocky with a slanted parallelogram outline, tabular, or bladed. Twinned crystals are common and frequently form characteristic "fishtails." Numerous transparent, swordlike selenite gypsum crystals 6½ft (2m) or more long can be found at the Cave of Swords, Chihuahua, Mexico, one of the world's most spectacular mineral deposits.

Gypsum occurs in extensive beds formed by the evaporation of ocean brine. It also occurs as an alteration product of sulfides in ore deposits and as volcanic deposits.

Cat's eye sheen
Satin spar, a fibrous variety of gypsum, can be cut into a cabochon gem with a cat's eye sheen.

massive habit

Massive melanterite
This nodule of melanterite shows typical massive form and some minor crystallization.

blue indicates presence of copper

PROFILE

Monoclinic

 2

1.9

Perfect

Conchoidal, brittle

White

Vitreous

 $FeSO_4 \cdot 7H_2O$

MELANTERITE

A hydrous iron sulfate, melanterite takes its name from the Greek word *melas*, which means "sulfate of iron." Melanterite is the iron analog of the copper sulfate chalcanthite, the two minerals having similar molecular structures. Most specimens of melanterite are colorless to white but can become green to blue as copper increasingly substitutes for iron. Melanterite is generally found in stalactitic or concretionary masses and rarely forms crystals. When crystals occur, they are short prisms or pseudo-octahedrons.

Melanterite is a secondary mineral formed by the oxidation of pyrite (p.62), marcasite (p.63), and other iron sulfides. It is frequently deposited on the timbers of old mine workings. Melanterite also occurs in the altered zones of pyrite-bearing rocks, especially in arid climates and in coal (p.253) deposits, where it is an alteration product of marcasite. Iron sulfate is used in water purification as a coagulant and also as a fertilizer.

kaolinite

crystalline chalcanthite

rock matrix

granular chalcanthite

Massive and crystalline chalcanthite
This specimen of chalcanthite occurs with patches of kaolinite. It exhibits both massive and crystalline forms of the mineral.

PROFILE

Triclinic

 2½

 2.3

 Not distinct

 Conchoidal

 Colorless

 Vitreous

VARIANT

Stalactite Chalcanthite in the form of a stalactitic aggregate

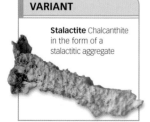

$CuSO_4 \cdot 5H_2O$

CHALCANTHITE

A hydrated copper sulfate, chalcanthite takes its name from the Greek words *khalkos*, which means "copper," and *anthos*, which means "flower." It used to be known as blue vitriol. It is commonly peacock blue, although some specimens are greenish. Natural crystals are relatively rare. Chalcanthite usually occurs in veinlets and as massive and stalactitic aggregates.

This widespread, naturally occurring mineral forms through the oxidation of chalcopyrite (p.57) and other copper sulfates that occur in the oxidized zones of copper deposits. Being a water-soluble mineral, it is often found forming crusts and stalactites on the walls and timbers of mine workings, where it crystallizes from mine waters. In arid areas, such as Chile, chalcanthite concentrates in sufficient quantities without being dissolved away to constitute an important ore of copper. Although chalcanthite is a sought-after collectors' mineral, its crystal structure disintegrates over time because it readily absorbs water.

PROFILE

Monoclinic

3½–4

4.0

Perfect

Uneven to subconchoidal

Pale green

Vitreous

Acicular brochantite
This brochantite specimen from
Chile has needlelike crystals on
a matrix of iron oxides.

iron-oxide matrix

*mass of needlelike
brochantite crystals*

VARIANT

*blue
azurite*

Brochantite on azurite
Green brochantite with
blue azurite

$Cu_4SO_4(OH)_6$

BROCHANTITE

A hydrous copper sulfate, brochantite is emerald
green, blue-green, or blackish green in color. It was
named in 1824 after the French geologist and mineralogist
A.J.M. Brochant de Villiers, who was the first pupil admitted
to the École des Mines, Paris, and who later became its
Professor of Geology and Mines. Brochantite usually forms
prismatic or needlelike crystals, which rarely exceed
a fraction of an inch in length. Twinning is common in
crystals. Brochantite is also found in tufts and druse
crusts and as fine-grained masses.

Brochantite forms in the oxidation zones of copper
deposits, especially those that occur in the arid regions
of the world. In these regions, brochantite is usually
associated with azurite (p.120), malachite (p.125), and
other copper minerals. In Arizona, and Chile, the
mineral is abundant enough to be an ore of copper.
Splendid specimens of brochantite come from Namibia,
and Bisbee, Arizona, where prismatic crystals may
exceed ⅜in (1 cm) in length.

PROFILE

Orthorhombic

2–2½

1.7

Perfect

Conchoidal

White

Vitreous to silky

vitreous to silky luster

fibrous strand

Fibrous epsomite
This epsomite specimen occurs
in a fibrous habit and shows a
vitreous to silky luster.

VARIANT

Powdery mass Epsomite
coating on a rocky matrix

$MgSO_4 \cdot 7H_2O$

EPSOMITE

Epsom salts is the common name for this hydrated
magnesium sulfate mineral. It was first found around
springs near the town of Epsom in Surrey, England, and
was named after that locality in 1805. It is colorless, white,
pale pink, or green. Epsomite crystals are rare; when
found, they are either prismatic or fibrous. Epsomite
usually occurs as crusts, powdery or
woolly coatings, or sometimes as
botryoidal or reniform masses.

Magnesium sulfate occurs
in solution in seawater, saline
lake water, and spring water.
When the water evaporates,
epsomite precipitates, forming
deposits. It is also found with
coal (p.253), in weathered
magnesium-rich rocks, sulfide ore
deposits, and dolomite (p.320)
and limestone caves.

Refined epsom salt
This widely used medication
is derived from epsomite.
One common use is as a
natural laxative.

PROFILE

Monoclinic

⬙ 2½–3

⬗ 2.8

▰ Perfect, indistinct

◩ Conchoidal

◪ White

⬈ Vitreous to waxy

Glauberite crystals
This group of dipyramidal glauberite crystals is from Ciempozuelos, Madrid, Spain.

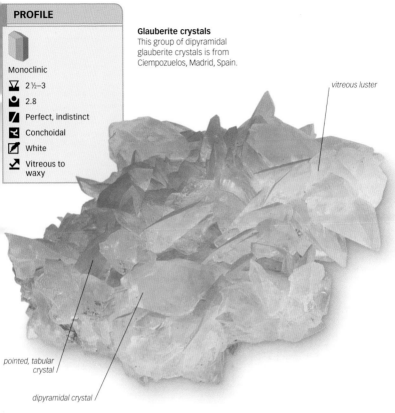

vitreous luster

pointed, tabular crystal

dipyramidal crystal

VARIANTS

Single crystal A single pyramidal crystal of glauberite

Pseudomorph A specimen with glauberite replaced by calcite

♣ $Na_2Ca(SO_4)_2$

GLAUBERITE

This mineral was named in 1808 for its similarity to another chemical, Glauber's salt, which in turn was named after the German alchemist Johann Glauber. Glauberite is a sodium calcium sulfate. It can be colorless, pale yellow, reddish, or gray, and its surface may alter to white, powdery sodium sulfate. Crystals can be prismatic, tabular, and dipyramidal, all with combinations of forms and all of which may have rounded edges. Glauberite crystal pseudomorphs form when other minerals, such as calcite (p.114) and gypsum (p.136), replace it. Glauberite has a slightly saline taste, turns white in water, and fuses to a white enamel.

This mineral forms under a variety of conditions. It is primarily an evaporite, forming in both marine and salt-lake environments. It is also found in cavities in basaltic igneous rocks and in volcanic fumaroles. Molds and casts of quartz (p.168) and prehnite (p.205) formed from glauberite are frequently found in basalt cavities in Patterson, New Jersey, USA.

PROFILE

Monoclinic

2½–3

6.0

Distinct in one direction

Conchoidal to uneven, brittle

Orange-yellow

Vitreous

Prismatic crystals
This spectacular specimen of orange crocoite shows partly striated, prismatic crystals.

elongated prismatic crystal ⎯⎯⎯

brilliant orange crocoite ⎯⎯⎯

VARIANTS

Red crocoite Red, prismatic crystals of crocoite in a rock matrix

Atypical crocoite
An almost reticulated growth of crocoite

$PbCrO_4$

CROCOITE

One of the most eye-catching of minerals, crocoite is bright orange to red in color. It takes its name from the Greek word *krókos*, which means "saffron." Crocoite crystals are prismatic, commonly square-sectioned, slender and elongated, and sometimes cavernous or hollow. They may be striated along their length and may rarely show distinct terminations. Crystals usually occur in radiating or randomly intergrown clusters. Crocoite can also occur in granular or massive forms. On exposure to light, much of the translucence and brilliance of the mineral is lost.

Crocoite is a rare mineral, as specific conditions—an oxidation zone of lead ore and the presence of low-silica igneous rocks that serve as the source of chromium—are required for its formation. It is the official mineral emblem of Tasmania, where exceptional crystals, 3–4 in (7.5–10 cm) long and having a brilliant luster and color, are found. Crocoite is identical in composition to the pigment chrome yellow.

tabular wulfenite crystal

iron oxide matrix

PROFILE

Tetragonal

2½–3

6.5–7.0

Distinct

Subconchoidal to uneven

White

Subadamantine to greasy

Yellow wulfenite
The wulfenite crystals on this iron oxide matrix show classic, square, platy development.

VARIANTS

Square crystals Typical thin, tabular crystals of wulfenite

Red cloud wulfenite Crystals found in Red Cloud Mine in Arizona

$PbMoO_4$

WULFENITE

The second most common molybdenum mineral after molybdenite, wulfenite was named after F.X. Wülfen, an Austro-Hungarian mineralogist, in 1841. The color of specimens varies and can be yellow, orange, red, gray, or brown. Wulfenite usually forms as thin, square plates or square, beveled, tabular crystals. Crystals sometimes show different terminations on each end, probably due to twinning. Bright, colorful, and sharply formed crystals are popular with collectors. Wulfenite also occurs in massive, earthy, and granular forms.

Wulfenite is a minor source of molybdenum. Tungsten substitutes for the molybdenum, although in most specimens it is present only in trace amounts. Wulfenite is a secondary mineral formed in the oxidized zones of lead and molybdenum deposits, and it occurs with other minerals, including cerussite (p.119), pyromorphite (p.151), and vanadinite (p.155). It is relatively widespread and is often found in superb crystals, occasionally up to 4 in (10 cm) on an edge.

Hübnerite crystals
In this specimen, translucent hübnerite crystals grow on a quartz matrix with tarnished tetrahedrite.

prismatic hübnerite crystal

adamantine luster

quartz matrix

tarnished tetrahedrite

PROFILE

Monoclinic

 4–4½

 7.3

 Perfect

Uneven

Yellow to brown

Submetallic/adamantine to resinous

 MnWO₄

HÜBNERITE

Named after the German mineralogist Adolf Hübner, who first described it in 1865, hübnerite is an important ore of tungsten. It is found as prismatic, long prismatic, tabular, or flattened crystals with striations and is commonly twinned. It can also form groups of parallel or subparallel crystals or radiating groups. Hübnerite is generally reddish brown. In transparent crystals, it can change color when viewed from different directions and show strong internal reflection.

Hübnerite is the manganese end member of a manganese–iron solid-solution series. It occurs in granitic pegmatites (p.260) and in thermal veins at high temperatures (1,065°F/575°C or above). The mineral is also recovered from alluvial gravels, in which it can concentrate.

Bulb filament
Hübnerite is an ore of tungsten, which is mainly used in light bulb filaments.

Ferberite crystal
This ferberite crystal is from
Cinovec, Czech Republic. It shows
the prismatic habit of the mineral.

submetallic luster

*opaque gray
ferberite*

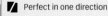

 FeWO₄

FERBERITE

The principal ore of tungsten, ferberite is an iron tungstate. It was named in 1863 after Moritz Rudolph Ferber, a German industrialist and mineralogist. Ferberite forms black crystals, which are commonly elongated or flattened with a wedge-shaped appearance. Twinning and striations are common in crystals. Ferberite is also found as granular masses.

Ferberite is the iron end-member of a solid-solution series it forms with hübnerite (p.144), the manganese end-member. Together, they constitute the mineral formerly called wolframite. Ferberite occurs in hydrothermal veins at high temperatures (1,065°F/ 575°C or above) and in granitic pegmatites (p.260) with other minerals.

Tungsten steel
Rocket nozzles, such as those used in Saturn V, are made of heat-resistant, hard, and strong tungsten steel.

Bipyramidal scheelite
This group of orange-yellow scheelite crystals clearly shows a tetragonal bipyramidal habit.

magnetite matrix

bipyramidal scheelite crystal

PROFILE

Tetragonal

 4½–5

6.1

 Distinct

 Uneven to subconchoidal

 White

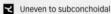 Vitreous to greasy

 CaWO$_4$

SCHEELITE

Named in 1821 after the Swedish chemist C.W. Scheele, scheelite is calcium tungstate. Its crystals are generally bipyramidal and twinned but also form in granular or massive aggregates. Irregular masses of colorless, gray, orange, or pale brown scheelite can be difficult to spot, but they fluoresce vivid bluish white under a short-wave ultraviolet light. Scheelite is sometimes associated with native gold (p.42), and its fluorescence is used by geologists in their search for gold deposits.

Scheelite commonly occurs in contact with metamorphic deposits, in hydrothermal veins formed at high temperatures (1,065°F/575°C or above), and less commonly in granitic pegmatites (p.260). Opaque crystals weighing up to 15½ lb (7 kg) come from Arizona. Scheelite is a major source of tungsten.

Brilliant cut scheelite
Transparent scheelite is relatively rare. Stones faceted from it are only for gem collectors.

PHOSPHATES, VANADATES, AND ARSENATES

The phosphate, arsenate, and vanadate minerals are grouped together because their crystal structures are similar. The phosphates are the most numerous of the three groups, with more than 200 known minerals.

COMPOSITION

Phosphates contain phosphorus and oxygen in a 1:4 ratio, written as PO_4. The combined atoms act as a single unit that in turn combines with other elements to form phosphate minerals. Arsenates have a basic structural unit of arsenic and oxygen, written as AsO_4, which combines with other elements to form arsenate minerals. Most arsenates are rare and many are brilliantly colored. Vanadates mostly contain the same type of structural tetrahedra as the phosphates and arsenates, written as VO_4. The structures of vanadates are complex, and these minerals are relatively rare.

OCCURRENCE

Primary phosphates usually crystallize from aqueous fluids derived from igneous crystallization; secondary phosphates, when primary phosphates are altered in the presence of water; and rock phosphates, from phosphorus-bearing organic material.

USES

Phosphates are of major economic importance as fertilizers. Vanadates are minor ores of vanadium and have no other economic importance. The only exception is carnotite, an important source of uranium.

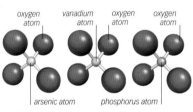

oxygen atom   vanadium atom   oxygen atom   oxygen atom

arsenic atom   phosphorus atom

Crystal structure
The arsenate (AsO_4), vanadate (VO_4), and phosphate (PO_4) ions consist of a metal atom bonded to four oxygen atoms. Each ion acts as a single unit.

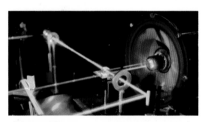

High-speed laser
Garnet-containing yttrium, which is derived from the yttrium phosphate xenotime, is used to make lasers. The direction of the laser beams is changed using mirrors.

Colorado Plateau
Spread across the Colorado Plateau in western Colorado, USA, are extensive deposits of carnotite (a phosphate of uranium, vanadium, and potassium).

PROFILE

Monoclinic

Apatite crystals
These spectacular apatite crystals from Panasqueira Mine, Beira Baixa, Portugal, occur with muscovite and a small amount of arsenopyrite.

5

3.1–3.2

Indistinct, variable

Conchoidal to uneven

White

Vitreous, waxy

color-zoned crystal

prismatic crystal

hexagonal, transparent crystal

VARIANTS

albite

Chlorapatite crystal
Double-terminated chlorapatite

Brilliant apatite
A single yellow crystal of hydroxylapatite

Hydroxylapatite A specimen with a waxy luster

$Ca_5(PO_4)_3(F,OH,Cl)$

APATITE

A series of calcium phosphate minerals that differ in composition are known as apatites. The name apatite is derived from the Greek *apate*, which means "deceit"— a reference to its similarity to crystals of aquamarine, amethyst, and olivine (p.232). Apatites can occur as green, blue, violet-blue, purple, colorless, white, yellow, pink, or rose-red specimens. All the apatites are structurally similar and are commonly found as transparent, well-formed, glassy crystals and in masses or nodules. Crystals are short to long prismatic, thick tabular, or prismatic with complex forms.

Apatites occur in marbles (p.301), skarns (p.302), and other metamorphic rocks. Rich deposits of apatite also occur in sedimentary rocks. As an accessory mineral, it occurs in a wide range of igneous rocks and in hydrothermal veins.

Step-cut gemstone
Owing to the brittleness of apatite, an edge of one facet of this blue gemstone has become chipped.

tabular, twinned
crystal aggregate

Tabular crystals
Thin, tabular, twinned
crystals characteristic of
autunite are clearly visible in
this lemon-yellow specimen.

vitreous luster

PROFILE

Tetragonal

 2–2 ½

 3.1–3.2

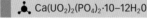 Perfect basal

 Uneven

 Pale yellow

Vitreous to pearly

$Ca(UO_2)_2(PO_4)_2 \cdot 10–12H_2O$

AUTUNITE

A popular collector's mineral, autunite is a calcium
uranium phosphate. Greenish or lemon yellow in color,
autunite specimens fluoresce green under ultraviolet
light. Crystals of autunite have a rectangular or octagonal
outline. Coarse groups are found, but scaly coatings are
more common. Autunite is also found as crusts with
crystals standing on edge, giving a serrated appearance.

Autunite is named after Autun, France, where this
mineral was discovered. It is formed in the oxidation
zones of uranium ore bodies as an alteration product
of uraninite (p.83) and other uranium-bearing minerals.
It also occurs in hydrothermal veins and in pegmatites
(p.260). Since autunite contains uranium and is
radioactive, it must be stored carefully and handled as
little as possible. When mildly heated, tetragonal autunite
dehydrates into orthorhombic meta-autunite. Most
museum and collector specimens of autunite have been
converted to meta-autunite. A moist atmosphere helps
prevent dehydration.

PROFILE

Monoclinic

⊽ 5

◍ 4.6–5.4

▧ Perfect, good, poor

◩ Conchoidal to uneven, brittle

◪ White

⬈ Resinous, waxy, or vitreous

Monazite crystal
This striated crystal of monazite is from Arendal, Aust-Agder, Norway, which is an important monazite locality.

termination

prism face

striation

VARIANT

Monazite fragment A brown crystal fragment showing growth lamellae

♣ (Ce,La,Th,Nd)PO$_4$

MONAZITE

The monazite group consists of three different phosphate minerals, all sharing the same crystal structure. The most widespread is monazite-(Ce), cerium phosphate, which is yellowish or reddish brown to brown, greenish, or nearly white. Monazite-(Ce) forms prismatic, flattened, or elongated crystals, which are occasionally large, coarse, and commonly twinned. Two other species of monazite are monazite-(La), which is lanthanum phosphate, and monazite-(Nd), which is neodymium phosphate.

Monazite is a common accessory mineral in granites (pp.258–59) and gneisses (p.288) and in pegmatites (p.260) and fissure veins. Detrital monazite can accumulate as monazite sands. Lanthanum is used in oil refining. Neodymium is used for coloring glass.

Cerium oxide
Monazite-(Ce) is a source of cerium. Cerium oxide is used for polishing glass, stone, and gemstones.

PROFILE

Hexagonal

⊠ 3½–4

◓ 7.0

▰ Poor

⤴ Uneven to subconchoidal, brittle

▱ White

⤢ Resinous

goethite matrix

resinous luster

barrel-shaped crystal

Barrel-shaped crystals
This mass of pyromorphite on a goethite matrix shows its typical barrel-shaped crystals.

VARIANTS

Lime-green crystals Crystals showing pyromorphite's intense coloration

prismatic crystal

Yellow-green crystals
A specimen of pyromorphite with yellow-green prismatic crystals

⚛ Pb₅(PO₄)₃Cl

PYROMORPHITE

A minor ore of lead but a popular collector's mineral, pyromorphite forms a continuous chemical series with mimetite (p.164) in which phosphorus and arsenic replace each other. Pyromorphite gets its name from the Greek words *pyr*, which means "fire," and *morphe*, which means "form"—an allusion to its property of becoming crystalline on cooling after it has been melted to a globule. It is dark green to yellow-green, shades of brown, a waxy yellow, or yellow-orange. Crystals may be either simple hexagonal prisms or rounded and barrel-shaped, spindle-shaped, or cavernous. Some crystals exhibit different colors when viewed from different directions and some produce electricity on application of mechanical stress. The mineral can also be globular, reniform, or granular in habit.

Pyromorphite occurs as a secondary mineral in the oxidized zones of lead deposits with galena (p.54), goethite (p.102), cerussite (p.119), smithsonite (p.124), and vanadinite (p.155). Pseudomorphs of pyromorphite after galena are common.

Torbernite crystals
In this specimen, tabular
crystals of torbernite rest
on an iron-rich matrix.

*iron-stained
rock matrix*

*tabular torbernite
crystal*

PROFILE

Tetragonal

 2–2½

 3.2

 Perfect, basal

 Uneven

 Pale green

Vitreous to
subadamantine

VARIANT

Metatorbernite Green
sheaves of metatorbernite
crystals in rock matrix

$Cu(UO_2)_2(PO_4)_2 \cdot 8–12H_2O$

TORBERNITE

Named in 1793 after the Swedish mineralogist Torbern
Olaf Bergmann, torbernite is a uranium-bearing mineral
and a minor ore of uranium. Torbernite forms thin to thick
tabular crystals that are commonly square in outline,
foliated micalike masses, sheaflike crystal groups, or
scaly coatings. Specimens are bright mid-green, emerald
green, leek green, or grass green in color. Torbernite
is chemically unstable, and with increased hydration it
transforms to metatorbernite. In fact, all specimens are
probably metatorbernite. It is also radioactive and needs to
be handled with appropriate care.

Torbernite is found as a secondary mineral formed in
the oxidation zones of deposits containing uranium and
copper and is associated with other phosphate minerals.
It forms as an alteration product of uraninite (p.83) or other
uranium-bearing minerals. Torbernite is also associated
with uraninite, autunite (p.149), and carnotite (p.159). Fine
specimens occur in Cornwall, England, in the Flinders
Range of Australia, and elsewhere.

quartz

Massive aggregate
This specimen of massive triplite is from Megiliggar Rocks in Cornwall, England.

massive triplite

PROFILE

Monoclinic

 5–5½

 3.5–3.9

 Good in three directions

 Uneven to subconchoidal

White to brown

Vitreous to resinous

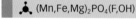

$(Mn,Fe,Mg)_2PO_4(F,OH)$

TRIPLITE

The first occurrence of triplite was described in 1813 in Chanteloube, Limousin, France. Although it is a fluoridated manganese phosphate, in most triplite samples iron partially replaces manganese. Triplite takes its name from the Greek word *triplos,* which means "triple"—a reference to its three cleavages oriented at right angles to each other. Its crystals are typically rough and poorly developed but may have many indistinct forms. Triplite is more commonly nodular or massive. Specimens may be chestnut brown, reddish brown, flesh red, or salmon pink in color. If altered, they may be brownish black to black. Translucent crystals may also exhibit different colors when viewed from different directions (a phenomenon known as pleochroism), going from yellow-brown to reddish brown.

Triplite is a primary mineral in granite pegmatites (p.260) with complex zones and in some hydrothermal tin veins. It may be accompanied by sphalerite (p.53), pyrite (p.62), apatite (p.148), and tourmaline (p.224).

Blue turquoise
In this specimen, nodular masses of light blue turquoise rest in a matrix of iron oxide.

turquoise

iron-oxide matrix

PROFILE

Triclinic

5–6

2.6–2.8

Good

Conchoidal

White to green

Waxy to dull

VARIANTS

Turquoise vein Massive turquoise in a small vein

Green turquoise A hard, green nugget from the USA

Turquoise in rock Blue-green, massive turquoise in rock

$CuAl_6(PO_4)_4(OH)_8 \cdot 4H_2O$

TURQUOISE

One of the first gemstones to be mined, turquoise is a hydrous copper aluminum phosphate. Beads made of turquoise that date back to c.5000 BCE have been recovered in Mesopotamia (present-day Iraq). This mineral usually occurs in massive or microcrystalline forms, as encrustations or nodules, or in veins. Crystals are rare; when found, they occur as short, often transparent prisms. Turquoise varies in color from sky-blue to green, depending on the amount of iron and copper it contains.

"Turquoise" is derived from the French word for "Turkey," because it was first transported to Europe through Turkey. Turquoise occurs in arid environments as a secondary mineral probably derived from the decomposition of apatite (p.148) and some copper sulfides.

Carved elephant
Turquoise is a favorite of Chinese stone carvers, who produced this turquoise elephant.

Red vanadinite
Vanadinite crystals are often brilliantly colored in shades of red and yellow. This specimen has smooth-faced, prismatic crystals.

adamantine luster

prismatic crystal

rock matrix

PROFILE

Hexagonal

 3

6.9

None

Uneven, brittle

Whitish yellow

Adamantine

$Pb_5(VO_4)_3Cl$

VANADINITE

A relatively rare mineral, vanadinite is a lead chloro-vanadate. The bright red or orange-red colors of vanadinite make it popular among mineral collectors, although it is sometimes brown, red-brown, gray, yellow, or colorless. Crystals are usually in the form of short, hexagonal prisms but can also be found as hexagonal pyramids or as hollow prisms. They can also be needlelike. Small amounts of calcium, zinc, and copper may substitute for lead, and arsenic can completely substitute for vanadium in the crystal structure to form the mineral mimetite (p.164). The mineral is also found as rounded masses or crusts.

Vanadinite forms as a secondary mineral in oxidized ore deposits containing lead, often associated with galena (p.54), goethite (p.102), barite (p.134), and wulfenite (p.143). Vanadium from vanadinite is used to make strong vanadium steels.

Steel spanner
Vanadium imparts strength and hardness to steel that is used to make high-stress tools, such as this spanner.

Concretionary variscite
Variscite is often found in nodules and concretions like the sliced specimen shown here. It can be sometimes mistaken for turquoise.

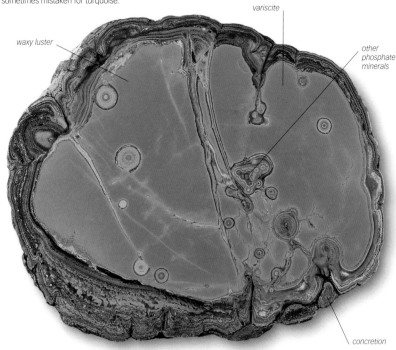

waxy luster

variscite

other phosphate minerals

concretion

PROFILE

Orthorhombic

 4½

2.6

Good but rarely visible

Splintery in massive

White

Vitreous to waxy

 $AlPO_4 \cdot 2H_2O$

VARISCITE

This mineral was named after Variscia, the old name for the German district of Voightland, where it was first discovered, in 1837. Variscite is pale to apple green in color. It is predominantly found as cryptocrystalline or fine-grained masses and in veins, crusts, or nodules. It rarely forms crystals.

Variscite forms in cavities produced by the action of phosphate-rich waters on aluminous rocks. It commonly occurs in association with apatite (p.148) and wavellite (p.158). It is valued as a semiprecious gemstone and is used for carvings and as an ornamental material. Variscite is porous, and, when worn next to the skin, tends to absorb body oils, which discolor it. A mineral that appears to be turquoise (p.154) but is actually variscite is sometimes marketed by the name variquoise.

Cabochon
Variscite can be polished into inexpensive gems, but their softness makes them vulnerable to wear.

PROFILE

Monoclinic

1½–2

2.7

Perfect

Uneven

Bluish white

Vitreous to earthy

Needlelike vivianite
This specimen of radiating vivianite crystals is set on a rock matrix.

radiating, bladed crystal

n, transparent crystal

crystals in cavity left by fossil shell

vitreous luster

VARIANT

Prismatic crystal Blue-black, elongated prismatic crystals of vivianite

$Fe_3(PO_4)_2 \cdot 8H_2O$

VIVIANITE

Named in 1817 after the English mineralogist John Henry Vivian, vivianite occurs as elongated, prismatic, or bladed tabular crystals. Specimens may be rounded, corroded, concretionary, earthy, or powdery in form. Vivianite can also form starlike groups or encrustations or occur in massive or fibrous forms. Sometimes colorless when freshly exposed, vivianite becomes either pale blue to greenish blue or indigo blue on oxidation. Before the development of modern synthetic chemicals, vivianite was the source of the sought-after blue paint pigment blue ocher.

Vivianite is a widespread secondary mineral, forming in the weathered zones of iron ore and phosphate deposits and in complex granite pegmatites (p.260).

Blue ocher
Powdered vivianite was used to make blue ocher, a rare and expensive pigment.

radiating wavellite crystals

unbroken spherule

vitreous luster

Radiating crystals
Needlelike crystals of wavellite form radiating aggregates on this rock matrix.

PROFILE	
Orthorhombic	
	3½–4
	2.4
	Good
	Subconchoidal to uneven
	White
	Vitreous to resinous

 Al$_3$(PO$_4$)$_2$(OH,F)$_3$·5H$_2$O

WAVELLITE

Named in 1805 after the amateur English mineralogist William Wavell, wavellite is a hydrated aluminum phosphate. Specimens are usually green but can also be white, greenish white, green-yellow, yellowish brown, turquoise-blue, brown, or black. They may exhibit color zoning. Crystals are uncommon but when found are short to long prismatic, elongated, and striated parallel to the prism faces. Wavellite is commonly found as translucent, greenish, globular aggregates of radiating crystals up to 1¼ in (3 cm) in diameter, as crusts, or as stalactitic deposits.

Wavellite is a secondary mineral that forms in low-grade aluminous, metamorphic rocks; goethite (p.102) and phosphate rock deposits; and, rarely, in hydrothermal veins. It is also found in areas where phosphate minerals have been weathered in granites (p.258) and granitic pegmatites (p.260).

Match production
Phosphorous sulfate derived from wavellite and other phosphates is a major component of matches.

Carnotite crust
A crust of vivid yellow, powdery radioactive carnotite coats this fragment of sandstone.

powdery coating

crust of carnotite

$K_2(UO_2)_2(VO_4)_2 \cdot 3H_2O$

CARNOTITE

A radioactive mineral, carnotite was named in 1899 after the French chemist and mining engineer Marie-Adolphe Carno. It is bright to lemon yellow or greenish yellow. Carnotite is generally found as powdery or microcrystalline masses; tiny, disseminated grains; or crusts. Crystals are platy, rhombohedral, or lathlike.

Carnotite is a secondary mineral formed by the alteration of primary uranium-vanadium minerals. It occurs chiefly in sandstone (p.308), either disseminated or in concentrations around fossil wood or other fossilized vegetable matter. Pure carnotite contains about 53 percent uranium by weight, which is used to generate nuclear energy and in atomic weapons. It has also been mined for vanadium and radium, from World War II onward.

Radium dial
Sourced from carnotite, radium has been used to create illuminated watch hands and dials.

rounded crystal cluster

vitreous luster

Adamite crystals
Rounded, whitish crystal clusters of adamite rest on a rock matrix in this specimen.

PROFILE

Orthorhombic

 3½

4.4

Good

Subconchoidal to uneven, brittle

White

Vitreous

VARIANTS

Reddish adamite Adamite crystals on a reddish orange iron-oxide matrix

adamite crystal

Spheroidal adamite A cluster of yellow, spheroidal adamite crystals on a goethite matrix

$Zn_2AsO_4(OH)$

ADAMITE

Named in 1866 after the French mineralogist G.J. Adam, who discovered adamite in Chile, this mineral is a zinc arsenate hydroxide. It is rarely colorless or white, and many specimens fluoresce green under ultraviolet light. Adamite is often brightly colored due to traces of other elements: copper commonly substitutes for zinc to yield yellow or green crystals depending on its concentration; manganese may substitute for zinc to yield crystals that are pink or violet. Adamite crystals are elongated, tabular, or blocky. This mineral also occurs as rosettes and spherical masses of radiating crystals.

Adamite forms as a secondary mineral in the oxidized zones of zinc and arsenic deposits, often associated with goethite (p.102), azurite (p.120), smithsonite (p.124), mimetite (p.164), scorodite (p.165), hemimorphite (p.227), and olivenite. Although adamite has no commercial uses, its bright and lustrous crystals are highly sought after by mineral collectors.

Clinoclase rosettes
In this specimen, rosettes of clinoclase crystals are seen with associated olivenite.

rosette of radiating
clinoclase crystals

olivenite

Monoclinic

2½–3

4.3

Perfect

Uneven, brittle

Bluish green

Vitreous to pearly

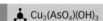 $Cu_3(AsO_4)(OH)_3$

CLINOCLASE

Discovered in 1830 in the Wheal Gorland mine in Cornwall, England, clinoclase was named in 1868. It takes its name from the Greek *me klísi*, which means "to incline," and *gia na spásei*, which means "to break"—a reference to its oblique basal cleavage. The vitreous crystals of clinoclase are translucent dark blue to dark greenish blue. They can be elongated or tabular or occur as single, isolated crystals that appear rhombohedral. Specimens can also form rosettelike aggregates or occur as crusts or coatings with a fibrous structure.

Clinoclase forms as a secondary mineral in the oxidized zones of deposits containing copper sulfides. Associated minerals include goethite (p.102), azurite (p.120), malachite (p.125), brochantite (p.139), adamite (p.160), quartz (p.168), and olivenite. Specimens come from Broken Hill, New South Wales, Australia; Tintic district, Utah, and Majuba Hill, Nevada, USA; the Vosges, France; and the Tsumeb Mine, Namibia.

Tabular chalcophyllite
A mass of vivid blue, tabular chalcophyllite crystals rests on a rock matrix.

rock matrix

tabular chalcophyllite crystal

$Cu_{18}Al_2(AsO_4)_2(SO_4)_3(OH)_{27}\cdot33H_2O$

CHALCOPHYLLITE

A vivid blue-green in color, chalcophyllite takes its name from the Greek words *chalco*, which means "copper," and *phyllon*, which means "leaf"—an allusion to its copper content and its common foliated habit. Chalcophyllite was first described after material collected in Germany and named in 1847. Translucent crystals exhibit a blue-green color when viewed from one direction and appear almost colorless from another direction. Crystals are platy, six-sided, and flattened and may have triangular striations. Chalcophyllite may also be rosettelike, tabular, drusy, or massive.

This mineral occurs in hydrothermal copper deposits, often accompanied by cuprite (p.87), azurite (p.120), malachite (p.125), brochantite (p.139), and clinoclase (p.161).

Statue of Lamma
Chalcophyllite was used as an ore of copper when this copper statue was made in the period 1800–1600 BCE.

PROFILE

Monoclinic

1½–2½

3.1

Perfect

Uneven, sectile

Pale red

Adamantine to vitreous, pearly

Acicular crystals
These brightly colored, needlelike crystals of erythrite are from Bou Azzer, Morocco.

rock matrix

purplish pink erythrite

needlelike crystal

VARIANT

Erythrite crust A thin crust of erythrite on a brown rock base

$CO_3(AsO_4)_2 \cdot 8H_2O$

ERYTHRITE

Although of little commercial value, erythrite is an important tool for prospectors looking for cobalt and related silver deposits. The bright purplish pink color of erythrite in a rock indicates the presence of cobalt. This explains why miners call erythrite "cobalt bloom." Erythrite is a cobalt arsenate hydrate. It forms a chemical replacement series with annabergite, in which nickel replaces cobalt in the erythrite structure. Its color may vary from crimson red to peach red, with the lighter colors indicating a higher nickel content. The coloration may also occur in bands. Well-formed crystals are rare, but when found they occur as deeply striated, prismatic to needlelike, commonly radiating, globular tufts of crystals, or as powdery coatings.

Erythrite is a secondary mineral found in the oxidized zones of cobalt-nickel-arsenic deposits. Fine specimens come from Canada and Morocco. Erythrite is also found in Mexico, France, southwestern USA, the Czech Republic, Germany, Australia, and elsewhere.

PROFILE

Hexagonal

⬙ 3½–4

⬙ 7.3

⬙ Poor

⬙ Conchoidal to uneven, brittle

⬙ White

⬙ Resinous

rounded masses of campylite

Mimetite on manganese oxide
This specimen from England contains "campylite"—a rounded variety of mimetite—and barite on nodules of manganese oxide.

barite

resinous luster

manganese-oxide matrix

VARIANTS

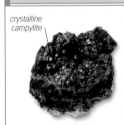

crystalline campylite

Campylite Massive and crystalline varieties of campylite set in a rock matrix

Prismatic crystals Mimetite in the form of prismatic, barrel-shaped crystals

$Pb_5(AsO_4)_3Cl$

MIMETITE

An arsenate mineral, mimetite is the end-member of a solid-solution series with pyromorphite (p.151). It is named after the Greek word *mimetes*, which means "imitator"—a reference to its resemblance to pyromorphite. Although similar in physical characterisitics and crystal form to pyromorphite, mimetite is a less common mineral. It forms heavy, barrel-shaped, hexagonal crystals or rounded masses, but is also found as botryoidal, granular, tabular, and needlelike aggregates. Mimetite specimens may be colorless or occur in shades of yellow, orange, brown, and green.

Mimetite is a secondary mineral, which forms in the oxidized zone of lead deposits and in other localities where the elements lead and arsenic occur together. Excellent specimens come from Chihuahua, Mexico; Saxony, Germany; Attica, Greece; Broken Hill, Australia; and Bisbee and Tombstone, Arizona, USA. A single crystal mined from Tsumeb in Namibia measured 2½ in (6.4 cm) in length.

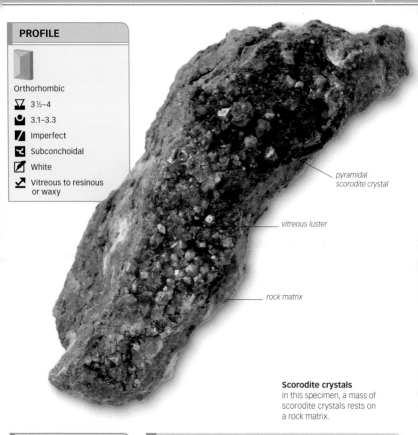

pyramidal
scorodite crystal

vitreous luster

rock matrix

Scorodite crystals
In this specimen, a mass of scorodite crystals rests on a rock matrix.

VARIANT

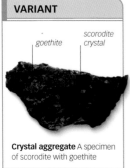

goethite

scorodite crystal

Crystal aggregate A specimen of scorodite with goethite

$FeAsO_4 \cdot 2H_2O$

SCORODITE

A hydrated iron arsenate mineral, scorodite takes its name from the Greek word *scorodion*, which means "garliclike"—an allusion to the odor emitted by the arsenic when specimens are heated. Scorodite can vary considerably in color depending on the light under which it is seen: pale leek green, grayish green, liver brown, pale blue, violet, yellow, pale grayish, or colorless. It may be blue-green in daylight but bluish purple to grayish blue in incandescent light; in transmitted light it may appear colorless to pale shades of green or brown. Crystals are usually dipyramidal, appearing octahedral, and may have a number of modifying faces. They may also be tabular or short prisms. Drusy coatings are common. Scorodite can also be porous and earthy or massive.

Scorodite is found in hydrothermal veins, hot spring deposits, and oxidized zones of arsenic-rich ore bodies. Associated minerals may be pharmacosiderite, vivianite (p.157), adamite (p.160), and various iron oxides.

SILICATES

The silicates constitute around 25 percent of all known minerals and nearly half of the most common ones. All silicates are built around a basic structure of silicon and oxygen. They are a major component of Earth and occur in lunar samples and meteorites.

COMPOSITION

The silicates make up about 95 percent of the crust and upper mantle of Earth. All silicates contain silicon and oxygen. Silicon is a lightweight, shiny metal; oxygen is a colorless, odorless gas.

In silicates, silicon and oxygen combine to form structural tetrahedra, each with a silicon atom in the center and oxygen atoms at the corners. Silicate tetrahedra may exist as discrete, independent units and connect only with other silicate tetrahedra (as in quartz), or they may link with other elements such as iron, magnesium, and aluminum. Tetrahedra may also share their oxygen atoms at corners, edges, or, more rarely, faces, creating various structures. The different linkages also create voids of different sizes, which are occupied by ions of various metals. Substitutions can occur where atoms are of a relatively similar size. Silicates are divided into six main groups

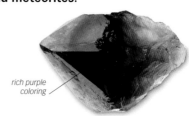

rich purple coloring

Amethyst crystal
The tectosilicate mineral quartz occurs in several differently colored varieties. These include amethyst (above), rock crystal, smoky quartz, and citrine.

(see panel, below) according to the structural configurations that result from the different ways in which tetrahedra and other elements are linked. Within these main groups are further subdivisions based on chemistry—that is, the type and location of other atoms in the structure. Many groups are solid-solution series, such as the feldspars (see panel, opposite) and the garnets, in which the ions of various metals and semimetals substitute for each other within the silicate structure.

SILICATE GROUPS

The six silicate groups are based on the different ways in which the basic silica tetrahedra are linked. These differing linkages create voids of different sizes and configurations that allow positively charged atoms of different sizes to fit into the structure.

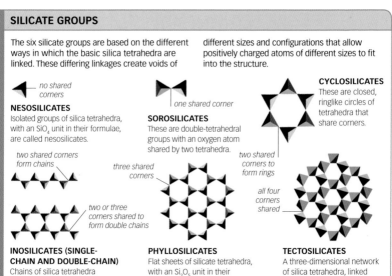

no shared corners

NESOSILICATES
Isolated groups of silica tetrahedra, with an SiO_4 unit in their formulae, are called nesosilicates.

one shared corner

SOROSILICATES
These are double-tetrahedral groups with an oxygen atom shared by two tetrahedra.

CYCLOSILICATES
These are closed, ringlike circles of tetrahedra that share corners.

two shared corners form chains

three shared corners

two shared corners to form rings

all four corners shared

two or three corners shared to form double chains

INOSILICATES (SINGLE-CHAIN AND DOUBLE-CHAIN)
Chains of silica tetrahedra with Si_2O_6 groups are called single-chain inosilicates.

PHYLLOSILICATES
Flat sheets of silicate tetrahedra, with an Si_2O_5 unit in their chemical formulae, are called phyllosilicates.

TECTOSILICATES
A three-dimensional network of silica tetrahedra, linked at each corner, makes up a tectosilicate.

THE FELDSPARS

The feldspars are a group of aluminosilicate minerals that contain calcium, sodium, or potassium. As shown here, there are three major solid-solution series within the group. Feldspars are the most abundant mineral in Earth's crust.

ALKALI FELDSPARS

ORTHOCLASE
$KAlSi_3O_8$

SANIDINE
$(K,Na)ALSi_3O_8$

ALBITE (Ab)
$NaAlSi_3O_8$

MICROCLINE
$KAlSi_3O_8$

ANORTHOCLASE
$(Na,K)ALSi_3O_8$

PLAGIOCLASE FELDSPARS

OLIGOCLASE
$(Na,Ca)(Al,Si)$
$AlSi_3O_8$

ANDESINE
$NaAlSi_3O_8-$
$CaAl_2Si_2O_8$

LABRADORITE
$(Ca,Na)Al(Al,Si)$
Si_2O_2

ANORTHITE (An)
$CaAl_2Si_2O_8$

BYTOWNITE
$(NaSi,CaAl)Al_2Si_2O_8$

OCCURRENCE AND USES

The ultimate source of all silicates is igneous rock in which tectosilicate feldspar minerals are the major component. Silicates are found not only on Earth but also on the Moon and in meteorites. After feldspar, quartz is the most abundant mineral in the crust and upper mantle. It occurs in nearly all high-silica igneous, metamorphic, and sedimentary rocks. In silica-poor rocks where quartz does not form, other silicate minerals develop. Since many silicates, especially quartz and its varieties, are resistant to weathering, they form the major component of most detrital sediments. There are numerous uses of silicates. Quartz and its varieties find use as gemstones, in electronic and optical applications, and as abrasives. The feldspars are used in glass and ceramics, as gemstones, and as abrasives. Other silicates are ores, and yet others are important gem, ornamental, and industrial minerals. The tough rocks formed from silicate minerals are used as major building and industrial materials.

Jadeite mask
The inosilicate jadeite was one of the first minerals used by humans. Although difficult to shape, it has been used for tools and ornaments.

The Ural Mountains
Located in west-central Russia, the Ural Mountains are a treasure trove of silicate minerals, which are used in industry and as gemstones.

PROFILE

Hexagonal

⛏ 7

💧 2.7

🪨 None

✴ Conchoidal

▦ White

↗ Vitreous

rhombohedral termination

prismatic crystal

striation on prism face

Prismatic quartz
This group of long, prismatic quartz crystals is from the Dauphiné province of France.

VARIANTS

Pyramidal amethyst
An amethyst specimen with pyramidal terminations

milky quartz termination

smoky quartz

Smoky quartz Double-terminated smoky quartz in milky quartz

termination

Milky quartz
A white, terminated quartz prism

🜨 SiO_2

QUARTZ

One of the most common minerals in Earth's crust, quartz has two forms: macrocrystalline (with crystals that can be seen by eye) and cryptocrystalline (formed of microscopic crystals). Macrocrystalline quartz is usually colorless and transparent, as in rock crystal, or white and translucent, as in milky quartz. Colored varieties include: pink and translucent rose quartz; transparent to translucent lavender or purple amethyst; transparent to translucent black or brown smoky quartz; and transparent to translucent yellow or yellow-brown citrine. All crystalline varieties form hexagonal prisms and pyramids.

Cryptocrystalline varieties of quartz include chalcedony (p.169), agate (p.170), and jasper (p.171). Quartz occurs in nearly all silica-rich sedimentary, igneous, and metamorphic rocks.

Oval citrine
This large, oval-cut citrine is set in a silver brooch. It is encircled by silver leaves and faceted amethysts.

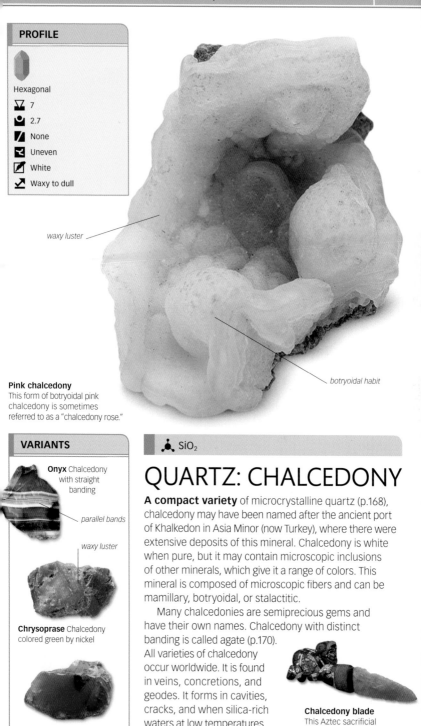

PROFILE

Hexagonal

7

2.7

None

Uneven

White

Waxy to dull

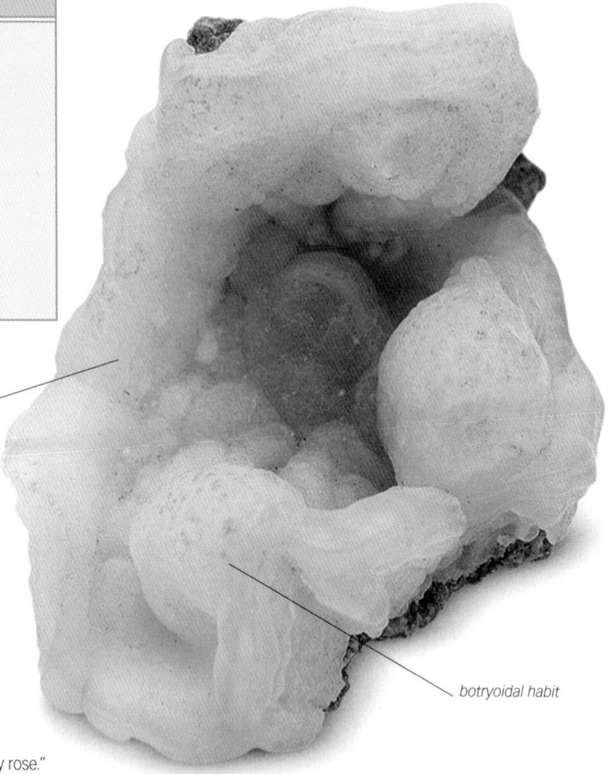
waxy luster
botryoidal habit

Pink chalcedony
This form of botryoidal pink chalcedony is sometimes referred to as a "chalcedony rose."

VARIANTS

parallel bands

Onyx Chalcedony with straight banding

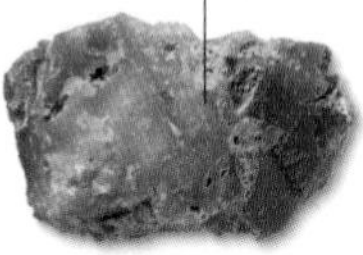
waxy luster

Chrysoprase Chalcedony colored green by nickel

Carnelian A piece of red-orange chalcedony

SiO_2

QUARTZ: CHALCEDONY

A compact variety of microcrystalline quartz (p.168), chalcedony may have been named after the ancient port of Khalkedon in Asia Minor (now Turkey), where there were extensive deposits of this mineral. Chalcedony is white when pure, but it may contain microscopic inclusions of other minerals, which give it a range of colors. This mineral is composed of microscopic fibers and can be mamillary, botryoidal, or stalactitic.

Many chalcedonies are semiprecious gems and have their own names. Chalcedony with distinct banding is called agate (p.170). All varieties of chalcedony occur worldwide. It is found in veins, concretions, and geodes. It forms in cavities, cracks, and when silica-rich waters at low temperatures (up to 400°F/200°C) percolate through existing rocks.

Chalcedony blade
This Aztec sacrificial knife has a finely chipped chalcedony blade and a mosaic handle.

PROFILE

Hexagonal

7

2.7

None

Conchoidal

White

Vitreous to waxy

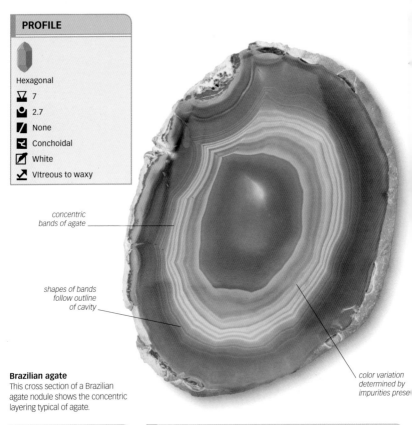

concentric bands of agate

shapes of bands follow outline of cavity

color variation determined by impurities prese[...]

Brazilian agate
This cross section of a Brazilian agate nodule shows the concentric layering typical of agate.

VARIANT

concentric bands

Fortification agate
Banded agate with angular bends

SiO_2

CHALCEDONY: AGATE

A common, semiprecious chalcedony, agate has been worked since prehistoric times. It is a compact, microcrystalline variety of quartz (p.168), and it has the same physical properties as quartz. Agate is characterized by concentric color bands in shades of white, yellow, gray, pale blue, brown, pink, red, or black.

Other names often precede the word agate to indicate the mineral's visual characteristics or place of origin. One of these is fire agate, which has inclusions of reddish to brown hematite that give an internal iridescence to polished stones. Another is fortification agate, which has concentric bands of color resembling an aerial view of an ancient fortress. Most agates are found in cavities in ancient lavas or other extrusive igneous rocks.

Snuff bottle
The 19th-century Chinese snuff bottle seen here has been carved from agate. It has a jade stopper.

PROFILE

Hexagonal

⬙ 7

◗ 2.7

▰ None

◲ Conchoidal

▱ White

⬦ Vitreous

Color variation
Hematite colors this example of jasper brownish red. Threads of white quartz veins make a crisscross pattern on this specimen.

brownish red jasper

white quartz vein

color variation due to other minerals

VARIANTS

Mammillary jasper Red jasper in mammillary form

Ribboned jasper
A specimen of jasper with parallel, reddish bands

♣ SiO₂

QUARTZ: JASPER

An impure variety of cryptocrystalline quartz (p.168), jasper takes its name from the Greek word *iaspis*, which is probably of Semitic origin. It is fine-grained or dense, and it contains various amounts of other materials, which give it opacity and color. Hematite (p.91) gives jasper a brick-red to brownish red color; clay a yellowish white or gray color; and goethite (p.102) a brown or yellow hue.

Jasper forms when silica-rich waters at low temperatures (up to 400°F/200°C) percolate through cracks and fissures in other rocks, incorporating a variety of materials and leaving behind deposits. It is found worldwide wherever cryptocrystalline quartz occurs. The classification and naming of jasper varies greatly and often incorporates place names or colors. Only some of these are formally recognized as varieties of jasper, leaving great latitude in defining which jasper is which. Color names such as "red" or "green" can apply to a range of shades, while locality names, such as "Bruneau jasper" after a canyon in Idaho, tend to be more specific.

PROFILE

Crystal system	Amorphous
⚡	5–6
⬤	1.9–2.3
▮	None
◩	Conchoidal
▧	White
⚡	Vitreous

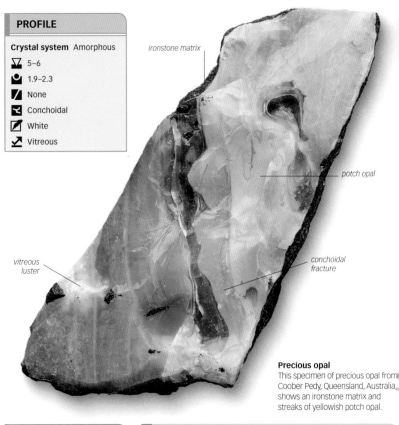

ironstone matrix

potch opal

vitreous luster

conchoidal fracture

Precious opal
This specimen of precious opal from Coober Pedy, Queensland, Australia, shows an ironstone matrix and streaks of yellowish potch opal.

VARIANTS

Boulder opal
Blue mass of opal in an iron-oxide nodule

Opal pseudomorph Crystals of glauberite replaced by opal

Fire opal Noniridescent, transparent opal

⚛ $SiO_2 \cdot nH_2O$

OPAL

Known since antiquity, opal derives its name from the Roman word *opalus,* which means "precious stone." Although it is colorless when pure, the vast majority of common opal occurs in opaque, dull yellows and reds. It varies from essentially amorphous to partially crystalline. Precious opal is the least crystalline form of the mineral, consisting of a regular arrangement of tiny, transparent, silica spheres. Regularly arranged spheres of a particular size create a diffraction effect called color play.

Opal is widespread and is deposited at low temperatures (up to 400°F/200°C) from silica-bearing, circulating waters. It is found as nodules, stalactitic masses, veinlets, and encrustations in most kinds of rocks. Opal constitutes important parts of many sedimentary accumulations, such as diatomaceous earth.

Victorian ring
Some cut opal dries and cracks with age and needs to be kept moist. The opal in this ring is well preserved.

PROFILE

Monoclinic

▽ 6–6 ½

● 2.5–2.6

✔ Perfect

✦ Subconchoidal to uneven, brittle

✔ White

⟋ Vitreous

Orthoclase prisms
In this specimen, white, blocky prisms of orthoclase are associated with cleavelandite albite and set in pegmatite.

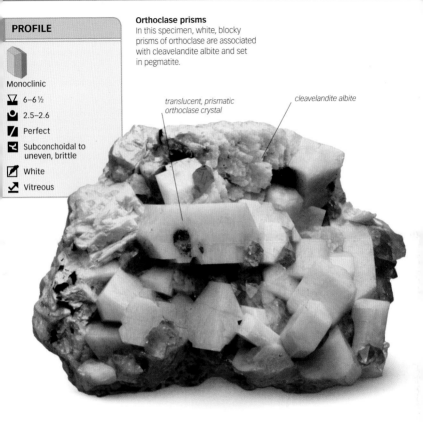

translucent, prismatic orthoclase crystal

cleavelandite albite

VARIANTS

Yellow orthoclase A crystal of yellow orthoclase

Moonstone rough An opalescent variety of orthoclase

twinned crystal

prismatic crystal

Orthoclase crystals Twinned orthoclase with smaller prism

♣ $KAlSi_3O_8$

ORTHOCLASE

An important rock-forming mineral, orthoclase is the potassium-bearing end member of the potassium—sodium feldspar solid-solution series. It is a major component of granite (pp.258–59)—its pink crystals give granite its typical color. Crystalline orthoclase can also be white, colorless, cream, pale yellow, or brownish red. Orthoclase appears as well-formed, short, prismatic crystals, which are frequently twinned. It may also occur in massive form. Moonstone is a variety of orthoclase that exhibits a schiller effect.

Pure orthoclase is rare— some sodium is usually present in the structure. Specimens are abundant in igneous rocks rich in potassium or silica, in pegmatites (p.260), and in gneisses (p.288). This mineral is important in ceramics, to make the item itself and as a glaze.

Moonstone-set brooch
Orthoclase exhibits the schiller effect which creates the shimmer seen on the moonstones in this brooch.

Prismatic sanidine
This single, well-formed prismatic crystal of sanidine rests in a matrix of the volcanic rock trachyte.

square cross section

translucent sanidine crystal

trachyte matrix

PROFILE

Monoclinic

6–6½

2.6

Perfect, good

Conchoidal to uneven

White

Vitreous

(K,Na)AlSi$_3$O$_8$

SANIDINE

A member of the solid-solution series of potassium and sodium feldspars, sanidine is the high-temperature form of potassium feldspar, forming at 1,065°F (575°C) or above. Crystals are usually colorless or white, glassy, and transparent, but they may also be gray, cream, or occur in other pale tints. They are generally short prismatic or tabular, with a square cross section. Twinning is common. Crystals have been known to reach 20 in (50 cm) in length. Sanidine is also found as granular or cleavable masses.

A widespread mineral, sanidine occurs in feldspar- and quartz-rich volcanic rocks, such as rhyolite (p.278), phonolite, and trachyte (p.279). It is also found in eclogites (p.299), contact metamorphic rocks, and metamorphic rocks formed at low pressure and high temperature. Sanidine forms spherular masses of needlelike crystals in obsidian (p.280), giving rise to what is called snowflake obsidian. Significant occurrences of sanidine are at the Alban Hills near Rome, Italy; Mont St.-Hilaire, Canada; and Eifel, Germany.

PROFILE

Triclinic

⚡ 6–6½

🔘 2.6

▨ Perfect, good

✂ Conchoidal to uneven, brittle

◪ White

⚡ Vitreous, dull

Prismatic microcline
Numerous prismatic crystals of light-colored microcline sit atop a pegmatite matrix, along with smoky quartz.

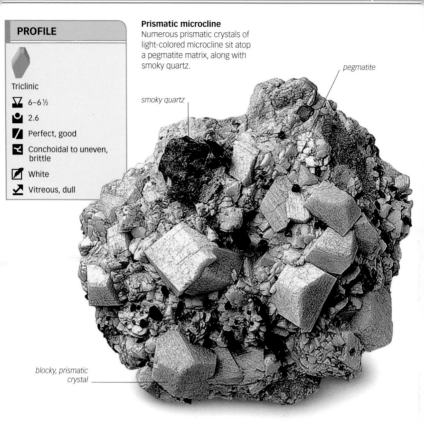

pegmatite

smoky quartz

blocky, prismatic
crystal

VARIANT

microcline   amazonite

Amazonite A single crystal of blue-green amazonite, a variety of microcline

🜨 $KAlSi_3O_8$

MICROCLINE

Used in ceramics and as a mild abrasive, microcline is one of the most common feldspar minerals. It can be colorless, white, cream to pale yellow, salmon pink to red, or bright green to blue-green. Microcline forms short prismatic or tabular crystals that are often of considerable size: single crystals can weigh several tons and reach yards in length. Crystals are often multiply twinned, with two sets of fine lines at right angles to each other. This gives a "plaid" effect that is unique to microcline among the feldspars. Microcline can also be massive.

The mineral occurs in feldspar-rich rocks, such as granite (pp.258–59), syenite (p.262), and granodiorite (p.263). It is found in granite pegmatites (p.260) and in metamorphic rocks, such as gneisses (p.288) and schists (p.291–92).

Amazonite cabochon
This Arts and Craft ring exhibits an asymmetrically set cabochon of amazonite in a rose-and-foliage design.

vitreous luster

single prismatic crystal

Prismatic anorthoclase
This specimen of pink and gray prismatic anorthoclase shows well-developed crystal faces.

PROFILE

Triclinic

 6–6½

 2.6

 Perfect, good

 Conchoidal to uneven, brittle

 White

 Vitreous

(Na,K)AlSi$_3$O$_8$

ANORTHOCLASE

This member of the sodium- and potassium-rich feldspar group takes its name from the Greek word *anorthos*, which means "not straight"—a reference to its oblique cleavage. Anorthoclase is colorless, white, cream, pink, pale yellow, gray, or green. Its crystals are prismatic or tabular and are often multiply twinned. Anorthoclase crystals can show two sets of fine lines at right angles to each other like microcline (p.175), but the lines are much finer. Specimens can also be massive or granular.

Anorthoclase forms in sodium-rich igneous zones. It commonly occurs with ilmenite (p.90), apatite (p.148), and augite (p.211). Much anorthoclase exhibits a gold, bluish, or greenish schiller effect, making it one of several feldspars known as moonstone when cut *en cabochon*. A type of the igneous rock syenite (p.262) called larvikite has large schillerized crystals of anorthoclase and is highly prized as an ornamental stone. Anorthoclase is widespread, but fine examples come from Cripple Creek, Colorado, USA; Larvik, Norway; and Fife, Scotland.

PROFILE

Triclinic

6–6½

2.6

Perfect, good

Conchoidal to uneven, brittle

White

Vitreous to pearly

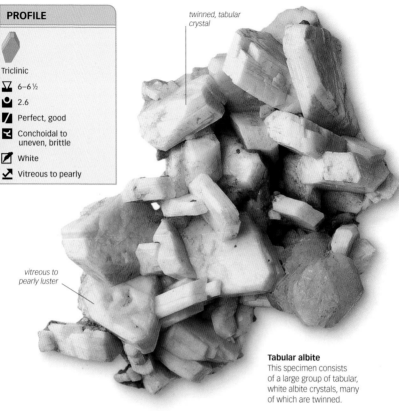

twinned, tabular crystal

vitreous to pearly luster

Tabular albite
This specimen consists of a large group of tabular, white albite crystals, many of which are twinned.

VARIANT

tourmaline

quartz

albite

Albite base Tourmaline and quartz crystals on albite

NaAlSi$_3$O$_8$

ALBITE

A rock-forming mineral, albite takes its name from the Latin word *albus*, which means "white"—a reference to its usual color. Specimens can also be colorless, yellowish, pink, or green. Albite occurs as tabular or platy crystals that are often twinned, glassy, and brittle. It can also be massive or granular. Albite was named in 1707.

This mineral is the solid-solution end member of both the plagioclase and the sodium- and potassium-rich feldspars. It occurs in pegmatites (p.260) and in some feldspar- and quartz-rich igneous rocks. Albite also forms through chemical processes in certain sedimentary environments and occurs in low-grade metamorphic rocks. The cleavelandite variety occurs in complex pegmatites as thin plates or scales.

Facet-grade albite
Faceted albite, although fragile, is sometimes used in jewelry, along with albite's moonstone variety.

PROFILE

Triclinic

- ▽ 6
- ☻ 2.6
- ◢ Perfect
- ◣ Conchoidal to uneven, brittle
- ◪ White
- ↗ Vitreous

Massive oligoclase
This typical massive specimen of oligoclase is from Penland, Mitchell County, North Carolina.

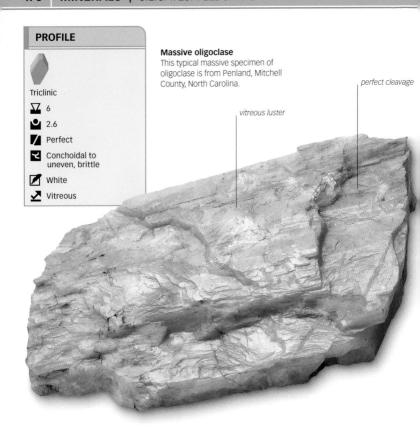

vitreous luster

perfect cleavage

VARIANTS

Sunstone rough
An uncut specimen of sunstone oligoclase

smoky quartz

Oligoclase crystal A pink crystal accompanied by smoky quartz

♣ (Na,Ca)Al$_2$Si$_2$O$_8$

OLIGOCLASE

In 1826, the German mineralogist August Breithaupt named this mineral after two Greek words: *oligos*, which means "little," and *clasein*, which means "to break"— because it was thought to have a less perfect cleavage than albite (p.177). Oligoclase can be gray, white, red, greenish, yellowish, brown, or colorless. Its usual habit is massive or granular, although it can form tabular crystals that are commonly twinned.

Oligoclase is the most common of the plagioclase feldspars. It occurs in granite (pp.258–59), granitic pegmatites (p.260), diorite (p.264), rhyolite (p.278), and other feldspar- and quartz-rich igneous rocks. It also occurs in high-grade, metamorphosed gneisses (p.288) and schists (pp.291–92).

Semiprecious oligoclase
Sunstone oligoclase, such as the oval example seen here, has hematite or goethite inclusions.

PROFILE

Triclinic

6–6½

2.7

Perfect

Conchoidal to uneven, brittle

White

Vitreous

vitreous luster

anorthite crystal

augite

Pink anorthite
In this specimen, pink crystals of anorthite occur with augite.

VARIANT

Anorthite aggregate A mass of blue-gray anorthite

 $CaAl_2Si_2O_8$

ANORTHITE

The calcium-rich end-member of the plagioclase-feldspar solid-solution series, anorthite takes its name from the Greek word *anorthos*, which means "not straight"—a reference to its triclinic form. Its brittle, short, glassy crystals are well-formed prisms that can be colored white or shades of gray, pink, or red. Specimens are also massive or granular. Anorthite is a calcium aluminosilicate and can contain up to 10 percent albite (p.177).

Anorthite is a major rock-forming mineral present in many magnesium- and iron-rich igneous rocks, contact metamorphic rocks, and chondroditic meteorites (p.337). Pure anorthite is uncommon; it weathers readily and is rare in rocks exposed at the surface for long periods. Anorthosite (p.261), a rock composed mainly of anorthite, makes up much of the lunar highlands. The so-called Genesis Rock, brought back by Apollo 15, is made of anorthosite and dates back to the formation of the Moon, which occurred about 4.1 billion years ago. Anorthite was also discovered in the comet Wild 2.

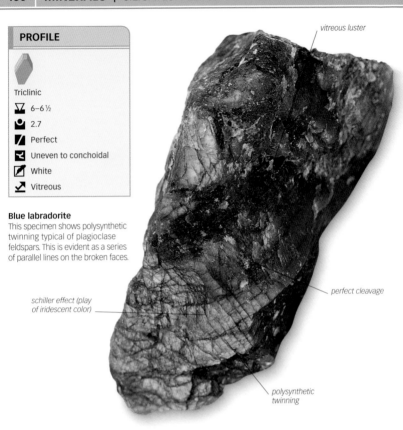

Triclinic

6–6½

2.7

Perfect

Uneven to conchoidal

White

Vitreous

Blue labradorite
This specimen shows polysynthetic twinning typical of plagioclase feldspars. This is evident as a series of parallel lines on the broken faces.

vitreous luster

perfect cleavage

schiller effect (play of iridescent color)

polysynthetic twinning

VARIANTS

Schiller effect Orange, purple, and blue flashes visible in a specimen of labradorite

Orange sunstone Labradorite "sunstone" from Oregon

$NaAlSi_3O_8$–$CaAl_2Si_2O_8$

LABRADORITE

The calcium-rich, middle-range member of the plagioclase feldspars, labradorite is characterized by its schiller effect—a rich play of iridescent colors, mainly blue, on cleavage surfaces. Specimens are generally blue or dark gray but can also be colorless or white. When transparent, labradorite is yellow, red, orange, or green. This mineral seldom forms crystals, but when crystals do occur, they are tabular. It most often forms masses with crystals that can be microscopic or up to 3ft (1m) or more wide.

Labradorite is a major constituent of certain medium-silica and silica-poor igneous and metamorphic rocks, including diorite (p.264), gabbro (p.265), basalt (p.273), andesite (p.275), and amphibolite (p.296). Gem-quality labradorite from Finland is known as spectrolite.

Semiprecious gemstone
The polished oval of labradorite in this choker beautifully displays the stone's rainbow iridescence.

blue porphyry

triclinic crystal

andesine crystal

Andesine crystals
This specimen has andesine crystals up to ¾ in (2 cm) long in blue porphyry. It was found in Estérel, Var, France.

VARIANT

Andesite porphyry Andesite is a major constituent of this porphyry rock

$NaAlSi_3O_8–CaAl_2Si_2O_8$

ANDESINE

The plagioclase feldspar andesine is named after the Andes Mountains in South America, where it is abundant in andesite lavas. A white, gray, or colorless mineral, andesine often forms well-defined crystals that usually exhibit multiple twinning. It can also be massive or occur as rock-bound grains.

A sodium calcium aluminosilicate, andesine is an intermediate member of the plagioclase solid-solution series. It occurs widely in igneous rocks of medium silica content, especially in andesite (p.275). Andesine is also found in other intermediate igneous rocks, such as syenite (p.262) and diorite (p.264). Specimens are commonly associated with magnetite (p.92), quartz (p.168), biotite (p.197), and hornblende (p.218). Andesine typically occurs in metamorphic rocks formed under high pressure and temperatures (1,065°F/575°C or above). It is also found as detrital grains in sedimentary rocks. The accurate identification of individual specimens involves detailed study and analysis.

Massive nepheline
This specimen of nepheline from Arkansas shows the mineral's most typical massive habit.

translucent with a vitreous luster

massive habit

VARIANT

rock matrix *nepheline prism*

Nepheline crystals Well-developed crystals within cavities in a rock matrix

(Na,K)AlSiO$_4$

NEPHELINE

The most common feldspathoid mineral, nepheline takes its name from the Greek word *nephele*, which means "cloud"—a reference to the fact that the mineral becomes cloudy or milky in strong acids. Specimens are usually white in color, often with a yellowish or grayish tint. They can also be colorless, gray, yellow, or red-brown. Nepheline is generally massive. Crystals usually occur as hexagonal prisms, although they can exhibit a variety of prism and pyramid shapes. Nepheline also forms large, tabular phenocrysts in igneous rocks.

This rock-forming mineral is found in iron- and magnesium-rich igneous rocks with perovskite (p.89), spinel (p.96), and olivine (p.232). It also occurs in intermediate igneous rocks with aegirine (p.209) and augite (p.211) and in some volcanic and metamorphic rocks.

Ceramic bowl
Nepheline is sometimes used as a substitute for feldspars in ceramics, such as this porcelain bowl.

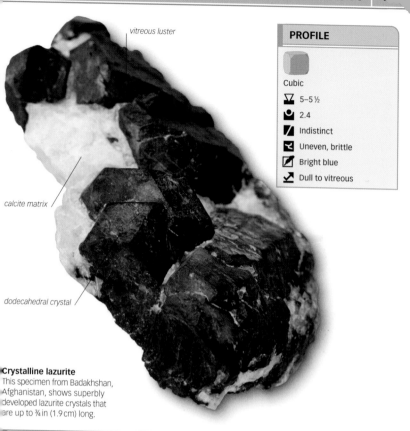

vitreous luster

calcite matrix

dodecahedral crystal

Crystalline lazurite
This specimen from Badakhshan, Afghanistan, shows superbly developed lazurite crystals that are up to ¾ in (1.9 cm) long.

VARIANTS

Polished slab A slice of lazurite showing intense color

Lapis lazuli An uncut piece of lapis lazuli streaked with calcite

marble

Lazurite in marble Lazurite dispersed in marble

$Na_3Ca(Al_3Si_3O_{12})S$

LAZURITE

A sodium calcium aluminosilicate, lazurite is the main component of the gemstone lapis lazuli and accounts for the stone's intense blue color, although lapis lazuli also typically contains pyrite (p.62), calcite (p.114), sodalite (p.184), and haüyne. Lazurite specimens are always deep or vibrant blue. Distinct crystals were thought to be rare until large numbers were brought out of mines in Badakhshan, Afghanistan, in the 1990s. These are usually dodecahedral and are much sought after. Most lazurite is either massive or occurs in disseminated grains.

Lapis lazuli is relatively rare. It forms in crystalline limestones (p.319) as a product of contact metamorphism. The best quality lapis lazuli is dark blue with minor patches of calcite and pyrite. In addition to its use as a gemstone, lapis lazuli was used as one of the first eye shadows.

Expensive pigment Powdered lapis lazuli was once used to make ultramarine, one of the most expensive pigments.

PROFILE

Cubic

- 5½–6
- 2.1–2.3
- Poor to distinct
- Uneven to conchoidal
- White to light blue
- Vitreous to greasy

Massive sodalite
This sodalite specimen shows intense blue color, which can sometimes lead to the mineral being mistaken for lapis lazuli.

vitreous luster

uneven fracture

massive habit

VARIANTS

Polished sodalite A specimen that has been polished to bring out its color

Indian sodalite A specimen of light blue sodalite found in India

$Na_4Al_3Si_3O_{12}Cl$

SODALITE

Named in 1811 after its high sodium content, sodalite is sodium aluminum silicate chloride. Specimens can be blue, gray, pink, colorless, or other pale shades. They sometimes fluoresce bright orange under ultraviolet light. Sodalite nearly always forms massive aggregates or disseminated grains. Crystals are relatively rare; when found, they are dodecahedral or octahedral.

Sodalite occurs in igneous rocks and associated pegmatites (p.260). It is sometimes found in contact metamorphosed limestones (p.319) and dolomites (p.320) and in rocks ejected from volcanoes. Rare crystals are found on the Mount Vesuvius volcano in Italy. Uncommon transparent specimens from Mont St.-Hilaire, Canada, are faceted for collectors.

Sodalite beads
This unusual modern Egyptian necklace has beads made of blue sodalite and red carnelian.

PROFILE

Cubic   Tetragonal

⬙ 5½–6

◗ 2.5

◤ Poor

✂ Conchoidal, brittle

◪ White

⬈ Vitreous

Leucite crystals
In this specimen formed at a high temperature, fine psuedotrapezohedral crystals of leucite rest in cavities in a rock matrix.

leucite pseudotrapezohedron

rock matrix

VARIANTS

Single crystal A single yellowish crystal of leucite

Italian leucite A crystal in pseudotrapezohedral form from Casserta, Italy

⚛ KAlSi$_2$O$_6$

LEUCITE

The name leucite comes from the Greek word *leukos*, which means "matt white"—a reference to the mineral's most common color. Specimens can also be colorless or gray. Crystals are common and can be up to 3½ in (9 cm) wide. More often, leucite occurs as massive or granular aggregates or as disseminated grains. It is tetragonal at temperatures below 1,155°F (625°C) and cubic with trapezohedral crystals at higher temperatures. The trapezohedral form is preserved as the mineral cools and develops tetragonal symmetry.

Leucite is found in potassium-rich and silica-poor igneous rocks. It is found with nepheline (p.182), sodalite (p.184), natrolite (p.186), analcime (p.190), and sodium- and potassium-rich feldspars, and occurs worldwide.

Potassium fertilizer
Because of leucite's high potassium content, the mineral is used as a fertilizer in some countries.

PROFILE

Orthorhombic

⬇ 5–5½

⬤ 2.3

◢ Perfect

✦ Uneven, brittle

◰ White

⬀ Vitreous to pearly

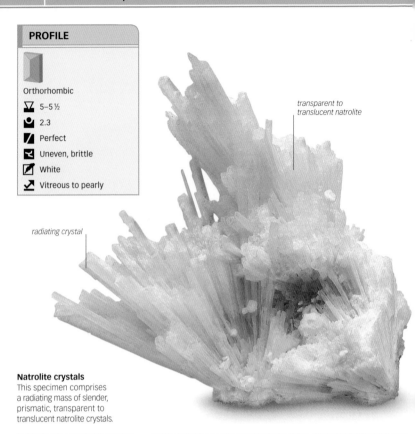

transparent to translucent natrolite

radiating crystal

Natrolite crystals
This specimen comprises a radiating mass of slender, prismatic, transparent to translucent natrolite crystals.

VARIANT

natrolite

calcite

Natrolite and calcite
A specimen including white calcite and light orange natrolite

 $Na_2Al_2Si_3O_{10}\cdot2H_2O$

NATROLITE

A hydrated sodium aluminosilicate, natrolite takes its name from the Greek word *natrium*, which means "soda"—a reference to the sodium content of this mineral. Natrolite can be pale pink, colorless, white, red, gray, yellow, or green. Some specimens fluoresce orange to yellow under ultraviolet light. Natrolite crystals are generally long and slender, with vertical striations and a square cross section. They may appear tetragonal and can grow up to 3 ft (1 m) in length. Natrolite is also found as radiating masses of needlelike crystals and as granular or compact masses. This mineral produces an electric charge in response to both pressure and temperature changes.

Natrolite is found in cavities or fissures in basaltic rocks (p.273), volcanic ash deposits, and veins in granite (pp.258–59), gneiss (p.288), and other rocks. It also occurs in altered syenites (p.262), aplites, and dolerites (p.268). Specimens are often associated with quartz (p.168), heulandite (p.187), apophyllite (p.204), and other zeolites.

PROFILE

Monoclinic

⬨ 3½–4

⬥ 2.2

⬧ Perfect

⬨ Uneven, brittle

⬧ Colorless

⬨ Vitreous to pearly

red heulandite crystal

basalt matrix

Red heulandite
In this specimen, tabular crystals of heulandite line a cavity in a basalt matrix.

VARIANT

Colorless crystals Typical, colorless, coffin-shaped heulandite crystals

$CaAl_2Si_7O_{18} \cdot 6H_2O$

HEULANDITE

The name heulandite is used to refer to a series of five zeolite minerals, all of which look the same but vary in composition. The group was named in 1822 after the British collector and mineral dealer J.H. Heuland. Heulandite is usually colorless or white but can also be red, gray, yellow, pink, green, or brown. When found, crystals are elongated, tabular, and widest at the center, creating a coffin shape. Occasionally, trapezohedral crystals are found. Heulandite specimens can also be granular or massive.

Heulandite forms at low temperatures (up to 400°F/200°C) in a wide range of environments: with other zeolites filling cavities in granites (pp.258–59), pegmatites (p.260), and basalts (p.273); in metamorphic rocks; and in weathered andesites (p.275) and diabases.

Oil refining
Heulandite and other zeolites are used to filter out unwanted molecules during oil refining.

PROFILE

Monoclinic

⬇ 5

🌡 2.3

▨ Perfect

▧ Uneven, brittle

▨ White

↗ Vitreous to silky

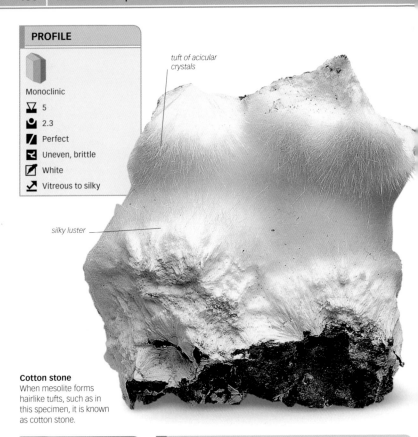

tuft of acicular crystals

silky luster

Cotton stone
When mesolite forms hairlike tufts, such as in this specimen, it is known as cotton stone.

VARIANTS

White mesolite Needles of mesolite on green apophyllite

Acicular mesolite
A radiating mass of needlelike crystals

🜨 $Na_2Ca_2(Al_6Si_9)O_{30}\cdot8H_2O$

MESOLITE

First described in 1816, mesolite takes its name from two Greek words: *mesos*, which means "middle," and *lithos*, which means "stone"—a reference to the fact that this mineral is chemically intermediate in composition between scolecite and natrolite (p.186). Mesolite is structurally identical and similar in appearance to scolecite and natrolite, which makes it difficult to identify in hand specimens. Specimens can be white, pink, red, yellowish, green, or pale colored. It occurs as long, slender needles, radiating masses, prisms, and, less commonly, compact masses or fibrous stalactites.

Mesolite is found in cavities in basalts (p.273) and andesites (p.275), where delicate, glassy prisms can occur with stilbite, heulandite (p.187), and green apophyllite (p.204). It is also found in hydrothermal veins. Exceptional specimens occur in Ahmadnagar and Poona, India; Neubauerberg, the Czech Republic; Naalsoy in the Faroe Islands; Victoria Land, Antarctica; and in the states of Washington, Oregon, and Colorado.

Pseudocubic chabazite
This group of pseudocubic chabazite crystals is from the Bay of Fundy in Nova Scotia, Canada.

pseudocubic chabazite crystal

basalt

PROFILE

Triclinic

4–5

2.0–2.2

Indistinct

Uneven, brittle

White

Vitreous

VARIANT

basalt

Chabazite in basalt A group of white chabazite crystals in a hollow in basalt

$(Na,Ca_{0.5},K)_4(Al_4Si_8O_{24})\cdot12H_2O$

CHABAZITE

This is a group of three common zeolite minerals that look alike but have distinct properties: chabazite-Ca, chabazite-K, and chabazite-Na. The name is derived from the Greek *chabazios* or *chalazios*, both of which mean "hailstone." Specimens are colorless, white, cream, pink, red, orange, yellow, or brown. Chabazite crystals occur as distorted cubes or pseudorhombohedrons consisting of multiple twins. They may also be prismatic. Twinning is common in all forms of chabazite.

Chabazite is found in cavities in pegmatites (p.260), basalt (p.273), andesite (p.275), volcanic ash deposits, and granitic (pp.258–59) and metamorphic (pp.288–303) rocks. It is widespread, with crystals that are 1–2in (2.5–5cm) long occurring in several locations. Chabazite and some other zeolites have an open crystal structure that is sievelike and permits small molecules to pass through, while preventing the passage of larger molecules. This structure, for example, helps filter methane from gases emitted by decaying organic waste matter.

PROFILE

Cubic

⊻ 5–5½

⬻ 2.3

▰ None

⬧ Subconchoidal, brittle

▱ White

⬈ Vitreous

Analcime trapezohedrons
This group of superbly crystallized analcime trapezohedrons from the Dean Quarry, Cornwall, England, rests on a bed of calcite crystals.

trapezohedral analcime crystal

calcite crystal

vitreous luster

VARIANT

Colorless analcime A single crystal of colorless analcime on a rock matrix

🔩 Na(AlSi$_2$)O$_6$·H$_2$O

ANALCIME

Formerly grouped with the feldspathoids, analcime is now classified as a zeolite. A sodium aluminum silicate, analcime is named after the Greek word *analkimos*, which means "weak"—a reference to the weak electrical charge that this mineral produces when it is heated or rubbed. Specimens are usually colorless or white but can also be yellow, brown, pink, red, or orange. Most analcime crystals are trapezohedral. Variations in the ratio and order of the sodium–aluminum portion in analcime can lead to structural variations and variation in crystal system.

Analcime occurs in seams and cavities in granite (pp.258–59), basalt (p.273), gneiss (p.288), and diabase, associated with calcite (p.114), prehnite (p.205), and other zeolites. It also occurs in extensive beds formed by precipitation from alkaline lakes.

Silica dessicator
Made from analcime, silica gel, such as in this dessicator, rapidly absorbs moisture and has many drying uses.

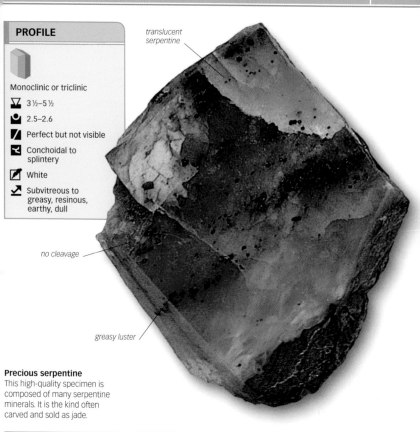

translucent serpentine

no cleavage

greasy luster

Precious serpentine
This high-quality specimen is composed of many serpentine minerals. It is the kind often carved and sold as jade.

VARIANTS

Lizardite A specimen of this fine-grained serpentine mineral from Cornwall, UK

platy mass

Antigorite A specimen of this serpentine mineral with characteristic, corrugated plates

$(Mg,Fe,Ni)_3Si_2O_5(OH)_4$

SERPENTINE

Resembling snakeskin in appearance, serpentine is a group of at least 16 white, yellowish, green, or gray-green magnesium silicate minerals. Although they usually form mixtures, individual members of the group can sometimes be distinguished. Four common serpentine minerals include chrysotile (p.192), antigorite, lizardite, and amesite, which occur in platy or pseudohexagonal, columnar crystals. Although their chemistry is complex, these minerals look similar.

Serpentines are secondary minerals derived from the chemical alteration of olivine (p.232), the pyroxenes, and the amphiboles. It is found in areas where highly altered, deep-seated, silica-poor rocks are exposed, such as along the crests and axes of great folds, in island arcs, and in Alpine mountain chains.

Williamsite cabochon
A variety of serpentine, williamsite is an ornamental stone that is sometimes cut as an inexpensive gem.

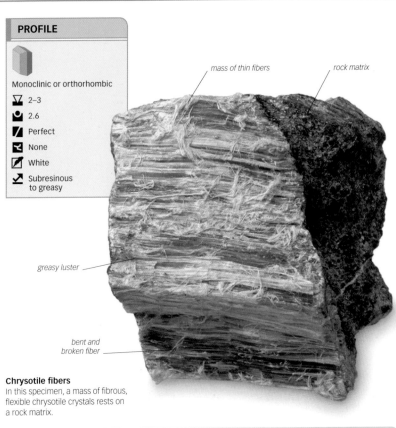

mass of thin fibers

rock matrix

greasy luster

bent and broken fiber

Chrysotile fibers
In this specimen, a mass of fibrous, flexible chrysotile crystals rests on a rock matrix.

🜨 $Mg_3Si_2O_5(OH)_4$

CHRYSOTILE

The fibrous serpentine mineral chrysotile is the most important asbestos mineral. Also known as white asbestos, it accounts for about 95 percent of all asbestos in commercial use. Chrysotile fibers are tubes in which the structural layers of the mineral are rolled in the form of a spiral. Individual chrysotile fibers are white and silky, while aggregate fibers in veins are green or yellowish. The fibers are generally oriented across the vein and less than ½ in (1.3 cm) in length, but they can be longer. The mineral sometimes appears golden, and its name is derived from the Greek for "hair of gold."

Chrysotile can take three different forms: clinochrysotile, orthochrysotile, and parachrysotile. These are chemically identical, but orthochrysotile and parachrysotile have orthorhombic rather than monoclinic crystals. These forms are indistinguishable in hand specimens, and clinochrysotile and orthochrysotile may occur within the same fiber. Specimens occur as veins in altered peridotite (p.266) with other serpentine minerals.

Foliated talc
This specimen of green, foliated talc exhibits its pearly luster and micalike cleavage.

greasy luster

micaceous cleavage

foliated talc

VARIANT

pearly luster

Pearly talc A pearly, toothlike piece of talc

$Mg_3Si_4O_{10}(OH)_2$

TALC

Easily distinguishable by its extreme softness, talc is white, colorless, pale to dark green, or yellowish to brown. Crystals are rare; talc is most commonly found in foliated, fibrous, or massive aggregates. It is often found mixed with other minerals, such as serpentine (p.191) and calcite (p.114). Dense, high-purity talc is called steatite.

Talc is a metamorphic mineral found in veins and magnesium-rich rocks. It is often associated with serpentine, tremolite (p.219), and forsterite (p.232) and occurs as an alteration product of silica-poor igneous rocks. Talc is widespread and is found in most areas of the world where low-grade metamorphism occurs. The name soapstone is given to compact masses of talc and other minerals due to their soapy or greasy feel.

Talcum powder
Talc is the principal mineral used to make talcum powder. It acts as an astringent on the skin.

Pyrophyllite stars
This aggregate of pyrophyllite displays radiating, starlike groups of laths with associated quartz.

radiating mass of pyrophyllite crystals

quartz crystal

pyrophyllite crystals

Pyrophyllite on rock Groups of pyrophyllite crystals on a rock matrix

⚛ $Al_2Si_4O_{10}(OH)_2$

PYROPHYLLITE

An aluminum silicate hydroxide, pyrophyllite takes its name from the Greek words *pyr* and *phyllon*, which respectively mean "fire" and "leaf"—a reference to the mineral's tendency to exfoliate when heated. Pyrophyllite can be colorless, white, cream, brownish green, pale blue, or gray. It is usually found in granular masses of flattened lamellae. Pyrophyllite rarely forms distinct crystals, although it is sometimes found in coarse laths and radiating aggregates. Specimens are often so fine-grained that the mineral appears textureless.

Pyrophyllite forms by the metamorphism of aluminum-rich sedimentary rocks, such as bauxite (p.101). It is a good insulator and is used in heat-resistant applications, such as in making fire bricks.

High gloss
Bright, reflective flakes of powdered pyrophyllite are added to lipstick to give it a high sheen.

Colorful fuchsite
Fuchsite is a minor variety of white muscovite. Specimens such as this one are colored by traces of chromium.

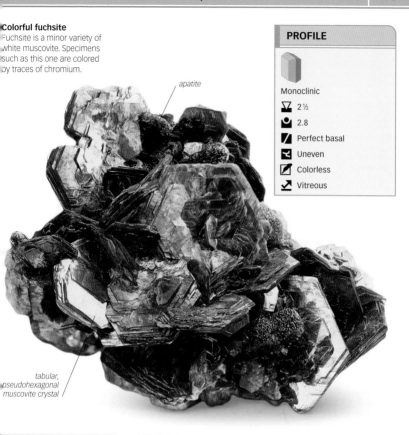

apatite

tabular, pseudohexagonal muscovite crystal

VARIANTS

Tabular crystals Silver-brown crystals of tabular muscovite

Platy muscovite Crystals of muscovite in a rock matrix

Green fuchsite Bright green fuchsite in a rock matrix

$KAl_2(Si_3Al)O_{10}(OH,F)_2$

MUSCOVITE

Also called common mica, potash mica, or isinglass, muscovite is the most common member of the mica group. Specimens are usually colorless or silvery white but can also be brown, light gray, pale green, or rose red. Muscovite typically occurs as tabular crystals with a hexagonal or pseudohexagonal outline. Crystals can be up to 9¾ft (3m) in diameter. Muscovite can also form thin, flat sheets and fine-grained aggregates. Fine-grained muscovite is called sericite or white mica, while bright green specimens rich in chromium are called fuchsite.

A common rock-forming mineral, muscovite occurs in metamorphic rocks, such as gneisses (p.288) and schists (pp.291–92), and in granites (pp.258–59), veins, and pegmatites (p.260). It is also found in some fine-grained sediments. Muscovite has considerable commercial importance. Its low iron content makes it a good electrical and thermal insulator. In Russia, thin, transparent sheets of muscovite, called muscovy glass, were used as window panes.

PROFILE

Monoclinic

⊻ 2

🔘 2.4–2.9

▰ Perfect basal

▰ Uneven

▰ Green

▰ Dull to earthy

aggregate of small grains

dull luster

Grainy glauconite
This typically massive specimen of glauconite includes grains and shows a dull luster.

VARIANTS

Glauconite sandstone
Sandstone with a high percentage of glauconite

Nodular glauconite Light green nodules of glauconite

🔬 (K,Na) (Mg,Al,Fe)$_2$(Si,Al)$_4$O$_{10}$(OH)$_2$

GLAUCONITE

A member of the mica group, glauconite was named in 1828 after the Greek word *glaukos*, which means "blue-green"—a reference to the mineral's usual color. Specimens can also be olive green to black-green. The mineral usually occurs as rounded aggregates or pellets of fine-grained, scaly particles. It weathers readily and easily crumbles to a fine powder.

A widespread silicate, glauconite forms in shallow marine environments, where it is used as a diagnostic mineral to identify continental-shelf deposits with slow rates of accumulation. The sedimentary rock greensand (p.309) is so called because of the green color imparted by glauconite pellets, which in turn, may incorporate other minerals. Glauconite can also be found in impure limestone (p.319), chalk (p.321), and sand and clay formations. The mineral has long been used as a pigment in artists' oil paint, especially in the paintings of Russian icons. It has also been used in wall paintings dating back to Roman Gaul.

PROFILE

Monoclinic

2–3 ⁹⁄₁₀

2.7–3.4

Perfect basal

Uneven

Colorless

Vitreous to submetallic

rock matrix

thin, flexible sheets of biotite

Black mica
In this specimen, iron-rich, tabular, pseudohexagonal crystals of a biotite-series mica rest on a rock matrix.

VARIANT

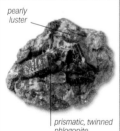
pearly luster

prismatic, twinned phlogopite crystals

Phlogopite Crystals of the magnesium end-member of the biotite solid-solution series

$KFe_3,Mg_3(AlSi_3O_{10})(OH,F)_2$

BIOTITE

Once considered a mineral in its own right, biotite is now recognized as a solid-solution series with the mineral annite as the iron end-member and phlogopite as the magnesium end-member. It was named in honor of the French physicist Jean-Baptiste Biot in 1847. Micas of the biotite series usually form large, tabular to short, prismatic crystals that are often pseudohexagonal in cross section. They also occur in thin layers or as scaly aggregates or disseminated grains. Specimens are black when iron-rich, and brown, pale yellow to tan, or bronze with increasing magnesium content. They readily cleave into thin, flexible sheets.

Biotite-series micas are widespread. They are a key constituent of many igneous and metamorphic rocks, including granites (pp.258–59), nepheline syenites (p.262), gneisses (p.288), and schists (p.291–92). They are also found in potassium-rich hydrothermal deposits and some clastic sedimentary rocks. Biotite is used extensively to date rocks.

PROFILE

Monoclinic

2½–3½

3.0

Perfect basal

Uneven

Colorless

Vitreous to pearly

Distinctive color
Numerous violet pseudohexagonal lepidolite crystals protrude from this pegmatite specimen.

vitreous luster

granitic pegmatite

tabular lepidolite crystal

VARIANT

Botryoidal lepidolite
Lepidolite in botryoidal habit

$K(Li,Al_3)(AlSi_3)O_{10}(OH,F)_2$

LEPIDOLITE

A light mica, lepidolite is Earth's most common lithium-bearing mineral. Its name is derived from two Greek words: *lepidos*, which means "scale," and *lithos*, which means "stone." Although typically pale lilac, specimens can also be colorless, violet, pale yellow, or gray. Lepidolite crystals may appear pseudohexagonal. The mineral is also found as botryoidal or kidneylike masses and fine- to coarse-grained, interlocking plates. Its perfect cleavage yields thin, flexible sheets.

Lepidolite occurs in granitic pegmatites (p.260), where it is associated with other lithium minerals, such as beryl (p.225) and topaz (p.234). The mineral is economically important as a major source of lithium, which is used to make glass and enamels. It is also a major source of the rare alkali metals rubidium and cesium.

Lithium battery
Extracted from lepidolite, the metal lithium has many industrial uses, such as in lithium batteries.

Vermiculite layers
This specimen of vermiculite, mined in Pennsylvania, shows the mineral's foliated habit.

pseudohexagonal outline

foliated habit

$(Mg,Fe,Al)_3(Al,Si)_4O_{10}(OH)\cdot 4H_2O$

VERMICULITE

The name vermiculite is applied to a group of mica minerals in which various chemical substitutions occur in the molecular structure. Vermiculite may be completely interlayered with other micas and claylike minerals. Specimens are green, golden yellow, or brown in color. Vermiculite usually forms tabular, pseudohexagonal crystals or platy aggregates.

Vermiculite occurs as large pseudomorphs replacing biotite (p.197), as small particles in soils and ancient sediments, and at the interface between feldspar-rich and iron- and magnesium-rich igneous rocks. It also forms by hydrothermal alteration of iron-bearing micas. When heated to nearly 572°F (300°C), vermiculite can expand quickly and strongly to 20 times its original thickness.

Potting soil
Expanded vermiculite is a good growing medium for new plants; it retains water and offers good aeration.

PROFILE

Monoclinic

⬒ 1–2

⬗ 2.1

▨ Perfect

▧ Uneven

▥ White to buff

⬏ Earthy

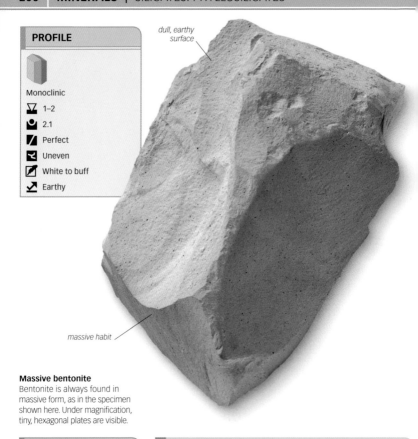

dull, earthy surface

massive habit

Massive bentonite
Bentonite is always found in massive form, as in the specimen shown here. Under magnification, tiny, hexagonal plates are visible.

VARIANTS

Desert cracking Loss of water from bentonite clays causes shrinkage and cracking

Bentonite sediments Layers of bentonite-rich clay

$(Na,Ca_{0.5})_{0.33}(Al,Mg)_2Si_4O_{10}(OH)_2 \cdot nH_2O$

BENTONITE

This group of minerals are all kinds of clay that expand as they absorb water and shrink as they dry. In regions underlain by bentonites, this property causes immense problems with building foundations. There are three bentonite minerals, each named after the respective dominant element: potassium bentonite, sodium bentonite, and calcium bentonite. The minerals are generally yellow, white, or gray in color. They occur as microscopic crystals and are earthy and frequently stained.

Although the term bentonite has been used for clay beds of uncertain origin, this mineral group generally forms from volcanic ash that has weathered in the presence of water. Important industrial minerals, bentonites are used as sealants and in oil drilling.

Potting clay
The potting clay used to make this bowl contains bentonite, which is also used in bricks and ceramics.

Triclinic

⛏ 2–2½

⚖ 2.6

▧ Perfect

▨ Unobservable

▧ White

⟋ Earthy

Powdery kaolinite
In this specimen, powdery
kaolinite coats a piece
of granite.

powdery kaolinite

earthy luster

VARIANTS

Blocky kaolinite Blocky,
typically white kaolinite

Iron staining A specimen of
kaolinite mixed with iron oxides,
which give it an orange color

⚛ $Al_2Si_2O_5(OH)_4$

KAOLINITE

Clay minerals are far removed in their outward
appearance from more attractive and glamorous
minerals, such as gold and diamond. Yet, by providing
the raw material for brick, pottery, and tiles, they have
played a vital part in the progress of human civilization.
Important among these minerals is kaolinite. Kaolinite
forms white, microscopic, pseudohexagonal plates in
compact or granular masses and in micalike piles.
Three other minerals—dickite, nacrite, and halloysite—
are chemically identical to kaolinite but crystallize in the
monoclinic system. All four have been found together
and are often visually indistinguishable.

Kaolinite is a natural product of the alteration of mica,
plagioclase, and sodium–potassium feldspars under the
influence of water, dissolved carbon dioxide, and organic
acids. It is used in agriculture; as a filler in food, such as
chocolate; mixed with pectin as an antidiarrheal; as a paint
extender; as a strengthener in rubber; and as a dusting
agent in foundry operations.

PROFILE

Monoclinic

1–2

2.6–2.9

Perfect

None

White

Dull

pale, earthy mass of illite

Illite mass
One of the major clay minerals, illite is usually found as pale, earthy masses.

VARIANT

Solid illite Solid masses of illite are occasionally found

$K_{0.65}Al_2Al_{0.65}Si_{3.35}O_{10}(OH)_2$

ILLITE

Once regarded as a clay mineral, illite is now classified as a group of mica minerals that bear many structural similarities to the white mica muscovite (p.195). Illite takes its name from its type location in Illinois. It is white, but impurities may tint it gray and other pale colors. It occurs as fine-grained aggregates. Individual hexagonal crystals can only be seen using an electron microscope. Because of its minute crystals, illite can only be positively identified by x-ray diffraction. The degree of crystallization of illite has been used as an indicator of metamorphic grade in clay-bearing metamorphic rocks.

Illite is found in sedimentary rocks and soils. It is the most abundant clay mineral in shales (pp.313–14) and clays. It appears to be derived from the weathering of muscovite and feldspar (pp.173–81).

Mud bricks
Ancient buildings, such as the Funerary Temple in Egypt, were often made from clays bearing illite.

Chrysocolla with azurite
In this specimen, chrysocolla can be seen with the carbonate mineral azurite in a rock matrix.

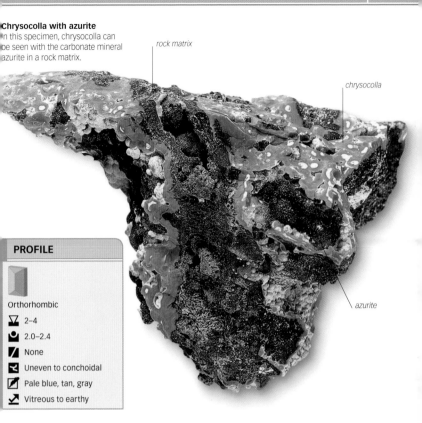

rock matrix

chrysocolla

azurite

PROFILE

Orthorhombic

▮ 2–4

🪨 2.0–2.4

⟋ None

◪ Uneven to conchoidal

▨ Pale blue, tan, gray

⤢ Vitreous to earthy

VARIANTS

Rough chrysocolla
A specimen intergrown with turquoise and malachite

chrysocolla

Cabochon Green chrysocolla within reddish iron oxide

⚛ $Cu_2H_2(Si_2O_5)(OH)_4 \cdot nH_2O$

CHRYSOCOLLA

The term chrysocolla was first used by the Greek philosopher Theophrastus in 315 BCE to refer to various materials used in soldering gold. The name is derived from two Greek words: *chrysos*, which means "gold," and *kolla*, which means "glue." A copper aluminum silicate, chrysocolla is generally blue-green in color. Specimens are commonly fine grained and massive. Crystals are very rare but when found occur as botryoidal, radiating aggregates.

An occasional ore of copper, chrysocolla is a decomposition product of copper minerals, especially in arid regions. It is frequently intergrown with other minerals, such as quartz (p.168), chalcedony (p.169), and opal (p.172), to yield a gemstone variety. Gemstones can weigh more than 5 lb (2.3 kg).

Chrysocolla bracelet
Rich blue-green chrysocolla, such as the cabochon in this antique bracelet, is highly prized as a gemstone.

Green apophyllite
In this specimen, green apophyllite occurs in a basalt matrix with a white zeolite mineral.

green apophyllite

white zeolite

basalt

VARIANTS

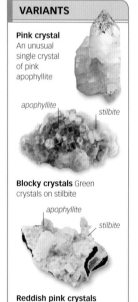

Pink crystal
An unusual single crystal of pink apophyllite

apophyllite *stilbite*

Blocky crystals Green crystals on stilbite

apophyllite *stilbite*

Reddish pink crystals
Apophyllite with white stilbite

$KCa_4Si_8O_{20}(F,OH)\cdot 8H_2O$ (fluorapophyllite)

APOPHYLLITE

The name apophyllite comes from the Greek words *apo* and *phyllazein*, which mean "to get" and "leaf" respectively—a reference to the way in which the mineral separates into flakes or layers when it is heated. Once considered to be a single mineral, apophyllite is now divided into two distinct species—fluorapophyllite and hydroxyapophyllite. These species form a solid-solution series in which fluorine can predominate over oxygen and hydrogen, and vice versa. Apophyllite specimens are green, pink, colorless, or white. Crystals are transparent or translucent and up to 8 in (20 cm) in length. They occur as square-sided, striated prisms with flat ends and may appear cubic. Apophyllite crystals may also show steep pyramidal terminations.

The mineral frequently occurs with zeolite minerals in basalt (p.273) and less commonly in cavities in granites (pp.258–59). It is also found in metamorphic rocks and in hydrothermal deposits. Colorless and green specimens from India are faceted as collectors' gems.

PROFILE

Orthorhombic

6–6½

2.9

Distinct basal

Uneven, brittle

White

Vitreous

Botryoidal prehnite
A group of radiating crystal masses of prehnite resting on a rock matrix gives a botryoidal form to this specimen.

radiating prehnite crystal

rock matrix

vitreous luster

VARIANT

calcite

prehnite

Green prehnite Spherical masses of prehnite occuring with white calcite on a rock matrix

$Ca_2Al_2Si_3O_{10}(OH)_2$

PREHNITE

A calcium aluminum silicate, prehnite was named in 1789 after its discoverer Hendrik von Prehn, a Dutch military officer. Specimens can be pale to mid-green, tan, pale yellow, gray, light blue, or white. Prehnite commonly occurs as globular, spherical, or stalactitic aggregates of fine to coarse crystals. Rare individual crystals are short prismatic to tabular with square cross sections. Many of these have curved faces.

Prehnite is often found lining cavities in volcanic rocks, associated with calcite (p.114) and zeolites (pp.185–90), and in mineral veins in granite (pp.258–59). Crystals up to several inches long come from Canada. Transparent specimens from Australia and Scotland are faceted for gem collectors.

White cabochon
Prehnite gems, such as this creamy white cabochon with dark inclusions, are almost too soft to wear.

Massive sepiolite
This specimen of massive sepiolite shows a characteristic dull, earthy luster.

massive habit

dull luster

Meerschaum A specimen of massive white sepiolite

$Mg_4Si_6O_{15}(OH)_2.6H_2O$

SEPIOLITE

A compact, claylike, often porous mineral, sepiolite is best known by its popular name *meerschaum*, which is the German word for "sea-foam." The name sepiolite comes from the mineral's resemblance to the light and porous bone of cuttlefish from the genus *Sepia*. Sepiolite is usually white or gray and may be tinted yellow, brown, or green. It is usually found in nodular masses of interlocking fibers, which give it a toughness contrary to its mineralogical softness. Sepiolite also occurs in porous aggregates.

Sepiolite is an alteration product of minerals such as magnesite (p.118) and rocks, such as serpentinite (p.298). It is found as irregular nodules in Turkey and elsewhere, and in large sedimentary deposits.

Meerschaum cigar holder
Sepiolite is used in carved tobacco pipes and cigar holders, which develop a brown patina when smoked.

Purple-brown pigeonite
This specimen of pigeonite comes from the Kovdor Pit, Kola Peninsula, Russia.

perfect cleavage

cleavable mass

PROFILE

Monoclinic

 6

 3.2–3.5

 Good

Uneven to conchoidal, brittle

White to pale brown

Vitreous

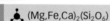 (Mg,Fe,Ca)$_2$(Si$_2$O$_6$)

PIGEONITE

A member of the pyroxene group of minerals, pigeonite is named after Pigeon Point, Minnesota, USA— the locality where it was first identified. Specimens are brown, purplish brown, or greenish brown to black in color. Pigeonite is generally found as disseminated grains. Well-formed crystals are relatively rare. An iron-rich variety of pigeonite is sometimes called ferropigeonite.

Pigeonite is an important mineral in lunar rocks and also occurs in meteorites (pp.335–37). It is found in lavas and smaller intrusive rock bodies as the dominant pyroxene and as an important component of dolerites (p.268) and andesites (p.275). The temperature limit of pigeonite formation indicates the crystallization temperature of the magma from which it has originated. Mare—the large, dark, flat areas of the Moon once believed to be seas—are in fact basalts (p.273) containing pigeonite. Notable localities on Earth include Skaergaard, Greenland; Mull, Scotland; Labrador, Canada; Mount Wellington, Tasmania; and Goose Creek, Virginia, and New Jersey, USA.

Prismatic crystals
This mass of small, prismatic enstatite crystals rests on a rock matrix.

small, prismatic crystals

rock matrix

VARIANTS

Single crystal A large crystal from Telemark, Norway

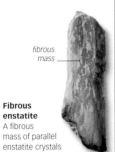

fibrous mass

Fibrous enstatite
A fibrous mass of parallel enstatite crystals

$Mg_2Si_2O_6$

ENSTATITE

The pyroxene mineral enstatite takes its name from the Greek word *enstates*, which means "opponent"— a reference to the use of this mineral as a refractory "opponent" of heat in the linings of ovens and kilns. Specimens are colorless, pale yellow, or pale green. They become darker and turn greenish brown to black with increasing iron content. Enstatite generally occurs as massive aggregates or disseminated grains. Well-formed crystals, when found, tend to be short prisms, often with complex terminations. Enstatite is also found as fibrous masses of parallel, needlelike crystals.

A widespread mineral, enstatite forms a solid-solution series with ferrosilite. The mineral usually occurs in magnesium- and iron-rich igneous rocks and in meteorites (pp.335–37).

Mixed-cut enstatite
Recovered from Myanmar and Sri Lanka, facet-grade enstatite, such as this gem, is mainly cut for collectors.

PROFILE

Monoclinic

⬡ 6

🔨 3.5–3.6

▨ Good to perfect

◩ Uneven

▨ Yellow-green to pale green

⬎ Vitreous

Terminated crystals
This specimen is composed of a group of prismatic aegirine crystals with feldspar. The crystals have full terminations.

prismatic crystal

feldspar

VARIANTS

Parallel crystals A mass of prismatic aegirine crystals aligned in parallel

Prismatic aegirine Prismatic crystals of aegirine in a rock matrix

$NaFe(Si_2O_6)$

AEGIRINE

The sodium iron silicate aegirine was discovered in Norway and named in 1835 after Aegir, the Scandinavian god of the sea. Aegirine is also known as acmite after the Greek word *acme*, which means "point" or "edge"— a reference to the mineral's typically pointed crystals. Specimens are dark green, reddish brown, or black in color. Aegirine occurs as needlelike or fibrous crystals that form attractive, radiating sprays. The crystals have steep or blunt terminations and are often striated along the length. Prism faces are often lustrous and striated, while the faces of terminations are often etched and dull.

A pyroxene, aegirine forms a solid-solution series with hedenbergite and diopside (p.210). It is found in magnesium- and iron-rich igneous rocks, especially syenitic pegmatites (p.260) and syenites (p.262). It is also found in schists (pp.291–92), metamorphosed iron-rich sediments, and metamorphic rocks altered by circulating fluids. Notable localities include Kongsberg, Norway, and Mont St.-Hilaire, Canada.

Prismatic diopside
This specimen of diopside in a rock matrix comes from St. Marcel, Valle d'Aosta, Italy.

quartz

prismatic diopside crystal

rock matrix

VARIANT

Violane A blue, crystalline variant of diopside

♣ $CaMg(Si_2O_6)$

DIOPSIDE

A member of the pyroxene family, diopside takes its name from the Greek for "double" and "appearance," a reference to the variable appearance of the mineral. Specimens can be colorless but are more often bottle green, brownish green, or light green in color. Diopside occurs in the form of equant to prismatic crystals that are usually nearly square in section. Crystals are less commonly tabular. This mineral can also form columnar, sheetlike, granular, or massive aggregates.

Most diopside is metamorphic and found in metamorphosed silica-rich limestones (p.319) and dolomites (p.320) and in iron-rich contact metamorphic rocks. It also occurs in peridotites (p.266), kimberlites (p.269), and other igneous rocks.

Chrome diopside
Emerald-green diopside, such as the gem shown here, is chromium-rich and is also known as chrome diopside.

PROFILE

Monoclinic

⚒ 5½–6

⚖ 3.3

▧ Distinct in two directions at almost right angles

▨ Uneven to subconchoidal

▨ Pale brown to greenish gray

⚒ Vitreous to dull

dark, nearly opaque crystal

Single crystal
In this specimen, a single, large, dark-colored augite crystal rests on a matrix of volcanic tuff.

good cleavage in two directions nearly at right angles

volcanic tuff

VARIANTS

Greenish black augite
A mass of greenish black, prismatic augite crystals

Prismatic crystal A short prismatic augite crystal from the Czech Republic

♣ $(Ca,Na)(Mg,Fe,Ti,Al)(Al,Si)_2O_6$

AUGITE

The most common pyroxene, augite is named after the Greek word *augites*, which means "brightness"—a reference to its occasional shiny appearance. Most augite has a dull, dark green, brown, or black finish. Augite occurs chiefly as short, thick, prismatic crystals with a square or octagonal cross section and sometimes as large, cleavable masses. It occurs in a solid-solution series in which diopside (p.210) and hedenbergite are the end-members.

Augite is common in silica-poor rocks and various other dark-colored igneous rocks, as well as igneous rocks of intermediate silica content. It also occurs in some metamorphic rocks formed at high temperatures (1,065°F/575°C or above). Augite is a common constituent of lunar basalts and some meteorites (pp.335–37). Notable crystal localities are in Germany, the Czech Republic, Italy, Russia, Japan, Mexico, Canada, and USA. Because it is difficult to distinguish between augite, diopside, and hedenbergite in hand specimens, all pyroxenes are often identified as augite.

PROFILE

Monoclinic

⛏ 6½–7

💧 3.0–3.2

▨ Perfect

✂ Subconchoidal to splintery

▱ White

⟋ Vitreous

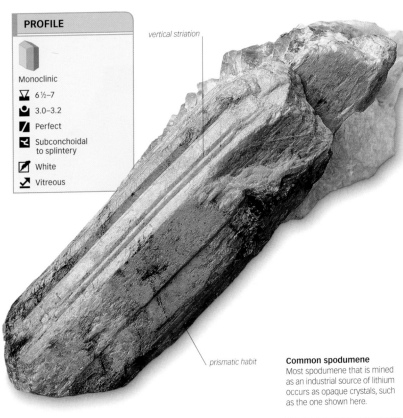

vertical striation

prismatic habit

Common spodumene
Most spodumene that is mined as an industrial source of lithium occurs as opaque crystals, such as the one shown here.

VARIANTS

subconchoidal fracture

Kunzite The lavender gemstone form of spodumene

elongate crystal

Hiddenite Green, gem-variety specimen of spodumene

♦ LiAl(Si$_2$O$_6$)

SPODUMENE

A member of the pyroxene group, spodumene is named after the Greek word *spodumenos*, which means "reduced to ashes"—a reference to the mineral's common ash-gray color. It can also be pink, lilac, or green. Crystals are prismatic, flattened, and typically striated along their length. Gem varieties of the mineral usually exhibit strong pleochroism.

Spodumene is an important ore of lithium. It occurs in lithium-bearing granite pegmatite dykes, often with other lithium-bearing minerals, such as eucryptite and lepidolite (p.198). One of the largest single crystals of any mineral ever found was a spodumene specimen from South Dakota, USA, 47 ft (14.3m) long and 90 tons in weight.

Strengthened glass
Spodumene is a key source of lithium, which forms the lithium fluoride that is used to add strength to glass.

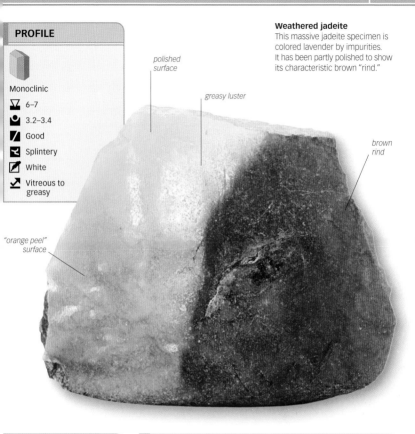

PROFILE

Monoclinic

6–7

3.2–3.4

Good

Splintery

White

Vitreous to greasy

polished surface

greasy luster

Weathered jadeite
This massive jadeite specimen is colored lavender by impurities. It has been partly polished to show its characteristic brown "rind."

brown rind

"orange peel" surface

VARIANTS

Lilac jadeite A rare and valuable variety of jadeite

polished surface

Imperial jade A rich green specimen of imperial jade

rough, violet mass

Violet jadeite A specimen of rare, valuable, violet jadeite

$Na(Al,Fe)Si_2O_6$

JADEITE

A pyroxene mineral, jadeite is one of the two minerals that are referred to as jade. The other is nephrite (p.217), which is a variety of either tremolite (p.219) or actinolite (p.220). Pure jadeite is white in color. Specimens can be colored green by iron, lilac by manganese and iron, or pink, purple, brown, red, blue, black, orange, or yellow by inclusions of other minerals. Jadeite is made up of interlocking, blocky, granular crystals and commonly has a sugary or granular texture. Crystals are short prisms. They are rare but when found are usually in hollows within massive material.

Jadeite occurs in metamorphic rocks formed at high pressure. Although usually recovered as alluvial pebbles and boulders, it is also found in the rocks in which it originally formed.

Jade mask
Jadeite, such as that used in this 18th-century mask, had cultural value for Central and South American Indians.

PROFILE

Triclinic

⬙ 4½–5

● 2.9

▨ Perfect

▧ Uneven to splintery

▨ White

⬈ Vitreous to silky

Crystalline wollastonite
The mass of parallel crystals in this specimen are shaped like coarse blades. They show silky luster and a splintery fracture.

fibrous mass of crystals

splintery fracture

VARIANTS

Massive wollastonite
A piece of massive wollastonite

Coarse crytals A mass of coarsely crystalline wollastonite from New York

♣ CaSiO₃

WOLLASTONITE

A valuable industrial mineral, wollastonite is white, gray, or pale green in color. It occurs as rare, tabular crystals or massive, coarse-bladed, foliated, or fibrous masses. Its crystals are usually triclinic, although its structure has seven variants, one of which is monoclinic. These variations are however, indistinguishable in hand specimens.

Wollastonite forms as a result of the contact metamorphism of limestones (p.319) and in igneous rocks that are contaminated by carbon-rich inclusions. It can be accompanied by other calcium-containing silicates, such as diopside (p.210), tremolite (p.219), epidote (p.230), and grossular garnet (p.245). Wollastonite also appears in regionally metamorphosed rocks in schists (pp.291–92), slates (p.293), and phyllites (p.294).

Ceramic tile
Wollastonite is widely used in ceramics, such as the tile shown here. It is also an ideal base for fluxes and glazes.

Triclinic

6

3.5–3.7

Perfect

Conchoidal to uneven

White

Vitreous

Massive rhodonite
This specimen of rough rhodonite shows the intense coloring and fine texture of the best gem-quality material.

vitreous luster

massive habit

uneven fracture

VARIANT

manganese-oxide matriz

tabular crystal

Tabular crystals Aggregates of tabular crystals

(Mn,Ca)$_5$(Si$_5$O$_{15}$)

RHODONITE

The semiprecious gemstone rhodonite takes its name from the Greek word *rhodon*, which means "rose"— a reference to the mineral's typical pink color. Crystals are uncommon but are rounded when found. Rhodonite usually occurs as masses or grains and is often coated or veined with manganese oxides.

Rhodonite is found in various manganese ores, often with rhodochrosite (p.121) or as a product of rhodochrosite that has undergone metamorphism. It has been used as a manganese ore in India but is more often mined as a gem and an ornamental stone. Rhodonite is primarily cut *en cabochon* as beads. Massive rhodonite is relatively tough and is good as a carving medium. Transparent rhodonite is rare. Although extremely fragile, it can be faceted for collectors.

Rhodonite box
Black-veined rhodonite, such as that used here, is relatively tough and is preferred by many carvers.

Radiating crystals
This specimen is a mass of fibrous, radiating crystals of anthophyllite with vitreous luster.

vitreous luster

mass of fibrous, radiating crystals

PROFILE

Orthorhombic

 5½–6

 2.8–3.6

 Perfect, imperfect

 Uneven

 Colorless to gray

Vitreous

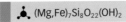 $(Mg,Fe)_7Si_8O_{22}(OH)_2$

ANTHOPHYLLITE

The name anthophyllite comes from the Latin word *anthophyllum*, which means "clove"—a reference to the mineral's clove-brown to dark brown color. Specimens can also be pale green, gray, or white. Anthophyllite is usually found in columnar to fibrous masses. Single crystals are uncommon; when found, they are prismatic and usually unterminated. The iron and magnesium content in anthophyllite is variable. The mineral is called ferroanthophyllite when it is iron-rich, sodium-anthophyllite when sodium is present, and magnesioanthophyllite when magnesium is dominant. Titanium and manganese may also be present in the anthophyllite structure.

Anthophyllite forms by the regional metamorphism of iron- and magnesium-rich rocks, especially silica-poor igneous rocks. It is an important component of some gneisses (p.288) and crystalline schists (pp.291–92) and is found worldwide. Anthophyllite is one of several minerals referred to as asbestos.

Polished nephrite
This small boulder of nephrite
has been sliced and polished
to reveal its quality.

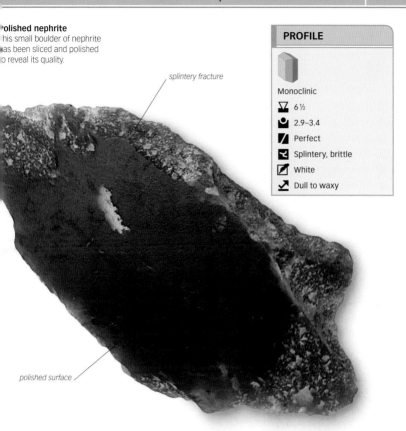

splintery fracture

polished surface

$Ca_2(Mg,Fe)_5(Si_8O_{22})(OH)_2$

NEPHRITE

Not a true mineral name, the term nephrite applies to
the tough, compact form of either tremolite (p.219) or
actinolite (p.220). Both are calcium magnesium silicate
hydroxides and structurally identical, except that in
actinolite some of the magnesium is replaced by iron.
Nephrite is dark green when iron-rich and creamy white
when magnesium-rich. Specimens are composed of a mat
of tightly interlocked fibers, creating
a stone that is tougher than steel.

Nephrite forms in metamorphic
environments, especially in
metamorphosed iron- and
magnesium-rich rocks, where it is
associated with serpentine (p.191)
and talc (p.193). It is also found
in regionally metamorphosed
areas where dolomites (p.320) are
intruded by iron- and magnesium-
rich igneous rocks.

Nephrite tiki
Hei tikis, such as this
one made of nephrite,
are worn by the Maori
of New Zealand.

prismatic
hornblende
crystal

vitreous luster

vertical
striation

Hornblende crystals
This specimen consists of a group
of prismatic hornblende crystals
embedded in a rock matrix.

VARIANTS

white rock
matrix

**Prismatic
hornblende**
Prismatic
crystals in a
rock matrix

**Massive
hornblende**
A piece of
massive
hornblende

six-sided
crystal

Single crystal
A single, short
prismatic crystal
of hornblende

⚛ eg: $Ca_2(Fe^2,Mg)_4(Al,Fe^3)(Si_7Al)O_{22}(OH,F)_2$

HORNBLENDE

The name hornblende is applied to a group of minerals
that can be distinguished from each other only by
detailed chemical analysis. The two end-member
hornblendes—iron-rich ferrohornblende and magnesium-
rich magnesiohornblende—are both calcium-rich and
monoclinic in crystal structure. Other elements, such
as chromium, titanium, and nickel, can also appear in
the crystal structures of the group. The concentrations
of these elements are an indicator of the metamorphic
grade of the mineral.

Specimens are green, dark green, or brownish green to
black in color. Hornblende crystals are usually bladed and
unterminated, and they often show a pseudohexagonal
cross section. Well-formed crystals are short to long
prisms. Hornblende also occurs as cleavable masses
and radiating groups. The mineral forms in metamorphic
rocks, especially gneisses (p.288), hornblende schists,
amphibolites (p.296), and magnesium- and iron-rich
igneous rocks.

Tremolite crystals
This specimen has plumelike aggregates of white, bladed tremolite crystals.

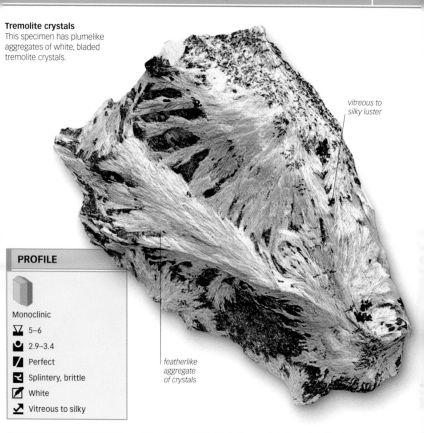

vitreous to silky luster

featherlike aggregate of crystals

VARIANTS

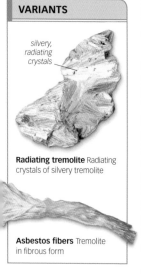

silvery, radiating crystals

Radiating tremolite Radiating crystals of silvery tremolite

Asbestos fibers Tremolite in fibrous form

$Ca_2(Mg,Fe^2)_5Si_8O_{22}(OH)_2$

TREMOLITE

A calcium magnesium silicate, tremolite forms a solid-solution series with ferroactinolite (p.220), where iron substitutes in increasing amounts for magnesium. The color of tremolite varies with increasing iron content from colorless to white in pure tremolite to gray, gray-green, green, dark green and nearly black in other specimens. Traces of manganese may tint tremolite pink or violet. When well-formed, crystals are short to long prisms. More commonly, tremolite forms unterminated bladed crystals, parallel aggregates of bladed crystals, or radiating groups. Tremolite and actinolite both form thin, parallel, flexible fibers up to 10 in (25 cm) in length, which are used commercially as asbestos. Tremolite is known as nephrite jade when it is massive and fine-grained.

The mineral is abundant and widespread. It is the product of both thermal and regional metamorphism and is an indicator of metamorphic grade because it converts to diopside (p.210) at high temperatures (1,065°F/575°C or above).

PROFILE

Monoclinic

5–6

2.9–3.4

Good, crossing at 56° and 124°

Splintery, brittle

White

Vitreous or silky

talc schist

thin, prismatic crystal

green, bladed crystal

Actinolite crystals
This specimen contains a group of thin, prismatic crystals of actinolite in a talc matrix.

VARIANT

Gray-green actinolite
Crystals of actinolite, some of which have been powdered

$Ca_2(Mg,Fe^{2+})_5Si_8O_{22}(OH)_2$

ACTINOLITE

Actinolite is an abundant mineral. It is in the middle of a solid-solution series of calcium, iron, and magnesium silicates that also includes ferroactinolite and tremolite (p.219). There is complete substitution in the series between iron and magnesium, but all have the same structure. Actinolite was named in 1794 after the Greek word *aktis*, which means "ray"—an allusion to its radiating, prismatic habit. Specimens range from green to dark green to black. Well-formed crystals are short to long prisms. Actinolite usually occurs as unterminated bladed crystals, parallel aggregates of bladed crystals, or radiating groups. It is sometimes found as needlelike or fibrous crystals up to 10 in (25 cm) long. When in this form, it is one of the minerals that are called asbestos. Massive, fine-grained actinolite and tremolite are both called nephrite jade.

Actinolite is an amphibole mineral and forms as a product of low- to medium-grade thermal and regional metamorphism. Good crystals come from Edwards, New York, USA, and Kantiwa, Afghanistan.

dark blue-green glaucophane

fuchsite

pyrite

Italian glaucophane
This specimen from Polloni in Piedmont, Italy, shows glaucophane with fuchsite and pyrite.

VARIANT

prismatic crystal

Glaucophane crystals
Crystals of glaucophane in a rock matrix

$Na_2(Mg_3Al_2)Si_8O_{22}(OH)_2$

GLAUCOPHANE

The mineral is named after two Greek words: *glaukos*, which means "bluish green"; and *phainesthai*, which means "to appear." Specimens can be gray, lavender blue, or bluish black. Crystals are slender, often lathlike prisms, with lengthwise striations. Twinning is common. Glaucophane can also be massive, fibrous, or granular. When iron replaces the magnesium in its structure, it is known as ferroglaucophane.

Glaucophane occurs in schists (pp.291–92) formed by high-pressure metamorphism of sodium-rich sediments at low temperatures (up to 400°F/200°C) or by the introduction of sodium into the process. Glaucophane is often accompanied by jadeite (p.213), epidote (p.230), almandine (p.243), and chlorite. It is one of the minerals that are referred to as asbestos. Glaucophane and its associated minerals are known as the glaucophane metamorphic facies. The presence of these minerals indicates the range of temperatures and pressures under which metamorphism occurs.

PROFILE

Monoclinic

⚒ 6

⚖ 3.3–3.4

▨ Perfect

⬗ Uneven

▧ Blue-gray

⬈ Vitreous, silky

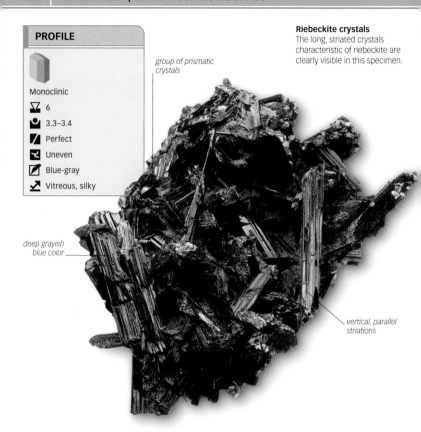

Riebeckite crystals
The long, striated crystals characteristic of riebeckite are clearly visible in this specimen.

group of prismatic crystals

deep grayish blue color

vertical, parallel striations

VARIANT

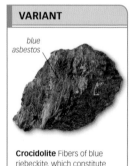

blue asbestos

Crocidolite Fibers of blue riebeckite, which constitute blue asbestos

⚛ $Na_2(Fe^{2+}_3Fe^{3+}_2)Si_8O_{22}(OH)_2$

RIEBECKITE

A sodium iron silicate, riebeckite is one of the several minerals called asbestos. It was named after Emil Riebeck, a 19th-century German explorer. Although riebeckite specimens are generally grayish blue to dark blue, their color can vary depending on the concentration of iron in their structure. Riebeckite can occur as prismatic, striated crystals or sometimes as massive or fibrous aggregates.

This mineral occurs in feldspar- and quartz-rich igneous rocks. These include granites (pp.258–59), syenites (p.262) and, feldspar- and quartz-rich volcanic rocks, especially sodium-rich rhyolites (p.278). Riebeckite granite is found on the island of Ailsa Craig in western Scotland and is locally known as ailsite. Ailsite is used to manufacture stones used in the sport of curling.

Tiger's eye ring
Crocidolite, a variant of riebeckite, forms the gemstone tiger's eye when it is silica-saturated.

PROFILE

Orthorhombic

7–7 ½

2.6

Moderate to poor

Conchoidal to uneven

White

Vitreous to greasy

Cordierite crystals
This group of short prismatic, dark gray cordierite crystals occurs in a rock matrix.

rock matrix

cordierite crystal

VARIANTS

Single crystal A large crystal of cordierite in matrix

Iolite A polished gemstone of cordierite called iolite

$(Mg,Fe)_2Al_4Si_5O_{18}$

CORDIERITE

The mineral is named after the French geologist Pierre L.A. Cordier, who first described it in 1813. Specimens can be blue, violet-blue, gray, or blue-green. Gem-quality blue cordierite or iolite is also known as water sapphire because of its color. Cordierite is pleochroic, exhibiting three different colors when viewed from different angles. Its crystals are prismatic, and the best blue color is seen along their length.

Cordierite occurs in high-grade, thermally metamorphosed, alumina-rich rocks. It is also found in gneisses (p.288) and schists (pp.291–92) and more rarely in granites (pp.258–59), pegmatites (p.260), and veins of quartz (p.168). Cordierite is important in the production of ceramics used in catalytic converters in cars.

Cordierite jewelry
A variety of cordierite, iolite is used in ornaments because of its color and brilliance.

PROFILE

Hexagonal or trigonal

7–7 ½

3.0–3.2

Indistinct

Uneven to conchoidal

Colorless

Vitreous

green or red crystal rim

Watermelon tourmaline
Color can vary either along or across a tourmaline crsytal. This zoning takes its most dramatic form in "watermelon" tourmaline.

crystal sliced across its width

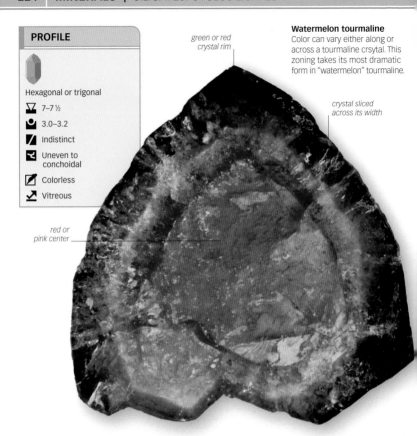

red or pink center

VARIANTS

Schorl Probably the most common tourmaline mineral

Elbaite A gemstone-quality variant of tourmaline

Indicolite A blue-colored variant of tourmaline

FeWO$_4$

TOURMALINE

Tourmaline is the name given to a family of minerals of complex and variable composition, but all members have the same basic crystal structure. The 11 minerals in the group include elbaite, schorl, dravite, and liddicoacite. Gemstone varieties based on their color are also recognized, including indicolite (blue), rubellite (pink or red), verdelite (green), and achroite (colorless). These variety names can be applied to more than one mineral. Most tourmaline is dark, opaque, and not particularly attractive, but many of its transparent varieties are valued as gems.

Tourmaline is abundant, and its best formed crystals are usually found in pegmatites (p.260) and metamorphosed limestones (p.319) in contact with granitic magmas. It accumulates in gravel deposits and occurs as an accessory mineral in some sedimentary rocks.

Cut rubellite
This specimen shows the rich red coloration and transparency found in some specimens of rubellite.

PROFILE

Hexagonal or trigonal

🔽 7½–8

🔶 2.6–2.8

◪ Indistinct

◪ Uneven to conchoidal

◪ White

◪ Vitreous

Aquamarine
This mass of prismatic aquamarine crystals is from the Karakoram Range in Pakistan. The name aquamarine means "seawater."

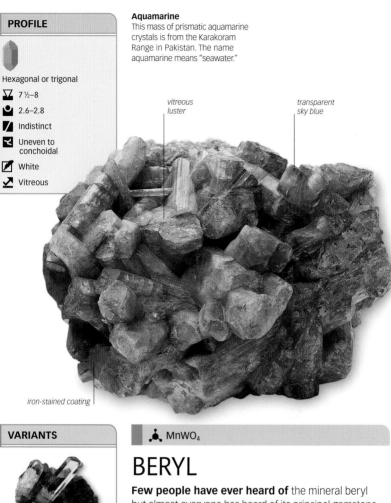

vitreous luster

transparent sky blue

iron-stained coating

VARIANTS

Heliodor Crystalline heliodor with hexagonal prisms

Emerald An unusually long prismatic crystal of emerald

Morganite A variant with crystals in shades of pink

⚛ MnWO₄

BERYL

Few people have ever heard of the mineral beryl but almost everyone has heard of its principal gemstone varieties—emerald and aquamarine. Before 1925, beryl's solitary use was as a gemstone but since then many important uses have been found for beryllium. As a result, common beryl, which is usually pale green or white, has become widely sought after as the ore of this rare element. Most beryl is found in granites (pp.258–59), granite pegmatites (p.260), and rhyolites (p.278), but it can also occur in metamorphic rocks, such as schists (pp.291–92).

Emerald owes its grass-green color to the presence of traces of chromium and sometimes vanadium. Flawless emeralds are rare, but since 1937 the manufacture of synthetic crystals has become possible. Aquamarine is the most common gemstone variety of beryl. Nearly always found in cavities in pegmatites or in alluvial deposits, it forms larger and clearer crystals than emerald. Other gemstone varieties of beryl include heliodor, morganite, and goshenite.

PROFILE

Hexagonal

5

3.3

Perfect

Uneven to conchoidal

Pale greenish blue

Vitreous to greasy

short, prismatic dioptase crystal

vitreous luster

chrysocolla matrix

Prismatic dioptase
This spectacular encrustation of dioptase crystals on quartz shows why it is a favorite with collectors.

VARIANTS

Clustered prisms A green dioptase specimen

Lustrous dioptase
A specimen found in Central Africa

 $CuSiO_2(OH_2)$

DIOPTASE

The bright green crystals of dioptase can superficially resemble emerald. Dioptase crystals mined from a rich deposit in Kazakhstan were wrongly identified as emerald when they were sent to Czar Paul of Russia in 1797. Were it not for its softness and good cleavage, dioptase would make a superb gemstone to rival emerald (p.225) in color. Its prismatic crystals, often with rhombohedral terminations, can be highly transparent. This explains why the name dioptase is derived from two Greek words: *dia*, which means "through," and *optazein,* which means "visible" or "to see." Transparent specimens of dioptase appear in different colors depending on the direction from which they are seen, and intensely colored specimens can be translucent. The mineral can also occur in granular or massive habits.

Dioptase forms in areas where copper veins have been altered by oxidation. Its vibrant color and its typical occurence as well-formed crystals make it popular with mineral collectors.

PROFILE

Orthorhombic

4½–5

3.4–3.5

Perfect, good, poor

Uneven, brittle

White

Vitreous

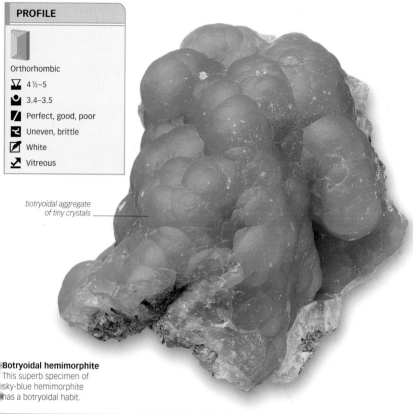

botryoidal aggregate
of tiny crystals

Botryoidal hemimorphite
This superb specimen of
sky-blue hemimorphite
has a botryoidal habit.

VARIANTS

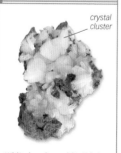

crystal
cluster

White hemimorphite Tabular
crystals on a rock matrix

rounded
mass

**Crystalline
aggregates**
A green
specimen
on a rock
matrix

$Zn_4Si_2O_7(OH)_2 \cdot H_2O$

HEMIMORPHITE

One of two minerals formerly called calamine in the
USA, hemimorphite takes its name from the Greek words
hemi, which means "half," and *morphe*, which means
"form"—a reference to its crystalline form. Hemimorphite
crystals are double-terminated prisms with a differently
shaped termination at each end—pointed at one and flat
at the other. Crystals are often grouped in fan-shaped
clusters. Hemimorphite can also be botryoidal, chalky,
massive, granular, fibrous, or form encrustations. Usually
colorless or white, specimens can also be pale yellow,
pale green, or sky blue. Some specimens show strong,
green fluorescence in shortwave ultraviolet light and weak,
light pink fluorescence in longwave ultraviolet light.

Hemimorphite is a secondary mineral formed in the
alteration zones of zinc deposits, especially as an alteration
product of sphalerite (p.53). It can be half zinc by weight
and is an important ore of that metal. Well-crystallized
specimens come from Algeria, Namibia, Germany, Mexico,
Spain, USA, and China.

PROFILE

Triclinic

6½–7

3.2–3.3

Good, poor

Uneven to conchoidal, brittle

Colorless to light brown

Vitreous

Axinite crystals
This mass of well-formed, transparent, wedge-shaped, tabular axinite crystals rests on a rock matrix.

vitreous luster

characteristic clove-brown color

VARIANTS

wedge-shaped axinite crystal

Gem quality Wedge-shaped crystals of brown axinite

distinctive axe shape

Unusual growth A small crystal growing on a larger one

$Ca_2FeAl_2(BSi_4O_{15})(OH)$

AXINITE

This group of minerals takes its name from the axehead shape of its crystals. Axinite minerals also occur as rosettes and in massive and granular forms. The most familiar color of axinite is clove brown. Varieties can also be gray to bluish gray; honey-, gray-, or golden-brown; violet-blue, pink, yellow, orange, or red. There are four minerals in the group: ferroaxinite, the most common; magnesioaxinite, in which magnesium replaces the iron in ferroaxinite; manganaxinite, in which manganese replaces the iron in ferroaxinite; and tinzenite, which is intermediate in composition between ferroaxinite and manganaxinite.

Axinite is commonly found in contact and low-temperature metamorphic rocks (those formed at up to 400°F/200°C) and in magnesium- and iron-rich igneous rocks.

Axinite gemstone
Brilliant-cut axinite crystals, such as this specimen in an unusual shade of violet, are popular with collectors.

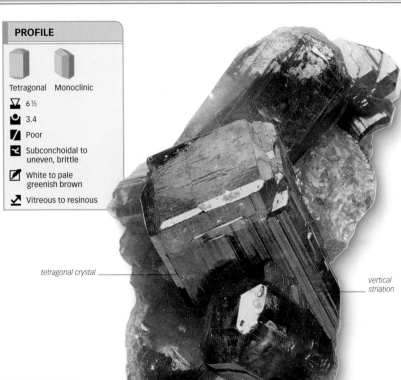

tetragonal crystal

vertical striation

Striated vesuvianite
This superb specimen consists of prismatic, vertically striated vesuvianite crystals.

VARIANTS

Cyprine A specimen of blue vesuvianite, or cyprine

Tetragonal crystal
A single, well-formed crystal of vesuvianite

$Ca_{10}(Mg,Fe)_2Al_4(SiO_4)_5(Si_2O_7)_2(OH,F)_4$

VESUVIANITE

Formerly called idocrase, vesuvianite is named after its place of discovery—Mount Vesuvius in Italy. Usually green or yellow-green, it can also be yellow to brown, red, black, blue, or purple. A greenish blue copper-bearing vesuvianite is called cyprine. An unusual bismuth-bearing vesuvianite from Langben, Sweden, is bright red. The mineral forms pyramidal or prismatic and glassy crystals. Crystals 2¾ in (7 cm) or more long have been found.

Elements such as tin, lead, manganese, chromium, zinc, and sulfur may substitute in the vesuvianite structure. The mineral is formed by the metamorphism of impure limestones (p.319). It is also found in granulites (p.297) and marbles (p.301) accompanied by calcite (p.114), diopside (p.210), wollastonite (p.214), and grossular (p.245).

Vesuvianite gem
Occasionally, vesuvianite is found in translucent to transparent crystals suitable for cutting into gems.

PROFILE

Monoclinic

⬦ 6–7

⬦ 3.4

⬦ Good

⬦ Uneven to splintery

⬦ Colorless or grayish

⬦ Vitreous

Epidote crystals
This superb group of striated epidote crystals, some reaching 1 in (2.5 cm) in length, shows typical prismatic development.

vitreous luster

prismatic crystal

striations

perfect cleavage

VARIANTS

Pistachio epidote Long, striated crystals from Peru

Acicular epidote Yellowish brown, needlelike crystals

$Ca_2Al_2(Fe,Al)(SiO_4)(Si_2O_7)O(OH)$

EPIDOTE

An abundant rock-forming mineral, epidote derives its name from the Greek word *epidosis*, which means "increase"—a reference to the fact that one side of the prism is always wider than the others. Epidote is most easily recognized by its characteristic color—light to dark pistachio green. Gray or yellow specimens are also found. Epidote is pleochroic, exhibiting different colors when viewed from different directions. The mineral frequently forms well-developed crystals. These may be columnar prisms or thick, tabular crystals with faces that are finely striated parallel to the crystal's length. Twinning is common. Specimens can also be needlelike, massive, or granular.

Epidote is found in low-grade, regionally metamorphosed rocks. It also occurs as a product of the alteration of plagioclase feldspars (pp.173–81).

Epidote gemstone
Clear, yellowish green to dark brown epidote gems are rare. Transparent crystals are cut for collectors.

perfect cleavage

deep vertical striation

Zoisite crystals
This specimen of ordinary zoisite shows a typical prismatic shape and vertical striations. The crystals are in a pegmatite matrix.

VARIANTS

Thulite A pink, manganese-rich variety of zoisite

Tanzanite A rich purple gem-quality zoisite variety

$Ca_2Al_3(SiO_4)_3(OH)$

ZOISITE

A calcium aluminum silicate hydroxide, most zoisite is gray, white, light brown, yellowish green, or pale greenish gray. A massive, pinkish red variety is called thulite. A lilac-blue to sapphire-blue variety of zoisite is called tanzanite and is sometimes mistaken for sapphire (p.95). Zoisite with inclusions of ruby is called ruby-in-zoisite. Zoisite crystals exhibit gray, purple, or blue colors depending on the angle from which they are viewed. Zoisite is found as deeply striated, prismatic crystals and also as disseminated grains and columnar or massive aggregates.

The mineral is characteristic of regional metamorphism and hydrothermal alteration of igneous rocks. It results from metamorphism of calcium-rich rocks and typically occurs in medium-grade schists (pp.291–92), gneisses (p.288), and amphibolites (p.296). It is also found in veins of quartz (p.168) and pegmatites (p.260).

Ruby-in-zoisite
Considered a good carving medium, ruby-in-zoisite has been used to make this 19th-century desk seal.

PROFILE

Orthorhombic

⚖ 6½–7

⬤ 3.3–4.3

▨ Imperfect

◧ Conchoidal

▨ White

↗ Vitreous

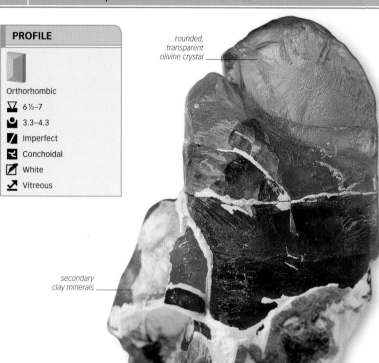

rounded, transparent olivine crystal

secondary clay minerals

Peridot crystal
This gem-quality specimen of olivine, or peridot, is from Pakistan. Other important sources include China and Myanmar.

VARIANTS

Forsterite Magnesium-rich olivine is called forsterite

tabular crystal

Fayalite Iron-rich olivine is called fayalite

$(Mg,Fe)_2SiO_4$

OLIVINE

The name olivine may be unfamiliar but most people know of its gemstone variety, peridot, which has been mined for over 3,500 years. The name olivine is applied to any mineral belonging to a solid-solution series in which iron and magnesium substitute freely in the structure. Fayalite is the iron end-member of the solid-solution series, and forsterite is the magnesium end-member.

Olivine specimens are usually yellowish green, but they can also be yellow, brown, gray, or colorless. Crystals are tabular, often with wedge-shaped terminations, although well-formed crystals of olivine are rare. Olivine may also occur in massive or granular habits. It is a major component of Earth's upper mantle.

Peridot gemstone
Green peridot, such as the one in this brooch, was used by Egyptians since the second millennium BCE.

PROFILE

Tetragonal

⬙ 7½

◗ 4.6–4.7

▸ Imperfect

▸ Uneven to conchoidal

▸ White

▸ Adamantine to oily

twinned zircon crystal

feldspar-and-biotite matrix

biotite

Afghan zircon
This specimen of zircon crystals in a feldspar-and-biotite matrix is from Afghanistan. The crystals are up to 1¼ in (3 cm) long.

VARIANTS

Purple zircon Crystals of zircon in a rock matrix

Crystalline cluster Zircon crystals that are embedded in pegmatite

$ZrSiO_4$

ZIRCON

A superb gem and one of the few stones to approach diamond (p.47) in fire and brilliance, zircon has a high refractive index and color dispersion. Known since antiquity, zircon takes its name from the Arabic word *zargun*, derived in turn from the Persian words *zar*, which means "gold," and *gun*, which means "color." Specimens can also be colorless, yellow, gray, green, brown, blue, and red. Brown zircon is frequently heat-treated to turn it blue. The mineral forms prismatic to dipyramidal crystals. Single crystals can reach a considerable size: specimens weighing up to 4½ lb (2 kg) and 8¾ lb (4 kg) have been found in Australia and Russia, respectively.

Zircon is found in metamorphic rocks and silica-rich igneous rocks. It resists weathering and, because of its relatively high specific gravity, concentrates in stream and river gravels and beach deposits.

Zircon bracelet
Gem zircons, such as the colorless, faceted zircons in this bracelet, have been mined for over 2,000 years.

PROFILE

Orthorhombic

▽ 8

◔ 3.4–3.6

▰ Perfect basal

▱ Subconchoidal to uneven

▱ Colorless

↗ Vitreous

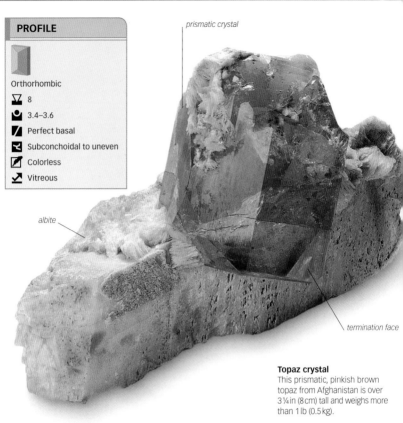

prismatic crystal

albite

termination face

Topaz crystal
This prismatic, pinkish brown topaz from Afghanistan is over 3¼ in (8 cm) tall and weighs more than 1 lb (0.5 kg).

VARIANTS

vitreous luster

Brown topaz
A fine, natural crystal of brown topaz

line of cleavage

Light blue topaz
A specimen of blue topaz

Imperial topaz
A golden imperial topaz from a deposit in Brazil

$Al_2SiO_4(F,OH)_2$

TOPAZ

The name topaz is thought to have been derived from the Sanskrit *tapaz*, which means "fire." Topaz occurs in a wide range of colors, with sherry-yellow and pink stones being particularly valuable. Colorless topaz has such a high refractive index that brilliant-cut specimens are mistaken for diamond (p.47). Well-formed prismatic crystals have a characteristic lozenge-shaped cross section and striations parallel to their length. The mineral is also found in massive, granular, and columnar habits.

Topaz is formed by fluorine-bearing vapors released in the late stages of crystallization of igneous rocks. It occurs in granites (pp.258–59), rhyolites (p.278), pegmatite dykes, and hydrothermal veins. Rounded pebbles are also found in river deposits. The world's largest faceted topaz weighs over 36,000 carats.

Pink topaz
A clear, octagonal step cut, pink topaz is set here in a gold ring. Natural pink topaz is rare.

Titanite crystals
These interpenetrating, wedge-shaped titanite crystals, 1½ in (3.5 cm) long, are from Russia.

wedge-shaped crystal

rock groundmass

vitreous luster

PROFILE

Monoclinic

5–5½

3.5–3.6

Imperfect

Conchoidal

White

Vitreous to greasy

VARIANT

Crystal group Wedge-shaped titanite crystals

$CaTiSiO_5$

TITANITE

Formerly called sphene, titanite is a calcium titanium silicate. The name sphene originates from the Greek word *sphen*, which means "wedge"—a reference to the typical wedge-shaped crystals of the mineral. Crystals can also be prismatic. Gem-quality crystals occur in yellow, green, or brown colors. Specimens can also be black, pink, red, blue, or colorless. Titanite is strongly pleochroic, exhibiting different colors when seen from different directions. The mineral can also be massive, lamellar, or compact. Faceted titanite is one of the few stones with a color dispersion higher than that of diamond (p.47).

Titanite is widely distributed as a minor component of silica-rich igneous rocks and associated pegmatites (p.260). It is also found in the metamorphic rocks gneiss (p.288), schist (pp.291–92), and marble (p.301).

Titanite ring
Faceted titanites, such as the brilliant cut set in this gold ring, have superb fire and intense colors.

Andalusite crystals
This group of prismatic andalusite crystals from the Austrian Tyrol is in a matrix of quartz.

prismatic andalusite crystal

quartz matrix

VARIANTS

Brown andalusite Prismatic crystals on a rock matrix

Chiastolite A yellowish brown andalusite crystal with cross-shaped inclusions of carbon

Al_2OSiO_5

ANDALUSITE

Named after the locality in Andalusia, Spain, where it was first described, andalusite is aluminum silicate. It is pink to reddish brown, white, gray, violet, yellow, green, or blue. Gem-quality andalusite exhibits yellow, green, and red colors when viewed from different directions. Andalusite crystals are commonly prismatic with a square cross section. They can also be elongated or tapered. Andalusite can also occur in massive form. A yellowish gray variety called chiastolite occurs as long prisms enclosing symmetrical wedges of carbon-rich material.

Andalusite is found in regional and low-grade metamorphic rocks, where it is associated with corundum (p.95), cordierite (p.223), sillimanite (p.237), and kyanite (p.238). It is rarely found in granites (pp.258–59) and granitic pegmatites (p.260) .

Rectangular step cut Relatively uncommon, transparent andalusite is too brittle to be worn. It is faceted for gem collectors.

PROFILE

Orthorhombic

- 7
- 3.2–3.3
- Perfect
- Uneven
- White
- Silky

vitreous luster

elongated, prismatic sillimanite crystal

rock matrix

Prismatic sillimanite
In this specimen, elongated, prismatic crystals of sillimanite can be seen in a rock matrix.

VARIANTS

Crystals in rock Sillimanite in a rock matrix

silky luster

Fibrous sillimanite A mass of parallel, fibrous crystals

Al_2OSiO_5

SILLIMANITE

Named after the American chemist Benjamin Silliman, sillimanite is one of three polymorphs of aluminum silicate. Commonly colorless to white, sillimanite can also be pale yellow to brown, pale blue, green, or violet. A single specimen may appear yellowish green, dark green, or blue when seen from different angles. The mineral occurs in long, slender, glassy crystals or in blocky, poorly terminated prisms.

Sillimanite is characteristic of clay-rich metamorphic rocks formed at high temperatures (1,065°F/575°C or above). The mineral is often found with corundum (p.95), cordierite (p.223), and kyanite (p.238). Specimens also occur in gneisses (p.288), sillimanite schists, hornfels (p.303), and detrital sediments.

Collectors' gem
Facet-grade sillimanite, such as this specimen, occurs in the gem gravels of Sri Lanka and Myanmar, and in Brazil.

Blady kyanite
This specimen of kyanite with quartz from northern Brazil shows the characteristic elongated, bladed habit of kyanite crystals.

vitreous luster

long, bladed crystal

rock matrix

quartz

VARIANT

rock matrix

kyanite

staurolite

Kyanite in rock Kyanite crystals with staurolite in a rock matrix

Al₂SiO₅

KYANITE

Named after the Greek word *kyanos*, which means "dark blue," kyanite is blue and blue-gray, the colors generally zoned within a single crystal. Kyanite can also be green, orange, or colorless. Specimens have variable hardness: about 4½ when scratched parallel to the long axis but 6 when scratched perpendicular to the long axis. Kyanite occurs mainly as elongated, flattened blades that are often bent and sometimes as radiating, columnar aggregates.

Kyanite is formed during the regional metamorphism of clay-rich sediments. It occurs in mica schists, gneisses (p.288), and associated hydrothermal quartz veins and pegmatites (p.260). It is used to estimate the temperature, depth, and pressure at which a rock has metamorphosed.

Spark plugs
Kyanite is mined for the aluminum silicate mullite, which is used in spark plugs.

PROFILE

Monoclinic

7–7 ½

3.7

Distinct

Conchoidal

Colorless to gray

Vitreous to resinous

prismatic staurolite crystal

twinned staurolite crystals

vitreous luster

mica schist matrix

Staurolite crystals
This is a specimen of staurolite in a mica schist matrix. Single and twinned crystals can be seen here.

VARIANTS

kyanite

staurolite

Staurolite in schist Kyanite and staurolite in schist

Fairy cross A twinned staurolite, or "fairy cross," crystal

$(Fe,Mg)_4Al_{17}(Si,Al)_8O_{45}(OH)_3$

STAUROLITE

A widespread mineral, staurolite takes its name from two Greek words: *stauros*, which means "cross," and *lithos*, which means "stone"—a reference to its typical crosslike twinned form. Cross-shaped penetration twins of the mineral are common and are in great demand as charms. Staurolite specimens are yellowish brown, reddish brown, or nearly black in color. The mineral normally occurs as prismatic crystals, which are either hexagonal or diamond-shaped in section and often have rough surfaces.

Staurolite occurs in mica schists, gneisses (p.288), and other metamorphosed, aluminum-rich rocks. It forms only under a specific range of pressure and temperature, which helps determine the various conditions under which the metamorphic rock formed.

Trapeze-cut staurolite
Transparent staurolite, as in this stone, is a rare faceting material because of its dark color and lack of brilliance.

PROFILE

Monoclinic

⊻ 7 ½

◖ 3.0

◪ Perfect

◪ Conchoidal, brittle

◪ White

◪ Vitreous

prismatic euclase crystal

rock matrix

striated crystal

Blue euclase
This mass of well-developed, prismatic crystals of blue euclase is on a rocky matrix.

VARIANT

Transparent euclase
A near-transparent, striated euclase crystal

♣ BeAlSiO₄(OH)

EUCLASE

Euclase takes its name from two Greek words: *eu*, which means "good," and *klasis,* which means "fracture"—a reference to its perfect cleavage. Generally white or colorless, euclase can also be pale green or pale to deep blue—a color for which it is particularly noted. It forms striated prisms, often with complex terminations. Massive and fibrous specimens are also found.

Euclase occurs in hydrothermal veins formed at low temperatures (up to 400°F/200°C), granitic pegmatites (p.260), and some metamorphic schists (pp.291–92) and phyllites (p.294). It is also found in stream gravels. Exquisite, colorless, and deep blue color-zoned crystals come from Karoi in Zimbabwe. Cut euclase resembles certain types of beryl (p.225) and topaz (p.234).

Euclase gemstone
This square-cut euclase gemstone shows small, dark inclusions of another mineral.

PROFILE

Orthorhombic

6–6 ½

3.2–3.3

Poor

Subconchoidal to uneven

Yellow to orange

Vitreous

yellowish brown humite crystal

Humite crust
In this specimen, a crust of yellowish brown humite crystals covers a rock matrix that also contains accessory mica.

rock matrix

VARIANTS

Yellow humite A specimen of massive, yellow humite

Orange humite Massive, orange humite with a brown weathering crust

$(Mg,Fe)_7(SiO_4)_3(F,OH)_2$

HUMITE

Named in 1813 after the English mineral and art collector Sir Abraham Hume (1749–1838), humite is a silicate of iron and magnesium. Manganese substitutes for iron in the structure to form a complete solid-solution series with manganhumite. Specimens are yellow to dark orange or reddish orange in color, tending toward brown with increasing manganese content. Humite is generally found in granular masses. Well-formed crystals are rare and grow in parallel with one another. Crystals rarely exceed ⅜ in (1 cm) in length and are occasionally twinned.

Humite is found with pyrite (p.62), cassiterite (p.79), hematite (p.91), quartz (p.168), tourmaline (p.224), and mica in contact and regionally metamorphosed limestones (p.319) and dolomites (p.320). Although this mineral occurs worldwide, noteworthy locations include Persberg and elsewhere in Sweden; Isle of Skye, Scotland; Mount Vesuvius, Italy; Valais, Switzerland; and Brewster, New York, USA.

PROFILE

Cubic

7–7 ½

3.6

None

Conchoidal, brittle

White

Vitreous

pyrope crystal

conchoidal fracture

rock matrix

Pyrope in matrix
This specimen from Mexico includes several pyrope garnets in a matrix. Most pyrope is found as pebbles in placer deposits with other gems.

VARIANT

Gemstone rough Water-rounded pyrope recovered from a placer deposit

$Mg_3Al_2(SiO_4)_3$

PYROPE

The magnesium aluminum garnet pyrope was named in 1803 after the Greek words *pyr* and *ōps*, which mean "fire" and "eye" respectively—a reference to the typical fiery color of specimens. Manganese, chromium, iron, and titanium substitute in the mineral's structure and act as coloring agents to some degree. Specimens can be rich red, dark red, violet-red, rose red, or reddish orange depending on the composition. Crystals are dodecahedral and trapezohedral, with hexoctahedra sometimes present. The mineral is most often found as rounded grains or pebbles.

Pyrope occurs as a high-pressure mineral in metamorphic rocks. It is also found in high-pressure, silica-poor igneous rocks and in detrital deposits derived from them.

Pyrope gemstones
Beautiful garnet jewelry comes from Bohemia, Czech Republic, where pyropes as big as hens' eggs are found.

modified dodecahedron

schist

well-formed crystal

Almandine crystal
This almandine in schist from an area near Wrangell, Alaska, USA, shows a modified dodecahedral form.

VARIANTS

schist

almandine crystal

Crystals in schist Numerous almandine dodecahedrons rest on schist

almandine crystal

Almandine in granulite
Crystals of almandine in a granulite matrix

$Fe_3Al_2(SiO_4)_3$

ALMANDINE

The most common garnet, almandine is named after Alabanda (now Araphisar) in Turkey, where it has been cut since antiquity. Almandine is always red, often with a pink or violet tinge. Specimens can sometimes be nearly black. This mineral tends to be a pinker red than other garnets. Crystals often have well-developed faces and are dodecahedral or trapezohedral or have other more complex forms. Massive aggregates and rounded grains are also found. Rutile (p.78) needles can show as a four-rayed star when almandine is cut *en cabochon*.

Almandine occurs worldwide. It is found in gneisses (p.288) and mica schists, igneous rocks (pp.256–57), and occasionally as inclusions in diamond (p.47). When it occurs in metamorphic rocks, its presence indicates the grade of metamorphism.

Faceted almandine
Three faceted almandine gems and a seed pearl create a central flower motif in this antique gold brooch.

Spessartine crystals
In this specimen from Norway, well-formed dodecahedral crystals encrust a rock matrix.

Cubic

7–7 ½

4.2

None

Conchoidal, brittle

White

Vitreous

rock matrix

uneven fracture

dodecahedral spessartine crystal

VARIANT

Translucent spessartine
An attractive crystal of translucent spessartine

 $Mn_3Al_2(SiO_4)_3$

SPESSARTINE

The manganese aluminum silicate spessartine is named after Spessart—the locality in Germany where it was first described. The mineral is pale yellow when nearly pure and orange to deep red, brown, or black in other specimens. A color change known as the alexandrite effect is occasionally found in spessartine grossular garnet. Crystals are dodecahedral or trapezohedral. Spessartine may also occur as either granular or massive aggregates.

Spessartine almost always contains some amount of iron (p.39). Pure spessartine is relatively rare and is found in manganese-rich metamorphic rocks, granites (pp.258–59), and pegmatite veins (p.260). The heaviest spessartine ever discovered weighs 6,720 carats.

Octagonal step cut
Because of spessartine's rich color, the liquid inclusions under the edge facets in this gem are not very noticeable.

Cubic

6½–7

3.6

None

Conchoidal

White

Vitreous

diopside

grossular crystal

Grossular on diopside
These grossular crystals from
Piedmont, Italy, are set on
a matrix of diopside.

Hessonite Reddish brown
dodecahedral grossular crystals

impure
marble

Pink grossular Rounded, pink
grossular crystals in marble

$Ca_3Al_2(SiO_4)_3$

GROSSULAR

The calcium aluminum silicate grossular, a type of
garnet, is named after the Latin word *grossularia*, which
translates into "gooseberry"—a reference to the mineral's
gooseberry-green color. Specimens can also be pale to
emerald green, white, colorless, cream, orange, red,
honey, brown, or black. Reddish brown or pink grossular
is called hessonite or cinnamon stone. Grossular is usually
translucent to opaque but can be transparent.

It occurs as rounded dodecahedral or
trapezohedral crystals that are up
to 5 in (13 cm) wide. Specimens can
also be granular or massive.

Grossular forms in impure
calcareous rocks that have
undergone regional or contact
metamorphism, in some schists
(pp.291–92) and serpentinites
(p.298), and occasionally in
meteorites (pp.335–37).

Grossular beads
This strung group is
made up of size-graded,
round, luminescent green
grossular beads.

ORGANICS

Generated by organic (biological) processes, the organics may or may not be crystalline. In some cases, they contain the same mineral matter—such as calcite or aragonite—as that generated through inorganic processes. Organics are sometimes used as gems.

COMPOSITION

The organics have a highly varied composition. Coral, pearl, and shell contain mineral matter generated by biological processes. Amber is fossilized resin, mainly from extinct coniferous trees, although amberlike substances from even older trees are also known. Copal is a modern equivalent of fossilized amber. Coal is derived from buried organic material, such as peat. Bitumen is a very heavy oil.

Shell
The shells of marine invertebrates capture large amounts of carbon in the form of aragonite. Their remains form extensive beds of carbonate rocks.

OCCURRENCE

The organics are relatively widespread. The shells of freshwater and marine organisms are part of a carbonate cycle that extracts carbon from the environment and returns it as carbonate sediment, either to be reincorporated into other organics or to be lithified. Other organics incorporate carbon in their essential composition.

USES

Coal and bitumen are the organics that find the widest use. Organically formed carbonate rocks are also extensively used as building stone and ballast and in the manufacture of cement. Other organics are used to make ornaments and jewelry.

Coral necklace
This branchlike Native American necklace is made from small, polished branches and tiny beads of red coral.

red coral

Coral reef
A coral reef forms in shallow ocean areas. Corals are the most important part of the reef and form its main structural framework. Coral skeletons are made of aragonite.

PROFILE

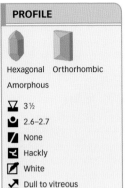

Hexagonal Orthorhombic

Amorphous

3½

2.6–2.7

None

Hackly

White

Dull to vitreous

wood-grain pattern

coral branch

Red coral
The use of red coral dates back to the Iron Age. This specimen from the Mediterranean has a wood-grain pattern on its branches.

VARIANTS

Blue coral
A type of coral used in artifacts and jewelry

Black coral
A variant that is polished to make jewelry

Brain coral
An elaborate confection of organic aragonite

Mostly CaCO₃

CORAL

According to Greek legend, coral came from the drops of blood shed when the mythic hero Perseus cut off the head of the monster Medusa. Coral is actually the skeletal material generated by marine animals also known as coral polyps. In most corals, this material is calcium carbonate, but in black and golden corals it is a hornlike substance called conchiolin. Coral has a dull luster when recovered, but it can be polished and brightened. It is sensitive even to mild acids and can become dull with extensive wear.

Coral is variable in color. Red and pink precious coral is found in the warm seas around Japan and Malaysia, in African coastal waters, and in the Mediterranean Sea. Black coral comes from the West Indies, Australia, and from around the Pacific Islands.

Coral necklace
This triple-stranded necklace from Morocco is made of coral, silver, and turquoise.

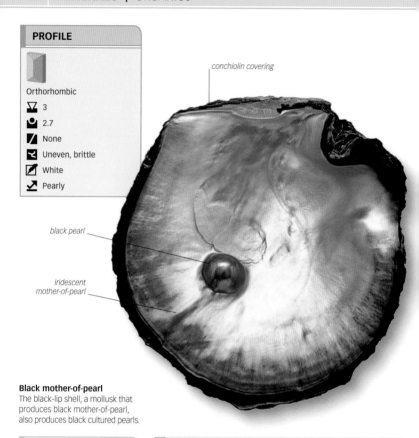

conchiolin covering

black pearl

iridescent mother-of-pearl

Black mother-of-pearl
The black-lip shell, a mollusk that produces black mother-of-pearl, also produces black cultured pearls.

VARIANTS

blister pearl

Blister pearls Attached to the shell, these are flat on one side

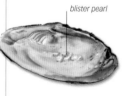

Freshwater pearls These have the same luster as marine pearls

♣ Mostly CaCO₃

PEARL

A concretion formed by a mollusk, a pearl consists mainly of aragonite (p.115), the same material as the animal's shell (p.249). The shell-secreting cells are located in a layer of the mollusk's body tissue called the mantle. When a foreign particle enters the mantle, the cells build up concentric layers of pearl around it. Colors vary with the mollusk and its environment and can be any delicate shade from black to white, cream, gray, blue, yellow, green, lavender, or mauve.

The finest pearls are produced by limited species of saltwater oysters and freshwater clams. A pearl is valued by its translucence, luster, color, and shape. The most valuable pearls are spherical or droplike, with a deep luster and good play of color. Rose-tinted Indian pearls are highly prized.

Pearl bracelet
This Cartier Art Deco bracelet has five strands of cultured pearls with a gold and oxidized-silver clasp.

PROFILE

Hexagonal Orthorhombic

Amorphous

2 ½

About 1.3

None

Conchoidal

White

Dull to vitreous

iridescent mother-of-pearl

inner surface of shell

Abalone shell
Found in warm seas, abalone shells, such as this one from New Zealand, are noted for their multicolored, iridescent, mother-of-pearl lining.

VARIANTS

Spider conch
A type of shell widely used for ornamental purposes

Tortoise shell The shell of a hawksbill turtle

Thorny oyster A shell made up of organic aragonite

$CaCO_3$

SHELL

Like coral (p.247), shell is mineral matter generated by biological processes. The mineral component of shell is either calcite (p.114) or aragonite (p.115), both of which are calcium carbonate. Shell forms as the hard outer covering of many mollusks. It is secreted in calcareous layers by cells in the mantle—a skinlike tissue in the mollusk's body wall. Mollusk shells differ in the composition, number, and arrangement of calcareous layers. These layers form as distinct microstructures with different mechanical properties and, in some shells, different colors.

Both marine and freshwater shells are used for ornamentation. Shells with different colored layers have been carved into cameos since antiquity. Pearly shells were used widely in button making around the 19th century.

Shell perfume bottle
This 19th-century perfume bottle is made of two shells glued together. It has a chain, ring, and pinchbeck stopper.

PROFILE

Crystal system None

▽ 2–2½

◉ About 1.1

▮ None

◈ Conchoidal

◼ White

◿ Resinous

translucent copal

golden-yellow color

conchoidal fracture

Copal nugget
This specimen of copal closely
resembles amber. Some copal
is used as an amber substitute
in jewelry.

VARIANTS

orange-yellow
gum

Kauri gum Resin
derived from the
Kauri conifer

Copal lumps Lumps of resin
from the Protium copal or
copal tree

👤 Various

COPAL

Named after the Nahuatl word *copalli*, which means
"resin," copal is a yellow to red-orange resin obtained from
various tropical trees. It can be collected from living trees
and from accumulations in the soil beneath the trees.
It can also be mined if it is buried. Copals from different
sources usually have different chemical properties but can
have similar physical properties. Copal has approximately
the same hardness as amber (p.251) but unlike amber
it is wholly or partially soluble in organic solvents.

Buried copal is the nearest
to amber in durability and is,
in many cases, virtually
indistinguishable from it.

Zanzibar in Tanzania is a major
source of buried copal. This
mineral is also found in China,
Brazil, and other South American
countries. It is used in varnishes,
lacquers, and inks.

Copal beads
In this necklace, beads of a
tough and compact form of
copal alternate with beads
carved from seeds.

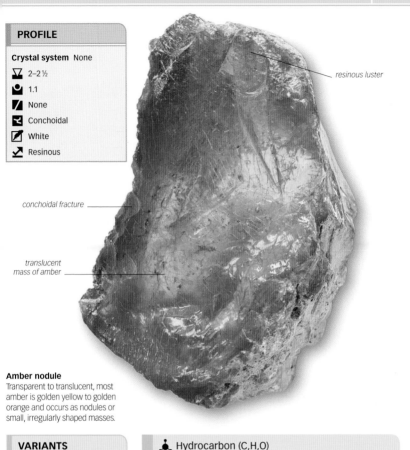

resinous luster

conchoidal fracture

translucent mass of amber

Amber nodule
Transparent to translucent, most amber is golden yellow to golden orange and occurs as nodules or small, irregularly shaped masses.

VARIANTS

Wave-rounded amber
A piece of wave-rounded Baltic amber

Lithuanian amber A group of amber pieces showing color variation

⚛ Hydrocarbon (C,H,O)

AMBER

The fossilized resin amber comes mainly from extinct coniferous trees, although amberlike substances from earlier trees are also known. It is generally found in association with lignite coal (p.253). Amber and other partially fossilized resins are sometimes given mineral-like names depending on where they are found, their degree of fossilization, or the presence of other chemical components. For example, resin that resembles copal (p.250) and comes from the London clay region is called copalite. At least 12 other names are applied to minor variants.

For thousands of years, the largest source of amber has been deposits along the Baltic coast, extending intermittently from Gdánsk right around to the coastlines of Denmark and Sweden. Amber has been traded since ancient times.

Preserved in amber
As resin dried 40–50 million years ago, insects were sometimes fossilized within the sticky substance.

PROFILE

Crystal system None

⬛ 2½

⬛ About 1.3

⬛ None

⬛ Conchoidal

⬛ Black to dark brown

⬛ Velvety, vitreous, or waxy

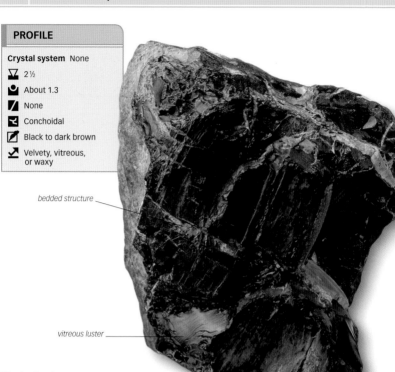

bedded structure

vitreous luster

Woody structure
This specimen of jet shows the layered, woody structure that is sometimes characteristic of the mineral.

VARIANT

fossil amonite

Jet fossil Jet with fossils of marine origin

⚛ Various

JET

Generally classified as a type of coal (p.253), jet has a high carbon content and a layered structure. It is black to dark brown in color. Specimens sometimes contain tiny inclusions of pyrite (p.62), which have a metallic luster. Jet is found in rocks of marine origin, perhaps derived from waterlogged driftwood or other plant material. It can occur in distinct beds, such as those at Whitby, England, from which jet has been extracted since the 1st century CE.

Jet has been carved for ornamental purposes since prehistoric times and has been found in prehistoric caves. The Romans carved jet into bangles and beads. In medieval times, powdered jet drunk with water or wine was believed to have medicinal properties.

Jet necklace
This Native American necklace is made of high-quality, fine-grained jet, which shows velvety luster.

PROFILE

Crystal system None

 2–2 ½

About 1.1

None

Conchoidal

Black

Nearly metallic

near-metallic luster

black surface is hard and clean to touch

Anthracite
Hard to the touch, anthracite is naturally shiny. It takes a brilliant polish and is used for decorative as well as practical purposes.

VARIANTS

Lignite A variant having a composition between peat and bituminous coal

Bituminous coal The most common form of coal

 Various

COAL

The fossilized remains of plants, coal usually occurs in layered, sedimentary deposits. It is brown or black and made up of an irregular mixture of chemical compounds called macerals, which are analogous to minerals in inorganic rocks. Unlike minerals, macerals have no fixed chemical composition and no definite crystalline structure.

Different varieties of coal are formed depending on the kinds of plant material, varying degrees of coalification (the process by which plant material is converted to coal), and the presence of impurities. Four varieties are recognized. Lignite is the lowest grade and is the softest and least coalified variety. It forms from peat under moderate pressure. Sub-bituminous coal is dark brown to black. Bituminous coal is the most abundant and is commonly burned for heat generation. Anthracite is the highest grade and the most highly metamorphosed form of coal. It contains the highest percentage of low-emission carbon and would be an ideal fuel if it were not relatively scarce.

ROCKS

IGNEOUS ROCKS

Igneous rocks are formed from magma—molten rock. They are classified as extrusive or intrusive depending on whether or not the magma emerged at Earth's surface before crystallizing. Extrusive rocks form on the surface; intrusive rocks form below it.

INTRUSIVE IGNEOUS ROCKS

Intrusive rocks are categorized as plutonic if formed deep inside the crust and hypabyssal if formed at shallow depths. Plutonic intrusive rocks are characterized by their large crystals and generally form geographically large bodies. For example, a batholith is a large igneous body with a surface exposure of at least 40 square miles (100 square km) and a thickness of about 6–9 miles (10–15 km). Batholiths form the cores of great mountain ranges, such as the Rockies and the Sierra Nevada in North America. Granite, diorite, peridotite, syenite, and gabbro are all plutonic igneous rocks.

Hypabyssal intrusive rocks are formed at shallower depths and are characterized by fine crystallization. They occur in sheetlike bodies called dikes and sills, volcanic plugs, and other relatively small formations. Dikes range from less than an

light plagioclase feldspar

dark pyroxene

Gabbro
Most gabbros form as plutonic intrusive rocks. This coarsely crystallized specimen contains light-colored crystals of plagioclase and dark crystals of pyroxene.

inch to many feet in thickness and can be hundreds of miles in length. Sills are similar to dikes, except that they form parallel to the enclosing rocks and intrude between two strata.

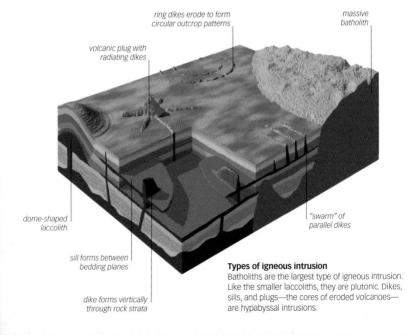

ring dikes erode to form circular outcrop patterns

massive batholith

volcanic plug with radiating dikes

dome-shaped laccolith

sill forms between bedding planes

dike forms vertically through rock strata

"swarm" of parallel dikes

Types of igneous intrusion
Batholiths are the largest type of igneous intrusion. Like the smaller laccoliths, they are plutonic. Dikes, sills, and plugs—the cores of eroded volcanoes— are hypabyssal intrusions.

EXTRUSIVE IGNEOUS ROCKS

Extrusive igneous rocks are also known as volcanic rocks. The principal rock types in this category include basalt, obsidian, rhyolite, trachyte, and andesite. All of these usually form from lava—a magma that has flowed either onto land or underwater. Other extrusive rocks, such as tuff and pumice, form in explosive volcanic eruptions. These "pyroclastic" rocks are porous because of the frothing expansion of volcanic gases during their formation. Basalt is the most common extrusive rock, forming the floor of most oceans and extensive plateaus on land, such as the Deccan Plateau of India and the Columbia River Basalts of Oregon, USA.

COMPOSITION OF IGNEOUS ROCKS

Igneous rocks form from magma, which is essentially a silicate melt. Igneous rocks are classified on the basis of silica content. Felsic rocks have over 65 percent silica, intermediate rocks 55–65 percent, mafic rocks 45–55 percent, and ultramafic rocks less than 45 percent silica. The silicate minerals that develop from the melt depend on factors such as silica concentration in the melt, the presence and concentration of other elements such as aluminum, iron, magnesium, calcium, sodium, and potassium within the melt, and the temperature and pressure at which crystallization takes place.

vesicle

light color similar to that of rhyolite

RHYOLITIC PUMICE

pale, fine-grained matrix of crystals

fine-grained matrix

LIGHT COLOR

phenocrysts of light plagioclase feldspar

MEDIUM COLOR

pyroxene phenocryst

PORPHYRITIC BASALT

fine matrix

DARK COLOR

Grain size
The origin of igneous rocks is generally indicated by the grain size of their minerals. Small or microscopic grains are found in extrusives; large grains in intrusives.

Color
Relatively few igneous rocks are identified by specific colors. Instead, they are generally described as light, intermediate, or dark.

Mount St. Helens
In 1980, Mount St. Helens in the USA erupted, sending thousands of tons of pyroclastic debris across northwestern USA. Extensive beds of pumice and tuff form from such eruptions.

potassium feldspar crystal

biotite

Dark granite
This specimen of granite is dominated by large crystals of potassium feldspar, quartz, and biotite.

VARIANTS

Pink granite Pink feldspars give this granite its color

White granite
A specimen dominated by light-colored minerals

Hornblende granite Granite with black hornblende

GRANITE

The most common intrusive rock in Earth's continental crust, granite is familiar as a mottled pink, white, gray, and black ornamental stone. It is coarse- to medium-grained. Its three main minerals are feldspar, quartz (p.168), and mica, which occur as silvery muscovite (p.195) or dark biotite (p.197) or both. Of these minerals, feldspar predominates, and quartz usually accounts for more than 10 percent. The alkali feldspars are often pink, resulting in the pink granite often used as a decorative stone.

Granite crystallizes from silica-rich magmas that are miles deep in Earth's crust. Many mineral deposits form near crystallizing granite bodies from the hydrothermal solutions that such bodies release.

Granite staircase
Granite is used as a building stone. This stairway made of granite ascends to the Bom Jesus Church in Portugal.

PROFILE

- ▲ Intrusive
- 🌐 Intrusive
- 🔍 Medium to coarse
- ▣ Quartz, feldspar, mica
- ▢ Hornblende, plagioclase
- ✳ Pink, white

pink orthoclase feldspar ____

Graphic granite
This specimen of granite shows simultaneous growth of quartz and feldspar, which produces a pattern.

VARIANTS

Porphyritic granite
A specimen in which large feldspar phenocrysts are set in granite

Orbicular granite Granite with spherical phenocrysts of feldspar

TEXTURED GRANITE

Granites with distinct patterns in their crystallization are known as textured granites and in some cases, graphic granites. Graphic granite consists of roughly 30 percent quartz (p.168) and 70 percent feldspar, with a few other minerals. These minerals are intergrown in such a way that straight-sided quartz crystals, which look like hieroglyphic characters, are set in a background of feldspar. The texture forms in pegmatites (p.260) when the main minerals crystallize from the magma at the same time.

Orbicular granite is an unusual but spectacular granite containing spheres (orbicules) of concentric layers of granitic minerals. The orbicules are about 2–4 in (5–10 cm) in diameter and often richer than the granite in darker minerals. They are usually restricted to small areas within the larger granite mass. In porphyritic granite, the feldspar crystals are larger and better formed than the surrounding mineral grains. These granites have been quarried and polished for use as ornamental and building stones.

PROFILE

- Feldspar-rich, plutonic
- Fluid-rich crystallization in the final stages of the formation of a granite
- More than $\frac{3}{16}$ in (5 mm) to many ft (m)
- Quartz, feldspar, mica
- Tourmaline, topaz
- White, pink

pink orthoclase feldspar

dark prismatic tourmaline crystal

Tourmaline pegmatite
This specimen contains crystals of black tourmaline in a matrix of pink feldspar and white quartz.

VARIANTS

Granitic pegmatite
A specimen with feldspar, quartz, biotite, and needle-shaped tourmaline

Blue topaz
A topaz crystal in a pegmatite matrix

Feldspar pegmatite
A pegmatite dominated by white feldspar, with amphibole

PEGMATITE

Important sources of many gemstones, pegmatites are very coarse-grained igneous rocks, mostly of a granitic composition. Although crystals can be huge—over 33 ft (10 m) in some specimens—individual crystals usually average 3¼–4 in (8–10 cm) in length. The large crystals are due to the considerable amount of water in the magma rather than slow cooling. The most perfect crystals are typically found in openings or pockets. Quartz (p.168) and feldspar dominate, but many other minerals can form large, beautiful crystals. Muscovite (p.195) and other micas commonly occur in pegmatites in large, flat sheets known as books.

Pegmatites are light-colored rocks and occur in small igneous bodies, such as veins and dykes, or sometimes as patches in larger masses of granite (pp.258–59). Several gemstones—such as tourmaline (p.224) group minerals, aquamarine (p.225), rock crystal, smoky quartz, rose quartz, and topaz (p.234)—are mined from pegmatites.

plagioclase
feldspar crystals

PROFILE

- Ultramafic, plutonic
- Crystallization of a silica-poor magma in a major intrusion
- 1⁄16–3⁄16 in (2–5 mm)
- Calcium plagioclase
- Olivine, pyroxene, garnet
- Light gray to white

Anorthosite
This specimen of anorthosite is dominated by light-colored plagioclase feldspars.

VARIANTS

Coarse anorthosite
A specimen with pyroxene and orthopyroxene

Lunar anorthosite Believed to be the first lunar rock to crystallize

ANORTHOSITE

An intrusive igneous rock, anorthosite is composed of at least 90 percent calcium-rich plagioclase feldspar—principally labradorite (p.180) and bytownite. Olivine (p.232), garnet, pyroxene, and iron oxides make up the remaining 10 percent. Anorthosite is coarse-grained and either white or gray. Specimens can also be green. Many anorthosites have an interesting "cumulate" texture, where well-formed crystals appear to have settled out of the liquid magma, in a similar way as large grains settling in a sediment.

Anorthosite is not a common rock, but where it does occur, it is found as immense masses, or as layers between iron- and magnesium-rich rocks, such as gabbro (p.265) and peridotite (p.266). Anorthosite is, however, common on the surface of the Moon.

Labradorite relief
Labrodorite occurs in anorthosite and is used in carvings, such as this 19th-century relief.

PROFILE

- ▲ Intermediate silica content, plutonic
- 🌐 Crystallization of an alkaline intermediate magma in a major intrusion
- 🔎 1/16–3/16 in (2–5mm)
- ⬛ Potassium feldspar
- ⬜ Sodium plagioclase, biotite, amphibole, pyroxene, hornblende, feldspathoids
- ✳ Gray, pink, or red

Pink syenite
The pink color of this syenite specimen is due to the presence of alkali feldspar, which predominates in syenite.

amphibole

feldspar

VARIANTS

Nepheline syenite Nepheline crystals with black hornblende

Syenite with zircon Zircon crystals in a syenite matrix

SYENITE

Visually similar to granite and often confused with it, syenites can be distinguished from granite by the absence or scarcity of quartz. A syenite is any one of a class of rocks essentially composed of: an alkali feldspar or sodium plagioclase (or both); a ferromagnesian mineral, usually biotite (p.197), hornblende (p.218), or pyroxene; and little or no quartz. The alkali feldspars can include orthoclase (p.173), albite (p.177), or less commonly, microcline (p.175). Syenites are attractive, multi-colored rocks—usually gray, pink, or red. Other minerals that occasionally occur in small amounts in syenite include titanite, apatite (p.148), zircon (p.233), magnetite (p.92), and pyrite (p.62). When syenites contain quartz, they are called quartz syenites.

Nepheline (p.182) and alkali feldspar are essential minerals in nepheline syenite, but this rock can contain other minerals, including unusual and attractive ones, such as eudialyte. If the rock includes a pyroxene, it is usually aegirine (p.209); if an amphibole it is usually arfvedsonite, both of which are rich in sodium.

PROFILE

- Feldspar-rich, plutonic
- Intrusive
- Coarse
- Plagioclase, alkali feldspar, quartz, mica
- Hornblende, augite
- Gray, white, or pink

dark, iron- and magnesium-bearing minerals

coarse texture

Speckled granodiorite
This pink granodiorite has a speckled appearance because of the presence of darker minerals, such as mica and hornblende.

VARIANT

Pink granodiorite A specimen of granodiorite with dark mica and hornblende

GRANODIORITE

Among the most abundant of intrusive igneous rocks, granodiorite is a medium- to coarse-grained rock that is similar to granite (p.258) in texture. Granodiorite can be pink or white, with a grain size and texture similar to that of granite, but abundant plagioclase generally makes it appear darker than granite. The biotite (p.197) and hornblende (p.218) give it a speckled appearance. The mica may occur in well-formed hexagonal crystals, and the hornblende may be present in needlelike crystals. Twinned plagioclase crystals are sometimes wholly encased by orthoclase.

The quartz (p.168) present in granodiorite can be gray to white. With increased amounts of quartz and alkali feldspar, granodiorite grades to granite. With less quartz and alkali feldspar, it becomes diorite (p.264). The volcanic equivalent of granodiorite is dacite (p.274). Two historic stones are granodiorite: the Rosetta Stone was carved from it, and the Plymouth Rock is a glacial erratic boulder of granodiorite.

PROFILE

 Intermediate silica content, plutonic

 Crystallization of a magma with intermediate silica content in a major intrusion

 ¹⁄₁₆–³⁄₁₆ in (2–5 mm)

Sodium plagioclase, hornblende

Biotite

Black or dark green mottled with gray or white

Two-toned diorite
This diorite specimen gets its two-toned appearance from light-colored plagioclase feldspar and black hornblende.

plagioclase feldspar

hornblende

VARIANTS

Light-colored diorite
A specimen of diorite with white plagioclase and a minor amount of hornblende

Fine-grained diorite
A specimen of fine-grained diorite with phenocrysts of hornblende

DIORITE

This medium- to coarse-grained intrusive igneous rock is sometimes sold as "black granite." In general, though, diorite is darker than granite (p.258). It is commonly composed of about two-thirds white plagioclase feldspar and one-third dark-colored minerals, such as biotite (p.197) and hornblende (p.218). The plagioclases in diorite—oligoclase (p.178) or andesine (p.181)—are rich in sodium. Diorite can be of uniform grain size or have large phenocrysts of plagioclase or hornblende.

The rock can occur as large intrusions or as smaller dykes and sills. Most diorite is intruded along the margins of continents. With small amounts of quartz (p.168) and alkali feldspar, it becomes a granodiorite (p.263); with larger amounts, it is classified as granite.

Neolithic axehead
Diorite can be extremely tough and was used to make ancient tools, such as this neolithic axehead.

PROFILE

- Mafic, plutonic
- Crystallization of a silica-poor magma in a major intrusion
- 1/16–3/16 in (2–5 mm)
- Calcium plagioclase feldspar, pyroxene, ilmenite
- Olivine, magnetite
- Dark gray to black

Coarse-grained gabbro
This specimen of gabbro has coarse grains, as produced by the formation of large crystals during slow cooling of a magma.

plagioclase feldspar

dark pyroxene

VARIANTS

Layered gabbro Bands of light plagioclase and dark ferromagnesian minerals

Leucogabbro A gabbro with feldspar-rich crystals

Olivine gabbro A gabbro containing olivine

GABBRO

Medium or coarse-grained rocks, gabbros consist principally of dark green pyroxene (augite and lesser amounts of orthopyroxene) plus white- or green-colored plagioclase and black, millimeter-sized grains of magnetite and/or ilmenite. A gabbro has an intermediate or low silica content and rarely contains quartz (p.168). Gabbro is essentially the intrusive equivalent of basalt (p.273), but unlike basalt gabbro has a highly variable mineral content. It often contains a layering of light and dark minerals (layered gabbro), a significant amount of olivine (olivine gabbro), or a high percentage of coarse crystals of plagioclase feldspar (leucogabbro).

Gabbros are widespread but not common on Earth's surface. They occur as intrusions and as uplifted sections of oceanic crust. Some gabbros are mined for their nickel, chromium, and platinum (p.38). Those containing ilmenite (p.90) and magnetite (p.92) are mined for their iron or titanium.

PROFILE

▲ Ultramafic, plutonic

🌐 Crystallization of a silica-poor magma in a major intrusion, or Earth's mantle

🔎 ¹⁄₁₆–³⁄₁₆ in (2–5 mm)

▪ Olivine, pyroxene

▫ Garnet, chromite

✳ Dark green to black

dark, olivine and pyroxene crystals

Coarse peridotite
This is a specimen of dark, olivine- and pyroxene-rich peridotite from Odenwald, West Germany.

VARIANTS

Green peridotite A specimen containing green olivine

Garnet peridotite Peridotite with red phenocrysts of pyrope garnet

PERIDOTITE

An intrusive igneous rock, peridotite is coarse-grained and dense. It is light to dark green in color. Peridotite contains at least 40 percent olivine (p.232) and some pyroxene. Unlike the olivine grains, the pyroxene grains in peridotite have a visible cleavage when viewed under a hand lens. Peridotite forms much of Earth's mantle and can occur as nodules that are brought up from the mantle by kimberlite (p.269) or basalt (p.273) magmas.

The rock is usually found interlayered with iron- and magnesium-rich rocks in the lower parts of layered igneous rock bodies, where its denser crystals first form through selective crystallization and then settle to the bottom of still-fluid or semi-solid crystallizing mushes. A peridotite specimen that has been altered by weathering becomes serpentinite (p.298). Peridotite and pyroxenite (p.267) form in similar environments, but pyroxenite contains a higher percentage of pyroxene. Peridotites are important sources of chromium and nickel.

Pyroxenite
Pyroxene, the main component of pyroxenite, can be seen in this specimen, along with smaller amounts of plagioclase feldspar and accessory sulfide minerals.

plagioclase feldspar

pyroxene

PYROXENITE

This is a coarse-grained, granular igneous rock that contains at least 90 percent pyroxene. Pyroxenite may also contain olivine (p.232) and oxide minerals when it occurs in layered intrusions or nepheline (p.182) when it occurs in silica-poor intrusions. A hard and heavy rock, it is light green, dark green, or black. Its surface often weathers to rusty brown. Individual crystals may be 3 in (7.5 cm) or more in length. Pyroxenites are usually found with gabbros (p.265) and peridotites (p.266). Unlike gabbros, pyroxenite contains almost no feldspars. Also, pyroxenite has less olivine than peridotites.

The principal minerals usually found accompanying pyroxenites, in addition to olivine and feldspar, are chromite (p.99) and other spinels (p.96), garnet, rutile (p.78), and magnetite (p.92). It has been proposed that large volumes of pyroxenite form in the upper mantle. Rare metamorphic pyroxenites are known and are described as pyroxene hornfels.

Dark gray dolerite
Dolerite's characteristic medium texture and dark color can be seen in this specimen.

medium texture

plagioclase feldspar

VARIANTS

Weathered dolerite A dolerite specimen showing surface flaking from weathering

Fine-grained dolerite A specimen of dolerite with fine-grained texture

DOLERITE

A medium-grained rock, dolerite has the same composition as gabbro (p.265): one- to two-thirds is calcium-rich plagioclase feldspar, and the remainder is mainly pyroxene. Specimens can have up to 55 percent silica and up to 10 percent quartz (p.168). Plagioclase crystals commonly occur as tiny rectangular crystals within larger pyroxene grains in dolerite. Olivine (p.232) can occur as a constituent in the form of rounded grains that are often weathered orange-brown.

An extremely hard and tough rock, dolerite occurs in dykes and sills intruded into fissures in other rocks. It is a heavy rock that is often polished for use as a decorative stone. Dolerite is also used in its rough state for paving and is crushed for road stone. It is a stone sold under the name "black granite."

Stonehenge, England
The inner circle at Stonehenge in England is made up of about 80 pieces of dolerite "bluestones."

PROFILE

- Silica-poor, volcanic
- Extrusion of a fluid part of Earth's mantle
- Wide range
- Olivine, pyroxene, mica, garnet, diopside
- Ilmenite, diamond, serpentine, calcite, rutile, perovskite, magnetite
- Dark gray

coarse texture

crystal of ferromagnesian minerals

dark matrix

Brecciated kimberlite
Kimberlite is named after Kimberley, the diamond industry center in South Africa. This is a typically heavy and fragmented specimen.

VARIANTS

Weathered kimberlite
Heavily weathered kimberlite from Kimberley, South Africa

Diamond in kimberlite
An octahedral diamond in a kimberlite matrix

KIMBERLITE

The major source of diamonds (p.47), kimberlite is a variety of peridotite (p.266). It is rich in mica, often in the form of crystals of phlogopite, a type of mica. Other abundant constituent minerals include chrome-diopside (p.210), olivine (p.232), and chromium- and pyrope-rich garnet. Lesser amounts of rutile (p.78), perovskite (p.89), ilmenite (p.90), magnetite (p.92), calcite (p.114), serpentine (p.191), pyroxene, and diamond can also be present.

Kimberlite is typically found in pipes—structures with vertical sides roughly circular in cross section. The rock may have been injected from the mantle into zones of weakness in the crust. Fragments of mantle rock are often brought to the surface in kimberlites, making them a valuable source of information about inner Earth.

Diamond ring
This ring has an emerald-cut diamond on a gold shank. Kimberlites are the primary source rock for diamonds.

PROFILE

▲ Extrusive

🌐 Crystallization of an alkaline magma in a minor intrusion

🔎 ½₅₆–¹⁄₁₆ in (0.1–2 mm)

◼ Orthoclase, plagioclase, biotite, hornblende

▢ Hornblende, magnetite, axinite, amphibole, pyroxene

✹ Dark brown to black

porphyritic texture

brown, weathered surface

Weathered lamprophyre
This weathered grayish brown specimen of lamprophyre has a porphyritic texture, with large crystals set in a fine matrix.

VARIANTS

Dark brown lamprophyre
A specimen of lamprophyre with mica flakes

Fine-grained lamprophyre
Lamprophyre with fine grains and no phenocrysts

LAMPROPHYRE

The term lamprophyre is used to refer to a group of igneous rocks with high potassium, magnesium, and iron content. Four minerals dominate these rocks: orthoclase (p.173), plagioclase, biotite (p.197), and hornblende (p.218). Amphibole and biotite tend to occur in a matrix of various combinations of plagioclase and other sodium- and potassium-rich feldspars, pyroxene, and feldspathoids (pp.182–84). Because of their relative rarity and varied composition, lamprophyres do not fit into standard geological classifications. In general, they form at great depth and are enriched in sodium, cesium, rubidium, nickel, and chromium, as well as potassium, iron, and magnesium. Some are also source rocks for diamonds.

The exact origin of lamprophyres is still debated. These rocks occur mainly in dykes, sills, and other small igneous intrusions. They form along the margins of some granites (pp.258–59) and are often associated with large bodies of intrusive granodiorite (p.263).

PROFILE

- ▲▲ Extrusive
- ⬡ Two-stage crystallization of an igneous rock
- ⊘ Less than $\frac{1}{256}$ in (0.1 mm); phenocrysts up to $\frac{3}{4}$ in (2 cm)
- ■ Various
- ◻ Various
- ✺ Red, green, purple

Rhomb porphyry
This porphyry has feldspar with rhombic cross sections in a fine-grained matrix.

fine grains

rhombic feldspar

VARIANTS

Quartz porphyry Porphyry with phenocrysts of quartz

fine, dark matrix

Feldspar porphyry
Phenocrysts of feldspar in a reddish brown matrix

PORPHYRY

The name porphyry is a general name and textural term for medium- to fine-grained igneous rocks that contain large crystals (phenocrysts) of other minerals, especially if these minerals are found in the smaller crystals of the matrix. It is most often used for rocks formed in lava flows or minor intrusions. The term porphyry is often prefixed with a reference to the minerals it contains, such as quartz–feldspar porphyry, which contains phenocrysts of the two minerals. Alternatively, the prefix can refer to the composition or texture of the rock. Examples are rhyolite porphyry or rhomb porphyry, respectively.

Porphyries form when crystallization begins deep in Earth's crust and cooling occurs quickly after rapid upward movement of magma. This results in the formation of very small crystals of the matrix. Historically, the name porphyry was used for the purple-red form of the rock, which has been valued since antiquity as an ornamental stone. Many Egyptian, Roman, and Greek sculptures used this type of porphyry.

carbonate minerals

Carbonatite
This carbonatite specimen contains a mixture of carbonates and other minerals.

VARIANT

Carbonatite with magnetite A specimen of carbonatite with accessory black magnetite

CARBONATITE

An unusual rock type, carbonatite consists of over 50 percent carbonate minerals—usually calcite (p.114), dolomite (p.117), or siderite (p.123). Most carbonatites also contain some portion of silicate minerals and may contain magnetite (p.92), the brown mica phlogopite, and rare-earth minerals such as pyrochlore (p.85). Specimens are typically cream-colored, yellow, or brown. Carbonatite looks similar to marble (p.301). It may be coarse-grained if intrusive and fine-grained if volcanic.

The process by which carbonatites form is still a matter of conjecture. They are usually found in areas of continental rifting in veins, dykes, and sills around intrusions of sodium- and potassium-rich igneous rocks. The geochemistry of carbonatites is complex and can vary considerably in specimens. Many contain scarce and valuable ores of rare elements, such as niobium, cesium, tantalum, thorium, and hafnium. Some carbonatites also contain significant amounts of platinum (p.38), gold (p.42), silver (p.43), and nickel.

PROFILE

- Mafic, volcanic
- Extrusion of a silica-poor magma
- Less than ½₅₆ in (0.1 mm)
- Sodium plagioclase, pyroxene, olivine
- Leucite, nepheline, augite
- Dark gray to black

Fine-grained basalt
This specimen of basalt shows its characteristic fine-grained texture.

fine grains

columnar-jointed, massive basalt

VARIANTS

Vesicular basalt A basalt specimen with holes left by gas bubbles during cooling

Amygdaloidal basalt
A specimen with zeolite crystals in vesicles

Porphyritic basalt
A basalt with phenocrysts of pyroxene

BASALT

Basalt is the most common rock on Earth's surface. Specimens are black in color and weather to dark green or brown. Basalt is rich in iron and magnesium and is mainly composed of olivine (p.232), pyroxene, and plagioclase. Most specimens are compact, fine-grained, and glassy. They can also be porphyritic, with phenocrysts of olivine, augite (p.211), or plagioclase. Holes left by gas bubbles can give basalt a coarsely porous texture.

Basalt makes up large parts of the ocean floor. It can form volcanic islands when it is erupted by volcanoes in ocean basins. The rock has also built huge plateaus on land. The dark plains on the Moon, known as maria, and, possibly, the volcanoes on Mars and Venus are made of basalt.

Basalt temple
This magnificent, thousand-pillared temple in Andhra Pradesh, India, is made of gray basalt.

Porphyritic dacite
This dacite specimen has a porphyritic texture, with prominent phenocrysts of plagioclase and biotite.

feldspar phenocryst

hornblende

VARIANTS

Fine-grained dacite A fine-grained specimen of dacite with small phenocrysts

blue-gray dacite

Blue-gray dacite A specimen of dacite with dark phenocrysts

DACITE

An extrusive igneous rock, dacite takes its name from Dacia (modern Romania)—the ancient Roman province where it was first found. The volcanic equivalent of granodiorite (p.263), dacite is usually pink or a shade of gray. It often has flowlike bands. Porphyritic varieties are common, with large crystals usually consisting of blocky plagioclase feldspar or rounded quartz (p.168), or both. Dacite matrix can be cryptocrystalline or glassy.

Dacite occurs with andesite (p.275) on continental margins, and with rhyolite (p.278) in continental volcanic districts. Along continental margins, dacite magmas form in areas where oceanic crust sinks beneath continental crust. Dacite magmas are chemically altered as they reach the mantle. Dacite lavas are quite viscous because of their moderate silica content, and thus can be quite explosive in eruptions. The explosion of Mount Saint Helens volcano in USA in 1980 was a result of dacite domes formed from previous eruptions. The mineral compositions of dacite lavas tell the history of the magma.

PROFILE

 Intermediate silica content, volcanic

 Extrusion of a magma with intermediate silica content

 Less than ¹⁄₂₅₆ in (0.1 mm)

 Plagioclase feldspars

 Pyroxene, amphibole, biotite

✷ Light to dark gray, reddish pink

Porphyritic andesite
This specimen of porphyritic andesite shows light feldspar phenocrysts in a dark andesite matrix.

fine-grained matrix

euhedral feldspar phenocrysts

VARIANTS

Fine-grained andesite
A specimen from the Solomon Islands, Pacific Ocean

small phenocrysts

Andesite with plagioclase
A specimen of andesite with phenocrysts of light plagioclase

Amygdaloidal andesite Vesicles of andesite filled with a zeolite

ANDESITE

This volcanic rock is named after the Andes Mountains. Intermediate in silica content, it is usually gray in color and may be fine-grained or porphyritic. Andesite is the volcanic equivalent of diorite (p.264). It consists of the plagioclase feldspar minerals andesine (p.181) and oligoclase (p.178), together with one or more dark, ferromagnesian minerals such as pyroxene and biotite (p.197).

Amygdaloidal andesite occurs when the voids left by gas bubbles in the solidifying magma are later filled in, often with zeolite minerals (pp.185–90). Andesite erupts from volcanoes and is commonly found interbedded with volcanic ash and tuff (p.282). Ancient andesites are used to map ancient subduction zones because andesitic volcanoes form on continental or ocean crust above these zones.

Volcanic andesite
Mount Fujiyama in Yamanashi Prefecture, Honshu, Japan, is the cone of an andesitic volcano.

PROFILE

▲ Extrusive

🌐 Rubbly top of an extruded, silica-poor magma

🔍 Less than ¹⁄₂₅₆ in (0.1 mm)

⬛ Plagioclase, pyroxene

⬜ Apatite, magnetite, olivine

✳ Dark brown, black, or red

Vesicular scoria
The large vesicles characteristic of scoria can be seen in this specimen.

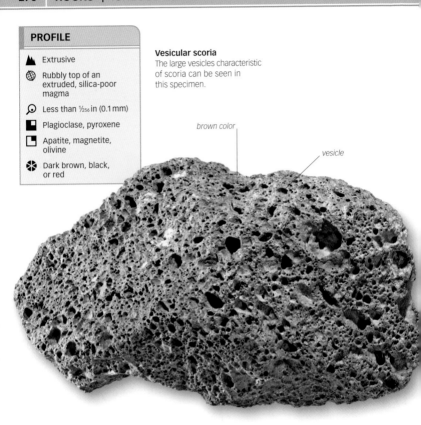

brown color

vesicle

VARIANT

Rubbly scoria A specimen of rubbly scoria from the top of a lava flow

SCORIA

The top of a lava flow is made up of a highly vesicular, rubbly material known as scoria. It has the appearance of vesicular lava. When fresh, scoria is generally dark in color—dark brown, black, or red. Weathered scoria has a medium-brown color and forms piles of loose rubble with small pieces. Most scoria is basaltic or andesitic in composition. This rock forms when gases in the magma expand to form bubbles as lava reaches the surface. The bubbles are then retained as the lava solidifies. Scoria is common in areas of recent volcanism, such as the Canary Islands and the Italian volcanoes.

This rock is of relatively low density due to its vesicles, but it is not as light as pumice (p.277), which floats on water. Scoria also differs from pumice in that it has larger vesicles with thicker walls. Scoria has commercial use as a high-temperature insulating material. It also has applications in landscaping and drainage.

PROFILE

- ▲ Volcanic
- 🌐 Solidification of a silica-rich lava with trapped gas bubbles
- 🔎 Less than ¹⁄₂₅₆ in (0.1 mm)
- ◼ Glass
- ▣ Feldspar, augite, hornblende, zircon
- ✳ Black, white, yellow, brown

Frothy pumice
The hollows (or vesicles) in this pumice clearly show its frothy nature. Vesicles may join together to form hollows or passages.

round vesicle

VARIANTS

Rhyolitic pumice A light-colored rhyolitic pumice with a frothy structure

Historic pumice A specimen of pumice from the Krakatoa eruption of 1883

PUMICE

A porous and frothlike volcanic glass, pumice is created when gas-saturated liquid magma erupts like a carbonated drink and cools so rapidly that the resulting foam solidifies into a glass full of gas bubbles. Pumices from silica-rich lavas are white, those from lavas with intermediate silica content are often yellow or brown, and rarer silica-poor pumices are black. The hollows in the froth can be rounded, elongated, or tubular, depending on the flow of the solidifying lava. The glassy material that forms pumice can be in threads, fibers, or thin partitions between the hollows.

Although pumice is mainly composed of glass, small crystals of various minerals occur. Pumice has a low density due to its numerous air-filled pores. For this reason, it can easily float in water.

Pumice stone
Pumice is soft and easily shaped. Mildly abrasive, it is often used to remove rough skin.

flow banding

hard, flinty
appearance

Banded rhyolite
This specimen of rhyolite has visible flow banding across its surface.

VARIANT

Porphyritic rhyolite
Light-colored rhyolite with phenocrysts of quartz

RHYOLITE

A rare volcanic rock, rhyolite is usually fine-grained. It is often composed largely of volcanic glass (pp.280–81). Individual grains of quartz (p.168), feldspar (pp.173–81), and mica may be present but are too small to be visible. The small size of these grains indicates that crystallization began before the lava flowed to the surface. Rhyolites sometimes have millimeter-scale phenocrysts of quartz, feldspar, or both. Specimens can also include iron- and magnesium-rich minerals, such as biotite (p.197) or pyroxene and amphibole. The granitic magma from which rhyolite crystallizes is very viscous. Therefore, flow banding is often preserved and can be seen on weathered surfaces. Banded rhyolites have few or no phenocrysts. A rhyolite variant with tiny crystals arranged in radiating spheres is called spherulitic rhyolite.

Rhyolite occurs with pumice (p.277), obsidian (p.280), and intermediate volcanic rocks, such as andesite (p.275). Rhyolites are almost exclusively confined to the interiors and margins of continents.

PROFILE

- ▲ Intermediate silica content, volcanic
- 🌐 Extrusion of an alkaline intermediate magma
- 🔍 Less than ½₂₅₆ in (0.1 mm)
- ▪ Sanidine, oligoclase
- ▫ Feldspathoids, quartz, hornblende, pyroxene, biotite
- ✳ Off-white, gray, pale yellow, pink

Porhyritic trachyte
This specimen of fine-grained trachyte has phenocrysts of a dark mineral.

fine-grained texture

dark phenocryst

VARIANTS

Gray trachyte A fine- to medium-grained specimen of trachyte

Porphyritic trachyte Light-colored trachyte with dark mineral phenocrysts

TRACHYTE

The name trachyte comes from the Greek word *trachys*, which means "rough"—a reference to the rock's typical rough texture. Trachyte's composition is dominated by alkali feldspar—a major component of the fine matrix and of the abundant phenocrysts that are common in the rock. Dark, iron- and magnesium-rich minerals, such as biotite (p.197), pyroxene, and amphibole, can be present in small quantities. Trachyte is similar to rhyolite (p.278) in color and occurence, but it contains little or no quartz (p.168).

Trachyte occurs on continents and oceanic islands with other volcanic rocks that are rich in alkali feldspars, have intermediate to high silica content, and are iron- and magnesium-rich.

Trachyte stonework
The cathedral in Morelia, in Mexico's Michoacán state, has ornate stonework of pink trachyte.

PROFILE

▲ Feldspar-rich, volcanic

🌐 Extrusion and rapid cooling of a silica-rich magma

🔍 Not granular

◼ Glass

◱ Hematite, feldspar

✴ Black, red, brown

Icelandic obsidian
This classic specimen of obsidian from Iceland perfectly demonstrates the rock's conchoidal fracture and vitreous luster.

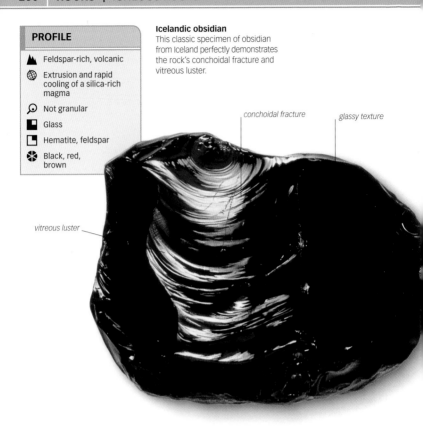

conchoidal fracture

glassy texture

vitreous luster

VARIANTS

Vesicular obsidian
A specimen with white, silicate-filled vesicles

Snowflake obsidian
A specimen with needlelike crystals in spherical aggregates

Banded obsidian
Obsidian with red hematite

OBSIDIAN

The natural volcanic glass obsidian forms when lava solidifies so quickly that crystals do not have time to form. Specimens are typically jet black, although the presence of hematite (p.90) can produce red and brown variants. The inclusion of tiny gas bubbles can sometimes create a golden sheen. Tiny crystals of feldspar (pp.173–81) and phenocrysts of quartz (p.168) can also be present. Obsidian can show flow banding.

Although obsidian can have any chemical composition, most specimens have a composition similar to rhyolite (p.278) and are found on the outer edges of rhyolite domes and flows. Like rhyolite, obsidian is also found along the rapidly cooled edges of sills and dykes. Most obsidian is relatively young, as the glass gradually crystallizes into minerals over a period of time.

Obsidian tear drop
These polished obsidian nodules are called Apache Tears after the tears of felled Apache warriors.

PROFILE

- ▲ Extrusive
- 🌐 Rapid cooling of basalt in a lava fountain
- 🔍 Up to ⅟₃₂ in (1 mm)
- ▪ Basaltic glass
- ▫ None
- ✾ Brown, black

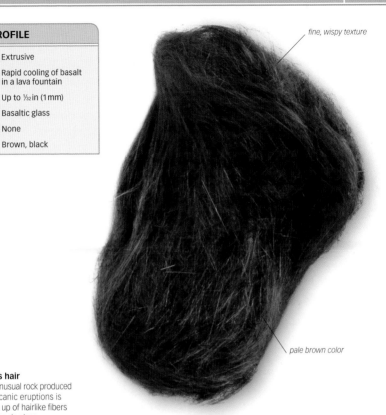

fine, wispy texture

pale brown color

Pele's hair
This unusual rock produced in volcanic eruptions is made up of hairlike fibers of volcanic glass.

VARIANTS

Pele's tear
A small blob of volcanic glass elongated by airflow

Golden hair A mass of fine, golden volcanic glass

Long strands Particularly long strands of Pele's hair

PELE'S HAIR AND TEARS

Two of the more unusual kinds of extrusive volcanic rock are named after Pele, the Hawaiian goddess of volcanoes. The first of these is Pele's hair, which refers to threads or fibers of volcanic glass (pp.280–81) formed when small droplets of molten basaltic material are blown into the air and spun out by the wind into long, hairlike strands. Specimens are usually emitted from lava fountains, lava cascades, vents, and vigorous lava flows. They are generally deep yellow or golden in color. A single strand of Pele's hair with a diameter of less than ⅟₁₆ in (0.5 mm) can be as long as 6½ ft (2 m). Strands can be blown tens of miles away from the vent or fountain where they originated.

The second variety of volcanic extrusive named after Pele is Pele's tears, which are small blobs of volcanic glass formed in much the same way as Pele's hair. Specimens occur as spheres or tear drops that are jet black in color. They are frequently found on one end of a strand of Pele's hair.

PROFILE

▲ Volcanic

🌐 Pyroclastic accumulation of fine material

🔎 $\frac{1}{256}$–$\frac{1}{16}$ in (0.1–2 mm)

◼ Glassy fragments

◻ Crystalline fragments

✸ Light to dark brown

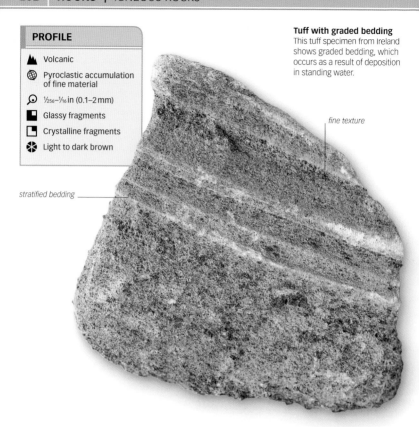

Tuff with graded bedding
This tuff specimen from Ireland shows graded bedding, which occurs as a result of deposition in standing water.

fine texture

stratified bedding

VARIANTS

Lithic tuff A specimen of tuff containing a high percentage of small rock fragments

Crystal tuff A specimen of tuff containing a predominance of crystal fragments

Bedded tuff A specimen of tuff that has fallen in distinct layers

TUFF

Any relatively soft, porous rock made of ash and other sediments ejected from volcanic vents that has solidified into rock is known as tuff. Most tuff formations include a range of fragment sizes and varieties. These range from fine-grained dust and ash (ash tuffs) to medium-sized fragments called lapilli (lapilli tuffs) to large volcanic blocks and bombs (bomb tuffs). Tuffs originate when foaming magma wells to the surface as a mixture of hot gases and incandescent particles and is ejected from a volcano.

The conditions under which the ejected ash solidifies determine the final nature of the tuff. Tuffs can vary both in texture and in chemical and mineralogical composition because of variations in the conditions of their formation and the composition of the ejected material. If the pyroclastic material is hot enough to fuse, a welded tuff (called ignimbrite) forms at once. Other tuffs lithify slowly through compaction and cementation, and can stratify when they accumulate under water.

PROFILE

▲ Extrusive

⊕ Mixing of liquid and solid material during crystallization of a basic magma

🔍 Less than ¹⁄₂₅₆ in (0.1 mm), clasts ³⁄₁₆–8 in (0.5–20 cm)

▪ Various

▫ Various

✳ Red, brown, black

Rhyolite breccia
This specimen of volcanic breccia incorporates angular fragments of reddish rhyolite.

vesicular lava

flow banding from original rhyolite deposit

reddish rhyolite fragment

VARIANT

Volcanic breccia A specimen of volcanic breccia that contains large clasts of other volcanics

VOLCANIC BRECCIA

These igneous rocks are formed either by the interaction of lava and scoria (p.276) or by the mixing of cooled lava and flowing lava. Volcanic breccia takes the form of inch-scale angular clasts, which may be rocks broken off the side of a magma conduit or rocks picked up off the surface during a pyroclastic or lava flow. In certain types of lavas, especially dacite (p.274) and rhyolite (p.278) lavas, thick and nearly solidified lava is broken into blocks and then reincorporated into the flow of liquid lava. Flowing lavas can also pick up surface rocks and incorporate them into a solidified breccia. In explosive volcanoes, solidified lava may be reshattered numerous times to be reconstituted as breccias.

Flowtop breccia commonly forms at the top of a lava flow where the moving lava picks up loose debris from previous eruptions and flows. It is especially common between basaltic lava flows, which may occur some time apart. Breccias are different from agglomerates (p.284), in which the clasts are rounded.

small, igneous clast

fine-grained ash

Agglomerate specimen
This specimen of agglomerate contains fine-grained ash and small clasts of other igneous rocks.

VARIANT

red dolomite

Carbonatite agglomerate
A specimen of carbonatite with clasts of red dolomite

AGGLOMERATE

An agglomerate is a pyroclastic rock in which coarse, rounded clasts up to several inches long are set in a matrix of lava or ash. The clasts are fragments that may be derived from lava, pyroclastic rock, or country rock (the rock that surrounds or lies beneath a volcano). The rounding of the clasts may have occurred either in the magma during eruption or by later sedimentary reworking. The rounded nature of these clasts is the key to designating the rock as an agglomerate rather than as a volcanic breccia (p.283). In a volcanic breccia, most of the clasts are angular.

One type of agglomerate, vent agglomerate, is the rock that plugs either the main vent or a satellite vent of a volcano. The outcrop of this rock is of limited extent and appears circular on a geological map. Like other agglomerates, vent agglomerate contains a variety of clasts of different sizes, shapes, and compositions from the lava, other volcanic rocks, or country rocks. These clasts lie in a matrix of fine-grained igneous rock.

green color from olivine

Olivine-rich bomb
Volcanoes that emit magnesium- and iron-rich lavas sometimes explosively hurl olivine-rich bombs, such as this one.

VARIANTS

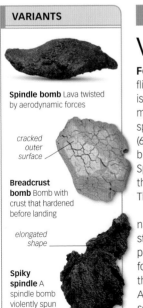

Spindle bomb Lava twisted by aerodynamic forces

cracked outer surface

Breadcrust bomb Bomb with crust that hardened before landing

elongated shape

Spiky spindle A spindle bomb violently spun after ejection

VOLCANIC BOMB

Formed by the cooling of a mass of lava while it flies through the air after eruption, a volcanic bomb is a pyroclastic rock. To be called a bomb, a specimen must be larger than 2½ in (6.5 cm) in diameter; smaller specimens are known as lapilli. Specimens up to 20 ft (6 m) in diameter are known. Volcanic bombs are usually brown or red, weathering to a yellow-brown color. Specimens can become rounded as they fly through the air, although they may also be twisted or pointed. They may have a cracked, fine-grained, or glassy surface.

There are several types of volcanic bomb, which are named according to their outward appearance and structure. Spherical bombs are spheres of fluid magma pulled into shape by surface tension. Spindle bombs are formed by the same process as spherical bombs, except that their rotation in flight leaves them elongated. A breadcrust bomb forms if the outside of the lava bomb solidifies during flight and develops a cracked outer surface while the interior continues to expand.

METAMORPHIC ROCKS

Metamorphism occurs when an existing rock is subjected to pressures or temperatures very different from those under which it formed. This causes its atoms and molecules to rearrange themselves into new minerals in the solid state, without melting.

DYNAMIC METAMORPHISM

There are three different ways in which metamorphic rocks are formed. The first of these is dynamic metamorphism. This occurs as a result of large-scale movements in Earth's crust, especially along fault planes and at continental margins where tectonic plates collide. The resulting mechanical deformation produces angular fragments to fine-grained, granulated, or powdered rocks. These rocks are characterized by a foliated appearance, in which mineral grains align as parallel plates.

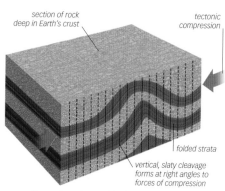

section of rock deep in Earth's crust

tectonic compression

folded strata

vertical, slaty cleavage forms at right angles to forces of compression

Dynamic metamorphism
Tectonic forces transform sedimentary rocks by dynamic metamorphism. Rock strata fold and cleavages develop as minerals align themselves due to the pressure.

REGIONAL METAMORPHISM

The second type of metamorphism is the formation of regional metamorphic rocks. These are associated with mountain building through the collision of tectonic plates. This process increases temperature and pressure over an area of thousands of square miles, producing widespread metamorphism. Important regional metamorphic rocks include slates, schists, and gneisses. Which rock forms depends on the existing rock, the temperatures and pressures to which it is subjected, and the time spent under those conditions. At the extremes, low temperature and pressure produces slates; high temperature and pressure produces gneisses.

Ancient metamorphic rocks
The Elk Mountains in Colorado, USA, have extensive areas of metamorphic rock, including schists and gneisses thought to have metamorphosed 1.7–1.9 billion years ago.

CONTACT METAMORPHISM

The third type of metamorphism is contact metamorphism or thermal metamorphism. This type occurs mainly as a result of increases in temperature, not in pressure. It is common in rocks near an igneous intrusion. Heat from the intrusion alters rocks to produce an "aureole" of metamorphic rock. The rocks nearest the intrusion are subjected to higher temperatures than those farther away, resulting in concentric zones of distinctive metamorphic rocks. The minerals of each zone depend on the original composition of the host rocks.

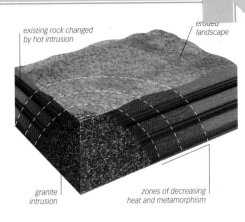

existing rock changed by hot intrusion

eroded landscape

granite intrusion

zones of decreasing heat and metamorphism

Contact metamorphism
A large intrusion of an igneous rock, such as granite, releases heat into the surrounding rocks, altering their mineral content.

CHANGING CHARACTERISTICS

Metamorphism is said to be low grade if it occurs at relatively low temperature and pressure and high grade at the intense end of the temperature and pressure range. The assemblages of minerals in rocks are affected differently depending on the grade of metamorphism and the relative importance of pressure and temperature in the reaction. In some low-grade reactions, the components of existing mineral assemblages are simply redistributed. In other reactions at higher temperatures and pressures, components combine with others present in the rock to form an entirely new set of minerals.

Shale to gneiss
This sequence shows how shale, a sedimentary rock, can be metamorphosed into various other rocks by the application of increasingly high degrees of heat and pressure (from left to right).

SHALE   SLATE   PHYLLITE   SCHIST   GNEISS

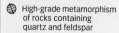

pale feldspar

dark biotite

Banded gneiss
This specimen of classic gneiss shows foliated banding of light and dark minerals.

GNEISS

Distinct bands of minerals of different colors and grain sizes characterize this metamorphic rock. In most gneisses, these bands are folded, although the folds may be too large to see in hand specimens. Gneiss is a medium- to coarse-grained rock. Unlike schist (pp.291–92), its foliation is well developed, but it has little or no tendency to split along planes. Most gneisses contain quartz (p.168) and feldspar (pp.173–81), but neither mineral is necessary for a rock to be called gneiss. Larger crystals of metamorphic minerals, such as garnet, can also be present.

Gneiss makes up the cores of many mountain ranges. It forms from sedimentary or granitic (pp.258–59) rocks at very high pressures and temperatures (1,065°F/575°C or above). A variety called pencil gneiss has rod-shaped individual minerals or mineral aggregates. In augen gneiss, the augens or "eyes" are single-mineral, eye-shaped grains that are larger than other grains in the rock. Orthogneiss is gneiss derived from igneous rock, and paragneiss is gneiss derived from sedimentary rock.

PROFILE

▲	Dynamic thrust zones
⊕	Stretching of a rock in a large fault
🌡	Low
⧳	Shearing stress
⊞	Streaked out
⦾	Less than 1/16 in (2 mm)
◼	As surrounding rock
▯	As surrounding rock
✿	As surrounding rock
◁◀	Surrounding rock

pale mylonite

Deformed mylonite
The folded bands in this mylonite specimen indicate that it has been subjected to extreme deformation.

VARIANT

fine grains

Granular mylonite
A specimen with stretched mineral grains

MYLONITE

The term mylonite refers to fine-grained rocks with streaks or rodlike structures produced by the ductile deformation, or stretching, of mineral grains. This classification is based only on the texture of the rock, and specimens can have different mineral compositions. Mylonite with a large percentage of phyllosilicate minerals, such as chlorite or mica, is known as phyllonite. When mylonite is hard, dark, and so fine that it has the appearance of streaky flint, it is known as ultramylonite. Although generally fine grained, a few mylonites are coarse grained and often sugary in appearance. These are referred to as blastomylonites.

There are many different views on the formation of mylonite. It is typically produced in a zone of thrusts or low-angle faults. Fine-grained mylonites may have been produced by recrystallization under pressure. The fact that mylonite grains are stretched rather than sheared makes it evident that the rock has softened in the metamorphic process.

PROFILE

- Regional metamorphic
- Partial melting of rocks containing quartz and feldspar
- High
- High
- Foliated, crystalline
- 1/16–3/16 in (2–5mm)
- Quartz, feldspar, mica
- Various
- Banded light and dark gray, pink, white
- Various, including granite

light quartz and feldspar

dark gneissose component

Mixed migmatite
The mixing of light igneous and dark metamorphic mineral elements is evident in this specimen of migmatite.

VARIANTS

Partial melting Migmatite with a snakelike vein of granite, which indicates partial melting

Migmatite folding
A specimen of migmatite with distortions produced by extreme temperatures

MIGMATITE

The term migmatite means "mixed rock" and refers to rocks that consist of gneiss (p.288) or schist (pp.291–92) interlayered, streaked, or veined with granite (pp.258–59). The granitic parts consist of granular patches of quartz (p.168) and feldspar (pp.173–81), and the gneissic parts consist of quartz, feldspar, and dark-colored minerals. The granite streaks are a result of the partial melting of the parent rock at temperatures below the melting point of the schist or gneiss. The layering may be tightly folded as a result of softening during heating. Migmatites occur at the borderline between igneous and metamorphic rocks.

The rock forms near large intrusions of granite when some of the magma has intruded into the surrounding metamorphic rocks. Commonly, migmatite occurs within extremely deformed rocks that once formed the bases of eroded mountain chains. It forms deep in the crust at high temperatures (1,065°F/575°C or above) and pressures.

PROFILE

- ▲ Regional metamorphic
- 🌐 Regional metamorphism of fine-grained sediments
- 🌡 Low to moderate
- 〰 Low to moderate
- ▦ Foliated
- ○ $\frac{1}{256}$–$\frac{1}{16}$ in (0.1–2 mm)
- ■ Quartz, feldspar, mica
- ▢ Garnet, hornblende, actinolite, graphite, kyanite
- ✳ Silvery, green, blue
- ◀◀ Mudstone, siltstone, shale, or felsic volcanics

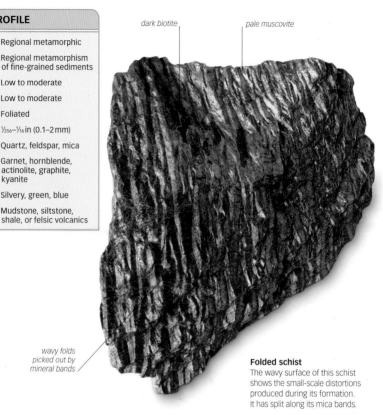

dark biotite *pale muscovite*

wavy folds picked out by mineral bands

Folded schist
The wavy surface of this schist shows the small-scale distortions produced during its formation. It has split along its mica bands.

VARIANTS

Muscovite schist A specimen of schist dominated by white muscovite mica

Blue schist Schist colored blue by glaucophane

Kyanite schist Small, blue blades of kyanite in schist

SCHIST

This metamorphic rock has a flaky and foliated texture. Specimens have wrinkled, wavy, or irregular sheets as a result of the parallel orientation of the component minerals. Schist shows distinct layering of light- and dark-colored minerals. The mineral assemblage varies, but mica is usually present. Most schists are composed of platy minerals, such as chlorite, graphite (p.46), talc (p.193), muscovite (p.195), and biotite (p.197). The mineral composition of a schist depends on its protolith or original rock and its metamorphic environment. The mineral assemblage can thus be used to determine the metamorphic history of the rock.

Indian schist carving
Although its texture and composition are often uneven, schist is sometimes used as a carving material.

PROFILE

🔺 Regional metamorphic

🌐 Medium-grade
   metamorphism
   of silica-rich rocks

🌡 Low to moderate

〰 Moderate

▦ Foliated

🔍 ¹⁄₁₆–³⁄₁₆ in (2–5 mm)

◼ Muscovite, biotite, garnet

▢ Feldspar, staurolite,
   sillimanite, kyanite,
   cordierite

✴ Light to dark

◀◀ Silica-rich rocks

wavy foliation

garnet
porphyroblast

Garnet porphyroblasts
Garnet is commonly present
in schists, forming large
crystals called porphyroblasts,
as seen here.

VARIANTS

Garnet-chlorite schist
Garnet porphyroblasts in
chlorite schist

**Garnet-muscovite-chlorite
schist** Garnet porphyroblasts
in a specimen of muscovite-
chlorite schist

GARNET SCHIST

Like other schists, garnet schist is a metamorphic rock
with a characteristic texture: wrinkled, irregular, or wavy
as a result of the parallel orientation of its component
minerals, such as chlorite, graphite (p.46), talc (p.193),
muscovite (p.195), and biotite (p.197). In garnet schist,
garnet occurs as porphyroblasts, which are large crystals
set in a metamorphic matrix with other smaller crystals.
The resulting texture is called porphyroblastic. The
equivalent texture in igneous rocks is called porphyritic.

Garnet schist is widespread and usually forms from
the metamorphism of fine-grained sediments, especially
during the formation of mountains. The mineral assemblage
in garnet schist, like in other schists, helps determine both
the environment in which the original rock formed and
its metamorphic history. Other porphyroblastic schists—
such as staurolite schist, corundum schist, kyanite
schist, muscovite schist, biotite schist, and schists of
other metamorphic minerals—are indicative of other
metamorphic histories.

PROFILE

- 🔺 Regional metamorphic
- 🌐 Low-grade regional metamorphism of fine-grained sediments
- 🌡 Low
- ≋ Low
- ⊞ Foliated
- 🔍 Less than ¹⁄₂₅₆ in (0.1 mm)
- ◼ Quartz, mica, feldspar
- ◻ Pyrite, graphite
- ✳ Various
- ◀◀ Mudstone, siltstone, shale, or felsic volcanics

Welsh slate
This dark gray specimen is from Wales, Britain's principal source of slate. In the USA, slate is quarried in Pennsylvania and Vermont.

fissile splitting

fine grains

foliated structure

VARIANTS

Chiastolite slate High-temperature slate with chiastolite crystals

Spotted slate Slate with small aggregates of carbon

Pyrite Slate with pyrite grains and porphyroblasts

SLATE

A fine-grained metamorphic rock, slate occurs in a number of colors that depend on the minerals in the original sedimentary rock and the oxidation conditions under which that rock formed. Slate has a characteristic cleavage that allows it to be split into relatively thin, flat sheets. This is a result of microscopic mica crystals that have grown oriented in the same plane. True slates split along the foliation planes formed during metamorphism, rather than along the original sedimentary layers.

Slate is common in regionally metamorphosed terrains. It forms when shale (p.313), mudstone (p.316), or volcanic rocks rich in silica are buried as well as subjected to low pressures and temperatures (up to 400°F/200°C). The ability of slate to split into thin sheets makes it ideal as a durable roofing material.

School slate
This child's school slate is from Victorian times. In the past, all school "blackboards" were made from slate.

PROFILE

- Regional metamorphic
- Regional metamorphism of fine-grained sediments
- Low to moderate
- Low
- Foliated
- Less than ½₂₅₆ in (0.1 mm)
- Quartz, feldspar, chlorite, muscovite mica, graphite
- Tourmaline, andalusite, cordierite, biotite, staurolite
- Silvery to greenish gray
- Mudstone, siltstone, shale, or felsic volcanics

sheen on surface

dark phyllite

flat surface

Irregular surface
This example of phyllite shows bands of minerals and a cleaved surface that is more irregular than that found in slate.

VARIANTS

Coarse foliation An example of coarsely foliated phyllite

Alternating minerals Phyllite with bands of minerals

Garnet porphyroblasts Small, dark garnets on foliated surface

PHYLLITE

Like slate (p.293), phyllite is a fine-grained metamorphic rock that is usually gray or dark green in color. It has a shinier sheen than slate because of its larger mica crystals. The rock has a tendency to split in the same manner as slate because of a parallel alignment of mica minerals. However, the split surfaces are more irregular than in slate, and phyllite splits into thick slabs rather than thin sheets. Many phyllite specimens have a scattering of large crystals called porphyroblasts, which grow during metamorphism. The rock is often deformed into folds a couple of inches wide and is veined with quartz (p.168). Biotite (p.197), cordierite (p.223), tourmaline (p.224), andalusite (p.236), and staurolite (p.239) are commonly found in phyllite.

This rock occurs in both young and old eroded mountain belts in regionally metamorphosed terrains. It forms when fine-grained sedimentary rocks, such as shales (p.313) or mudstones (p.316), are buried and subjected to relatively low pressures and temperatures (up to 400°F/200°C) for a long period of time.

PROFILE

▲	Regional metamorphic
⊕	Regional metamorphism of orthoquartzite
⧂	High
⊠	Low to high
⊞	Crystalline
⊘	¹⁄₁₆–³⁄₁₆ in (2–5 mm)
▣	Quartz
▢	Mica, kyanite, sillimanite
✳	Almost any
◀◀	Sandstone

interlocking grains

crystalline quartz

Crystalline metaquartzite
The metamorphic variety of quartzite is a crystalline rock with over 90 percent quartz.

VARIANTS

Pale metaquartzite
A specimen of metaquartzite with a very high percentage of quartz

Gray metaquartzite
A specimen that reflects the color of the original sandstone

QUARTZITE

This quartz-rich metamorphic rock is usually white to gray when pure. Specimens can be various shades of pink, red, yellow, and orange when mineral impurities are present. Quartzite is very hard and brittle and shows conchoidal fracture. It usually contains at least 90 percent quartz (p.168).

Metamorphic quartzite, or metaquartzite, forms when sandstone (p.308) is buried, heated, and squeezed into a solid quartz rock. It is found with other regional metamorphic rocks formed during the shifting of Earth's tectonic plates. Quartzite can also refer to sedimentary sandstone converted to a much denser form through the precipitation of silica cement in pore spaces. The two types of quartzite can be distinguished by examining the grains under a microscope: metamorphic quartzite consists of interlocking crystals of quartz, whereas sedimentary quartzite, or orthoquartzite, contains rounded quartz grains. Crushed quartzite is often used as railroad ballast and in the construction of roads.

PROFILE

- ▲ Regional metamorphic
- 🌐 High-grade metamorphism of silica-poor igneous rocks
- 🌡 Low to moderate temperatures (up to 1,065°F/575°C)
- 🌊 Low to moderate
- ▦ Foliated, crystalline
- ⌀ 1⁄16–3⁄16 in (2–5 mm)
- ◼ Hornblende, tremolite, actinolite
- ◻ Feldspar, calcite, garnet, pyroxene
- ✳ Gray, black, greenish
- ◀◀ Basalt, graywacke, dolomite

coarse texture

amphibole crystal

Amphibolite composition
Although it comprises mainly amphibole minerals, amphibolite can also contain feldspar, garnet, pyroxene, and epidote.

VARIANTS

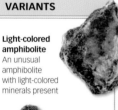

Light-colored amphibolite
An unusual amphibolite with light-colored minerals present

Hornblende-rich amphibolite
A hornblende-rich specimen of amphibolite

Green amphibolite
Amphibolite with many garnet porphyroblasts

AMPHIBOLITE

As the name suggests, amphibolites are dark-colored, coarse-grained rocks that are dominated by amphiboles: the black or dark green hornblende (p.218) and the green tremolite (p.219) or actinolite (p.220). Specimens may contain grains of calcite (p.114), feldspar (pp.173–81), and pyroxene and large crystals of minerals such as garnet. Except for garnet, the mineral grains in amphibolite are usually aligned. The rock can also show banding.

Amphibolites form from the metamorphism of iron- and magnesium-rich igneous rocks, such as gabbros (p.265), and from sedimentary rocks, such as graywacke (p.317). They comprise one of the major divisions of metamorphic rocks as classified by their mineral assemblages. These rocks form under conditions of low to moderate pressures and temperatures (up to 1,065°F/575°C). Amphibolites are used in building roads and in other aggregates where high degrees of strength and durability are required.

fine matrix

plagioclase feldspar

Unfoliated rock
Unlike many other regionally metamorphosed rocks, granulite is characterized by a lack of foliation.

VARIANT

porphyroblast

Light-colored granulite This specimen of granulite has numerous porphyroblasts

GRANULITE

This metamorphic rock is named for its even-grained, granular texture. Specimens are typically tough and massive. Granulite has a high concentration of pyroxene, with diopside (p.210) or hypersthene, garnet, calcium plagioclase, and quartz (p.168) or olivine (p.232). It has nearly the same minerals as gneiss (p.288) but is finer-grained and less perfectly foliated, and has more garnet.

Formed at high pressures and temperatures (1,065°F/575°C or above) deep in Earth's crust, granulites are characteristic of the highest grade of metamorphism. Rocks formed under these conditions belong to a category of metamorphic rocks known as the granulite facies. Mineral groups such as micas and amphiboles cannot survive at the high metamorphic grade under which granulites form and are converted into pyroxenes and garnets. Most granulites date from the Precambrian Age, which ended over 500 million years ago. They are of particular interest to geologists because many of them represent samples of the deep continental crust.

easily seen coarse grain

mottled, patchy texture

Grainy serpentinite
This example of serpentinite clearly shows its fine grains.

Alpine serpentine Red and green serpentinite streaked with calcite from the Alps

SERPENTINITE

An attractive rock, serpentinite is composed of serpentine (p.191) and other serpentine-group minerals. It commonly has flowing bands of various colors, especially green and yellow. Serpentine minerals form by a metamorphic process called serpentinization that alters olivine and pyroxene-rich, silica-poor igneous rocks. This process occurs at low temperatures (up to 400°F/200°C) and in the presence of water. The original minerals are oxidized to produce serpentine, magnetite (p.92), and brucite (p.105). The degree to which a rock undergoes serpentinization depends on the composition of the parent rock and the mineral composition of its components, especially its olivine (p.232). For example, fayalite-rich olivines serpentinize differently than forsterite-rich olivines.

Serpentinite is used as a decorative stone since it can be easily cut and polished. It is also mixed into concrete aggregate and used as a dry filler in the steel shielding jackets of nuclear reactors.

PROFILE

- ▲ Regional
- ⊕ High-pressure metamorphism of silica-poor igneous rocks
- 🌡 High temperatures (1,065°F/575°C or above)
- ⧖ High
- ▦ Foliated, crystalline
- 🔍 ¹⁄₁₆–³⁄₁₆ in (2–5 mm)
- ◼ Pyroxene, garnet
- ◰ Kyanite, quartz, olivine, diopside
- ✸ Various colors
- ◀◀ Silica-poor igneous rocks

Distributed eclogite grains
Eclogites, such as this one with red garnet and green pyroxene, are formed under great pressure, and are thought to originate in the mantle.

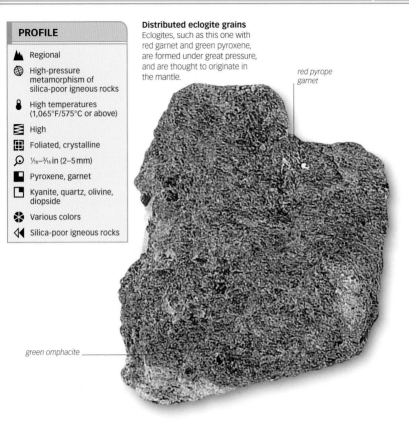

red pyrope garnet

green omphacite

VARIANTS

Mantle rock Eclogite with garnet porphyroblasts

Fine-grained eclogite
Garnet- and pyroxene-rich specimen of eclogite

ECLOGITE

A rare but important rock, eclogite is formed only by conditions typically found in the mantle or the lowermost and thickest part of the continental crust. Its overall chemical composition is similar to that of igneous basalt (p.273). It is a beautiful, coarse-grained, dense rock of bright red garnet and contrasting bright green omphacite—a pyroxene characteristic of high-temperature metamorphism. Diopside (p.210) and olivine (p.232) are commonly present as well. Eclogite grains may be evenly distributed or banded.

Eclogite forms at very high temperatures (1,065°F/575°C or above) and pressures from silica-poor igneous rocks. Many investigators believe that eclogite is characteristic of a considerable portion of the upper mantle. When brought upward into the crust, eclogites are mainly found as xenoliths (foreign inclusions) in igneous rocks and as isolated blocks up to 330 ft (100 m) wide in other metamorphic rocks. Although rare, diamonds (p.47) may occur in eclogites.

PROFILE

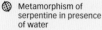

▲	Regional
🌐	Metamorphism of serpentine in presence of water
🌡	Low temperatures (up to 400°F/200°C)
☰	Low
⊞	Foliated
🔍	Less than 1/256 in (0.1 mm)
◼	Talc
◻	Chlorite, magnesite
✸	White, green, brown, black
◁◀	Serpentine

Soapstone specimen
This specimen of soapstone shows the foliation of the original talc.

greasy luster

massive habit

VARIANTS

Foliated soapstone
Soapstone with visible foliation

Flaky soapstone Soft soapstone with a flaky surface

Green soapstone
A specimen of soapstone consisting primarily of green talc

SOAPSTONE

Also known as steatite, soapstone is a fine-grained, massive rock. Talc (p.193), one of the softest minerals, is its principal component. Soapstone specimens are easily recognized by their softness: they have a greasy feel and can be scratched with a fingernail. Soapstone may also contain varying amounts of amphiboles, such as anthophyllite (p.216) and tremolite (p.219), and chlorites. Specimens can be green, brown, or black when polished, but they become white when scratched.

Soapstone is found associated with other metamorphosed silica-poor igneous rocks, such as serpentinite (p.298). It is used in fireplace surrounds because it absorbs and distributes heat evenly. It is also carved into molds for soft-metal casting.

Lion dog seal
Soapstone, such as that used in this Chinese seal, has been used to carve ornaments for millennia.

iron-oxide cement

Marble breccia
This specimen of marble has been cracked and shattered, the veins infilled, and fragments recemented with iron- and calcium-rich cement.

marble fragment

hematite vein

Olivine marble
Marble with small crystals of olivine

Green marble A specimen of marble colored by green silicate minerals

Gray marble Marble from relatively pure limestone

MARBLE

A granular metamorphic rock, marble is derived from limestone (p.319) or dolomite (p.320). It consists of a mass of interlocking grains of calcite (p.114) or the mineral dolomite (p.117).

Marbles form when limestone buried deep in the older layers of Earth's crust is subjected to heat and pressure from thick layers of overlying sediments. It may also form as a result of contact metamorphism near igneous intrusions. Impurities in the limestone can recrystallize during metamorphism, resulting in mineral impurities in the marble, most commonly graphite (p.46), pyrite (p.62), quartz (p.168), mica, and iron oxides. In sufficient amounts, these can affect the texture and color of the marble.

Taj Mahal, India
The Taj Mahal is built of Makrana—a white marble that changes hue with the angle of the light.

PROFILE

- ▲ Contact
- ⊕ Contact metamorphism of limestone
- 🌡 High temperatures (1,065°F/575°C or above)
- 〰 Low
- ▦ Crystalline
- 🔍 ½₂₅₆–¾ in (0.1–20mm)
- ■ Calcite
- ▢ Garnet, serpentine, forsterite, vesuvianite
- ✱ Variegated
- ◀◀ Limestone, dolomite

brown calcite

diopside and tremolite

Skarn specimen
This specimen of skarn with calcite and dark minerals shows the rock's typical veined and banded appearance.

VARIANT

Garnet in skarn A uvarovite garnet porphyroblast in a skarn matrix

SKARN

This rock is a product of the contact metamorphism of limestone (p.319) or dolomite (p.320) by an igneous intrusion, often granite (pp.258–59), with an intermediate or high silica content. Hot waters derived from the granitic magma are rich in silica, iron, aluminum, sulfur, and magnesium. When limestone or dolomite is invaded by this high-temperature hydrothermal solution, the carbonate minerals calcite (p.114) and dolomite react strongly with the slightly acid solution. The elements carried in the solutions combine with the calcium and magnesium in the parent rock to form silicate minerals, such as diopside (p.210), tremolite (p.219), and andradite. The resulting rock is usually a highly complex combination of calcium-, magnesium-, and carbonate-rich minerals.

Skarn minerals can be fine- to medium-grained. They also occur as coarse, radiating crystals or bands. Some skarns are rich in metallic ores and form valuable deposits of metals, including gold (p.42), copper, iron, tin, lead, molybdenum, and zinc.

PROFILE

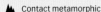
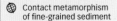

- ▲ Contact metamorphic
- ⊕ Contact metamorphism of fine-grained sediment
- 🌡 Moderate to high temperatures (400°F/ 200°C or above)
- 〰 Low to high
- ⊞ Crystalline
- 🔍 Less than 1/256 in (0.1 mm)
- ◼ Hornblende, plagioclase, andalusite, cordierite, and others
- ◻ Magnetite, apatite, titanite
- ✴ Dark gray, brown, greenish, reddish
- ◀◀ Almost any rock

dark, pyroxene crystals

Pyroxene hornfels
In this specimen of hornfels, dark porphyroblasts of pyroxene can be seen.

VARIANTS

Garnet hornfels
A specimen colored red by garnet crystals

Cordierite hornfels Hornfels with small grains of cordierite, quartz, and mica

Chiastolite hornfels Hornfels with elongated porphyroblasts of chiastolite (andalusite)

HORNFELS

Formed by contact metamorphism close to igneous intrusions at temperatures as high as 1,300°–1,450°F (700°–800°C), hornfels can form from almost any parent rock and is notoriously difficult to identify. Its composition depends on the parent rock and the exact temperatures and fluids to which the rock is exposed. Specimens are usually dense, hard, and hard to break. They are fine-grained and relatively homogeneous, with a conchoidal, flintlike fracture. The rock may sometimes appear glassy. The color is usually even throughout, although specimens may also be banded.

Hornfels is often categorized by the mix of minerals present in the specimen. Garnet hornfels, for example, is characterized by large crystals of garnet set into a rock matrix. Cordierite hornfels contains large crystals of cordierite (p.223) that can be up to several inches in diameter. An outcrop of hornfels rarely extends more than a few yards from the contact and may pass outward into spotted slate.

SEDIMENTARY ROCKS

Sedimentary rocks are formed at or near Earth's surface either by accumulation of grains or by precipitation of dissolved material. These rocks make up the majority of the rock exposed at Earth's surface, but are only about 8 percent of the volume of the entire crust.

LITHIFICATION

The transformation of loose grains of sediment into clastic sedimentary rock is known as lithification. The grains are often bound together by a cementing agent, which is generally precipitated from solutions that filter through the sediment. In some cases, the cementing agent is created at least in part by the breakdown of some rock particles of the sediment itself. The most common cement is silica (usually quartz), but calcite and other carbonates as well as iron oxides, barite, anhydrite, zeolites, and clay minerals also form cements. The cementing agent becomes an integral and important part of the sedimentary rock once it is formed. In some cases, clastic sedimentary rocks (see opposite) can also be formed by simple compaction—a process in which the grains bind together under extreme pressure.

Lithification can sometimes take place almost immediately after the grains have been deposited as sediment. In other cases, hundreds or even millions of years may pass by before lithification occurs. At any given time, there are large amounts of rock fragments that have been produced by weathering but have not been lithified and simply exist as a form of sediment.

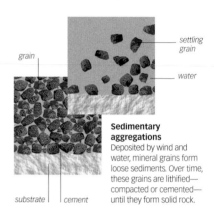

grain

settling grain

water

substrate | cement

Sedimentary aggregations
Deposited by wind and water, mineral grains form loose sediments. Over time, these grains are lithified—compacted or cemented—until they form solid rock.

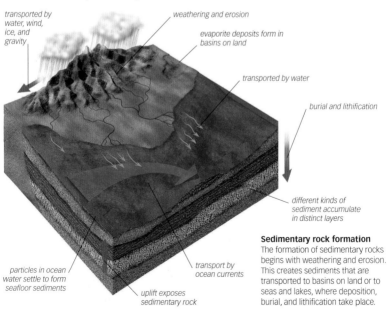

transported by water, wind, ice, and gravity

weathering and erosion

evaporite deposits form in basins on land

transported by water

burial and lithification

different kinds of sediment accumulate in distinct layers

particles in ocean water settle to form seafloor sediments

transport by ocean currents

uplift exposes sedimentary rock

Sedimentary rock formation
The formation of sedimentary rocks begins with weathering and erosion. This creates sediments that are transported to basins on land or to seas and lakes, where deposition, burial, and lithification take place.

CLASTIC ROCKS

Clasts are rock fragments ranging in size from boulders to microscopic particles. Clastic sedimentary rocks are grouped according to the size of the clasts from which they form. Larger clasts such as pebbles, cobbles, and boulder-sized gravels form conglomerate and breccia; sand becomes sandstone; and finer silt and clay particles form siltstone, mudstone, and shale. The mineral composition of clastic rocks can be subject to considerable change over time.

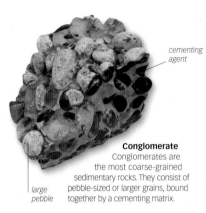

cementing agent

Conglomerate
Conglomerates are the most coarse-grained sedimentary rocks. They consist of pebble-sized or larger grains, bound together by a cementing matrix.

large pebble

CHEMICAL ROCKS

Chemical sedimentary rocks are formed by the precipitation of the transported, dissolved products of chemical weathering. In some cases, the dissolved constituents are directly precipitated as solid rock. Examples include banded iron formations, some limestones, and bedded evaporite deposits—rocks and mineral deposits of soluble salts resulting from the evaporation of water. In other sedimentary rocks, such as limestone and chert, solid material first precipitates into particles or becomes the shells of organisms, which are then deposited and lithified.

White Cliffs of Dover
Located near the town of Dover in Kent, England, the celebrated White Cliffs of Dover are spectacular deposits of chalk many feet thick.

FOSSILS

A fossil is a remnant, impression, or trace of an organism that lived in a past geologic age. Fossils are preserved almost exclusively in sedimentary rocks. The most common fossils are of aquatic plants and animals. After an organism dies, the soft parts decompose, leaving behind only the hard parts—the shell, teeth, bones, or wood. Buried in layers of sediment, the hard parts gradually turn to stone. In a process known as permineralization, water seeps through the rock, depositing mineral salts in the pores of the shell or bone, thereby fossilizing the remains. In some cases, the organic matter is completely replaced by minerals as it decays. In other cases, circulating acid solutions dissolve the original shell or bone, leaving a cavity of identical shape, which is filled in as new material is deposited in the cavity, creating a cast.

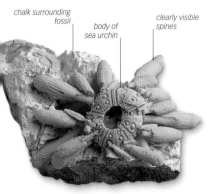

chalk surrounding fossil

body of sea urchin

clearly visible spines

Fossil in chalk
Large sea urchin fossils, such as this well-preserved example, are usually found in chalk, which is itself made up of the fossils of tiny marine organisms.

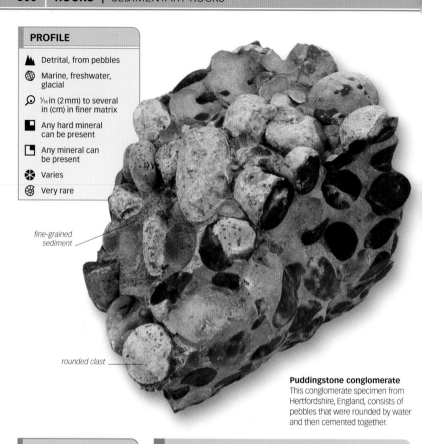

fine-grained sediment

rounded clast

Puddingstone conglomerate
This conglomerate specimen from Hertfordshire, England, consists of pebbles that were rounded by water and then cemented together.

VARIANTS

Quartz conglomerate
A specimen with large clasts of quartz

Polygenetic conglomerate
A specimen with clasts of various rock types

alluvial diamond

Alluvial diamond
A diamond cemented into a conglomerate

CONGLOMERATE

Rocks formed by the lithification of rounded rock fragments that are over 1/16 in (2mm) in diameter are known as conglomerates. They can be further classified by the average size of their constituent materials—pebble-conglomerate (fine), cobble-conglomerate (medium), and boulder-conglomerate (coarse). Conglomerate can also be known by the rock or mineral fragments in its composition; for example, a quartz pebble conglomerate.

Depending on the environment in which these fragments are deposited, these rocks may be of two types. Well-sorted conglomerates result from water flow over a long period. These have well-sorted pebbles (with a small size variation) generally of only one rock or mineral type, and a few small particles between the pebbles. Poorly sorted conglomerates form from rapid water flow and deposition. They have poorly sorted pebbles (of varying sizes) of mixed rock and mineral types with a number of small particles between the pebbles.

PROFILE

- ▲ Detrital, from coarse sediment
- 🌐 Marine, freshwater, glacial
- 🔎 ¹⁄₁₆ in (2 mm) to 1 in (several cm) in finer matrix
- ◼ Any hard mineral can be present
- ◻ Any mineral can be present
- ✸ Varies
- ✸ Very rare

angular fragment

gray, silica-rich fragment

Poorly sorted breccia
This specimen of breccia shows large and small angular fragments with no clear pattern of orientation.

VARIANTS

Limestone breccia
Fragments of limestone in breccia

Polygenetic breccia
A specimen with clasts of different types of rock

Fault breccia Cemented clasts shattered by faulting

BRECCIA

Lithified sediments with rock fragments that are more than ¹⁄₁₆ in (2 mm) in diameter but angular or only slightly rounded are called breccias. The lack of rounding indicates that little or no transportation took place before the fragments became incorporated in the rock.

Breccias can form in several ways. Rocks can shatter—for example, due to frost action or earth movement—and the fragments then become cemented in the new position. Shattered fragments may also move before being cemented—for example, they may accumulate at the base of a cliff or be carried by a flash flood. Breccias can also form in areas of active faulting. In areas where faulting occurs underwater, newly shattered material can also move in underwater landslides and become cemented to form breccia.

Breccia vase
This ancient Egyptian carved vase made of breccia or mottle stone was used to store liquids.

PROFILE

- ▲ Detrital, from sand
- ⊕ Terrestrial
- 🔍 1/256–1/16 in (0.1–2 mm)
- ◼ Quartz, feldspar
- ◻ Silica, calcium carbonate
- ✳ Cream to red
- ✸ Vertebrates, invertebrates, plants

Structure in sandstone
This sandstone from Yorkshire, England, is derived from deposits of wind-blown sand. The bedding planes, which slumped after deposition, are well preserved.

fine-grained texture

evidence of slumping

VARIANTS

Micaceous sandstone
A specimen with flakes of mica and patches of iron oxide

Goethite sandstone Sand grains with red goethite

Red sandstone
A specimen of quartz sandstone colored red due to the presence of iron oxides

SANDSTONE

The second most abundant sedimentary rock after shale (p.313), sandstone makes up about 10 to 20 percent of the sedimentary rocks in Earth's crust. Sandstones are classified according to texture and mineralogical properties into micaceous sandstone, orthoquartzite (p.310), and graywacke (p.317). They are usually dominated by quartz (p.168) and have visible sandy grains and other minerals present in varying amounts. Well-rounded grains are typical of desert sandstone, while river sands are usually angular, and beach sands somewhere in between.

Bedding is often visible in sandstones as a series of layers representing successive deposits of grains. Bedding surfaces may show either ripples or the cross bedding typical of dunes. Sandstone is an important indicator of deposition and erosion processes.

Sandstone platform
This platform in the center of the courtyard pool at Fatehpur Sikri, India, is made from red sandstone.

Marine greensand
This specimen is from the Atlantic coastal plain of North America, where greensand is a common type of rock.

well-sorted sediment

green coloring from glauconite

PROFILE

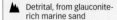

- ▲ Detrital, from glauconite-rich marine sand
- 🌐 Marine
- 🔍 ¹⁄₂₅₆–¹⁄₁₆ in (0.1–2 mm)
- ⬛ Quartz, glauconite
- ⬜ Feldspar, mica
- ✳ Green
- ✳ Vertebrates, invertebrates, plants

VARIANT

Greensand banding
A band of greensand within a rock outcrop

GREENSAND

A quartz sandstone with a high percentage of the green mica mineral glauconite (p.196) is known as greensand or glauconitic sandstone. The term glauconite is also loosely applied to any glauconitic sediment. Glauconite is believed to form in shallow, oxygen-poor marine environments that are rich in organic detritus. It forms as a result of a slow accumulation of sediments, by the replacement of calcite (p.114), or by primary deposition. It may contain shell fragments and larger fossils. Some glauconite pellets are biogenic, originating as fecal pellets.

Greensand tends to be weak and friable, although relatively hard greensand has been used as building stone. The soil derived from greensand varies, ranging from fertile to sterile. Glauconite is favored in organic cultivation as a natural source of potassium and phosphorus. Its potassium content is useful in radiometric age-dating. Due to its chemical-exchange properties, the glauconite in greensand is used as a water softener and in water-treatment systems.

quartz grains

Pink orthoquartzite
Although this specimen of pink orthoquartzite is composed almost entirely of quartz, it is colored by small amounts of iron oxide.

PROFILE

▲ Detrital

🌐 Terrestrial

🔍 ½₅₆–¹⁄₁₆ in (0.1–2 mm)

◼ Quartz

▢ Heavy minerals, such as zircon and rutile

✳ Light to medium

✳ Rare, vertebrates

VARIANT

Gray orthoquartzite
A specimen colored gray by quartz grains

ORTHOQUARTZITE

A pure quartz sandstone, orthoquartzite is usually composed of well-rounded quartz (p.168) grains cemented by silica. The high degree of rounding of the grains indicates that they have traveled some distance, which also accounts for the high degree of sorting. Some orthoquartzites are up to 99 percent quartz, with only minor amounts of iron oxide and traces of other erosion-resistant minerals, such as rutile (p.78), magnetite (p.92), and zircon (p.233). Lesser amounts of other minerals can color the generally white or pinkish specimens either gray or red. Orthoquartzites can be differentiated in hand specimens from other sandstones by their lighter color and absence of other minerals.

Orthoquartzites rarely preserve fossils, although the sedimentary structures are usually preserved. The presence of silica cement makes orthoquartzites durable. They tend to resist weathering and form prominent outcrops. Orthoquartzite is distinct from metamorphic quartzite, also known as metaquartzite (p.295).

Gray arkose
Darker variants of arkose, such as this specimen, tend to be older than pink arkose.

pinkish feldspar

quartz grains

PROFILE

▲	Detrital, from feldspar-rich sand
⊕	Terrestrial, marine, or freshwater
⊘	¹⁄₂₅₆–¹⁄₁₆ in (0.1–2 mm)
■	Quartz, feldspar
▢	Mica
✿	Pinkish, pale gray
⊕	Rare

VARIANT

Pink arkose A variant of arkose formed more recently than gray arkose

ARKOSE

A pink sandstone, arkose is colored by an abundance of feldspars (pp.173–81), especially pink alkali feldspars. Its high feldspar content (more than 25 percent of the sand grains) sets it apart from other sandstones. Arkose specimens are relatively coarse and consist primarily of quartz (p.168) and feldspar grains, with small amounts of mica. The grains tend to be moderately well sorted and angular or slightly rounded. They are usually cemented with calcite (p.114) or sometimes with iron oxides or silica. The flat cleavage faces and angular grain shape of the feldspars reflect light under a hand lens. Sandstones with a feldspar content of 5–25 percent are called subarkoses.

Arkose forms from the quick deposition of sand weathered from granites (pp.258–59) and gneisses (p.288). The development of arkoses is thought to indicate either a climatic extreme or a rapid uplift and high relief of the source area. Arkoses are common along the front ranges of the Rocky Mountains.

PROFILE

- Detrital, from grit
- Freshwater
- ⅟₃₂–³⁄₁₆ in (1–4 mm)
- Quartz, feldspar
- Garnet, rutile
- White, pink, gray
- Invertebrates, vertebrates, plants

reddish color from iron oxides

Quartz gritstone
Specimens of quartz gritstone, such as this, are composed of more than 75 percent quartz.

VARIANT

Feldspathic gritstone
A variant containing up to 25 percent feldspar

GRITSTONE

Providing material for grindstones and millstones, gritstone has, in the past, been a commercially important sedimentary rock. It is a porous rock composed of cemented, coarse, often angular sand grains, with occasional small pebbles. Quartz (p.168) is always the greatest component, but specimens often contain iron oxides that give them a yellow, brown, or red color. In some, the grains can be easily rubbed out; in others, strong cement makes the rock suitable for use as grinding stones.

Gritstones originate in river deposits and frequently show signs of cross-bedding or current bedding. The Millstone Grit, a gritstone deposit in northern England, was mined for millstones used in flour mills and for grindstones, which were used to make paper pulp from wood and sharpen tools. Gritstone is still quarried for use as building material worldwide. Large exposures of gritstone are favored by rock climbers because the rough surface provides outstanding friction, enabling them to grip the smallest features in the rock.

Gray shale
This specimen of shale from Runswick Bay, Yorkshire, England contains fossils of bivalves and ammonites.

fossilized ammonite

fissile sheets

fossilized bivalve

PROFILE

▲	Detrital, from mud, clay, or organic material
⊕	Marine, freshwater, glacial
◎	Less than $\frac{1}{256}$ in (0.1 mm)
■	Clays, quartz, calcite
▣	Pyrite, iron oxides, feldspar
✸	Various
⊛	Invertebrates, vertebrates, plants

VARIANTS

Fossiliferous shale Shale with numerous fossils of brachiopods

alum-rich mineral

Light-colored shale
A specimen with alum-rich, light-colored areas

SHALE

The most abundant sedimentary rock, shale makes up about 70 percent of all sedimentary rocks in Earth's crust. It consists of a high percentage of clay minerals, substantial amounts of quartz (p.168), and smaller amounts of carbonates (pp.114–25), feldspars (pp.173–81), iron oxides, fossils, and organic matter. Shales are colored reddish and purple by hematite (p.91) and goethite (p.102); blue, green, and black by ferrous iron; and gray or yellowish by calcite (p.114). They split easily into thin layers.

Shales consists of silt- and clay-sized particles deposited by gentle currents on deep ocean floors, shallow sea basins, and river floodplains. They occur thinly interbedded with layers of sandstone (p.308) or limestone (p.319) and in sheets up to several yards thick.

Fossil Trilobite
Preserved in gray shale, this fossil trilobite is more than 400 million years old.

Dark oil shale
This specimen of oil shale shows dark, kerogen-rich layers. When heated, the kerogen gives off a vapor that contains oil.

kerogen-rich rock

PROFILE

▲ Detrital

⊕ Inland seas

🔎 Less than ½₅₆ in (0.1 mm)

◼ Quartz, feldspar

▢ Alum

✵ Gray, black

⊕ Invertebrates, vertebrates, plants

VARIANT

Oily surface A specimen with condensed droplets of oil visible on the surface

OIL SHALE

The name oil shale is a general term for organic-rich sedimentary rocks that contain kerogen—a chemically complex mixture of solid hydrocarbons derived from plant and animal matter. When subjected to intense heat, these shales yield oil. Oil shales range from brown to black in color. They are flammable and burn with a sooty flame. Some oil shales are true shales in which clay minerals are predominant. Others are actually limestones (p.319) and dolomites (p.320). Much of the original organic material in oil shales is unrecognizable, but it is believed to be derived from plankton, algae, and microorganisms that live in fresh sediment.

In previous centuries, small amounts of oil have been successfully recovered from oil shales. During the past century, oil shales have been mined with rock types varying from shale (p.313) to marl (p.322) and other carbonate rocks. Various pilot plants have been built to extract oil from shales, but the commercial results have been modest so far.

Gray siltstone
The tiny grains that make up siltstone are too small to be seen without a microscope.

silt-sized grains

dark color from carbon

PROFILE

- ▲ Detrital, from silt
- ⊕ Marine, freshwater, glacial
- ⊙ Up to ⅟₂₅₆ in (0.1 mm)
- ◼ Quartz, feldspar
- ◻ Mica, chlorite, mica-rich clay minerals
- ✦ Gray to beige
- ⊕ Invertebrates, vertebrates, plants

VARIANT

Fossiliferous siltstone
A fern fossil enclosed in siltstone

SILTSTONE

Formed from grains whose sizes vary between that of sandstone (p.308) and mudstone (p.316), siltstone is a sedimentary rock. Like sandstone, it can form in different environments and have different colors and textures. Siltstones are typically red and gray with flat bedding planes. Plant fossils and other carbon-rich matter are common in darker-colored siltstones. Examples tend to be hard and durable and do not easily split into thin layers. However, the presence of mica may produce a siltstone that splits into thicker, flagstonelike sheets. In addition to mica, siltstone may contain abundant chlorite and other mica-rich clay minerals.

Although many shales (p.313) contain more than 50 percent silt, siltstones are usually chemically cemented and show cross-bedding, ripple marks, and internal layering. This indistinct layering tends to weather at oblique angles unrelated to bedding. Siltstone is less common than shale or sandstone and rarely forms thick deposits.

PROFILE

 Detrital, from mud

 Marine, freshwater, glacial

 Less than 1⁄256 in (0.1 mm)

 Clays, quartz

 Calcite

 Gray, brown, black

 Invertebrates, vertebrates, plants

curved fracture

mud-sized grain

Mudstone specimen
Mudstone is somewhat similar in appearance to siltstone, but its grains are smaller and it has a broken surface with a much finer texture.

VARIANTS

Fossiliferous mudstone
A specimen of mudstone with numerous invertebrate fossils

Calcareous mudstone
A mudstone variant with a substantial amount of calcite

MUDSTONE

A gray or black rock formed from mud, mudstone contains carbon-rich matter, clay minerals, and detrital minerals such as quartz (p.168) and feldspar (pp.173–81). Mudstones look like hardened clay and can show the cracks seen in sun-baked clay deposits.

As in shale (p.313), mudstone's individual grains are clay- and silt-sized particles that can only be seen under a hand lens. Mudstone generally has the same color range as shale, with similar associations between color and content. Unlike shale, mudstone is not laminated during lithification and is not easily split into thin layers. The lack of layering is either due to the original texture or the disruption of layering. Mudstone deposits may be up to 10 ft (several meters) in thickness.

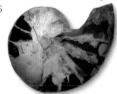

Nautiloid fossil
This fossil nautilus is preserved in mudstone. The iridescence of a part of its shell is still visible.

PROFILE

- ▲ Detrital, from muddy sand
- ⊕ Marine
- ⌀ ¹⁄₂₅₆–¹⁄₁₆ in (0.1–2mm)
- ■ Quartz, feldspar, mafic minerals
- ▨ Chlorite, biotite, clay, calcite
- ✺ Mostly gray or greenish gray; also brown, yellow, or black
- ⊛ Rare

poorly sorted minerals

fine-grained groundmass

Fine-grained graywacke
This specimen shows the poor sorting characteristic of graywacke. The angular clasts are set in a fine-grained matrix.

angular fragment

VARIANTS

Dirty sandstone A specimen from Canada with typical dirty appearance and poor sorting

Turbidite A graywacke formed by undersea avalanches

GRAYWACKE

Easily confused with igneous basalt (p.273), graywacke is a turbidite—a rock resulting from rapid deposition in a turbulent marine environment. It gets its name from the German word *grauwacke*, which signifies a gray, earthy rock. Also called dirty sandstone, graywacke is hard, and mostly gray, brown, yellow, or black.

Graywacke is composed of poorly sorted, coarse- to fine-grained quartz (p.168), feldspar (pp.173–81), and dark-colored minerals such as amphibole and pyroxene, set in a fine-grained matrix of clay, calcite (p.114), or quartz. Graywackes may occur in thick or thin beds along with slates (p.293) and limestones (p.319). In ancient Egypt, this stone was used to make sarcophagi, vessels, and statues.

Graywacke carving
This ancient Egyptian graywacke carving dates from 1370 BCE. It is an offering to the god of writing.

PROFILE

- ▲ Detrital
- ⊕ Glacial
- ○ From less than ½₂₅₆ in (0.1 mm) to many ft (m)
- ◼ Rock fragments
- ◻ Rock fragments
- ✳ Various
- ⊕ None

large clast

gray clay matrix

Tillite specimen
The large variation in clast sizes in tillites is evident in this specimen.

VARIANTS

oversized clast

Large clast Tillite with a large clast in a finer matrix

Differing clast sizes
A specimen of tillite with rounded clasts of differing sizes

TILLITE

Unsorted and unstratified rock material deposited by glacial ice that has later been lithified is called tillite. As glaciers move down valleys, they erode and transport rocks. On melting, they deposit this material, which is referred to as till. Glacial tills consist of preexisting rock fragments pushed forward or sideways by the glacier, newly eroded material ground or broken up by the glacier, or mixtures of the two.

Tillites are typically made of grains with a wide range of sizes. They include fragments ranging from clay-sized particles to large blocks. The largest pieces give rise to the rock's alternative name, "boulder clay." The matrix, which frequently comprises a large percentage of the rock, is often made from rock flour, an unweathered and finely ground rock powder. Matching beds of ancient tillites on opposite sides of the South Atlantic Ocean provided early evidence for continental drift—the idea that continents move relative to one another—which was an important precursor to the theory of plate tectonics.

Fossiliferous limestone
This limestone specimen from Oxfordshire, England, includes several fossil invertebrates.

fine texture

fossil of shell

PROFILE

▲	Chemical, organic
⊕	Marine
◯	Crystalline
■	Calcite
▣	Aragonite, dolomite, siderite, quartz, pyrite
✴	White, gray, pink
⊕	Marine and freshwater invertebrates

VARIANTS

Coral limestone Limestone formed from fossil coral

Freshwater limestone
Uncommon variant of limestone

Oolitic limestone Round ooliths set in calcite cement

LIMESTONE

Composed mainly of calcite (p.114), this abundant rock forms multiple layers that are thick and extensive. It can be yellow, white, or gray. Specimens can be identified by the rapid release of carbon dioxide and a fizzing sound when they react with dilute hydrochloric acid. Limestones can be compact, grainy, or friable. Many have cross-bedding or ripple marks. The texture of limestone ranges from coarse and fossil-rich to fine and microcrystalline.

Limestone generally forms in warm, shallow seas either from calcium carbonate precipitated from seawater or from the shells and skeletons of calcareous marine organisms. It is used in construction, as a raw material in the manufacture of glass, as a flux in metallurgical processes, and in agriculture.

Limestone mask
This face mask dating from the Neolithic Period has been carved out of mottled limestone.

PROFILE

- ▲ Chemical
- ⊕ Marine
- ⌕ Crystalline
- ▪ Dolomite
- ▫ Calcite
- ✸ Gray to yellowish gray
- ⊛ Invertebrates

fine-to-medium texture

compact carbonate rock

Dolomite rock
This specimen of dolomite has a uniform texture that is typical of the rock.

VARIANT

Red dolomite A specimen of dolomite colored with iron oxides and hydroxides

DOLOMITE

This rock, formed exclusively from the mineral dolomite (p.117), is also called dolostone. Most dolomite rocks are believed to be limestones (p.319) in which dolomite has replaced the calcite (p.114) in contact with magnesium-bearing solutions. This process is called dolomitization. Fresh dolomite looks similar to limestone, while weathered dolomite is yellowish gray. Dolomites have fewer fossils than limestones because fossils and other features are destroyed by the dolomitization process. Dolomite fizzes less violently than limestone when in contact with hydrochloric acid.

Dolomite typically occurs as massive layers. It is also present as thin layers or pods within limestone. Dolomite is used as a flux to make steel. It can also be used as a lightweight building aggregate, in cinder blocks, and in poured concrete.

Environment-friendly flux
In contrast to other steel-making fluxes, dolomite produces slag that can be reused.

Microscopic fossils
This specimen of chalk, which is almost entirely calcite, is made up of tiny fossils of marine organisms.

soft, white, powdery texture

fine, white grain

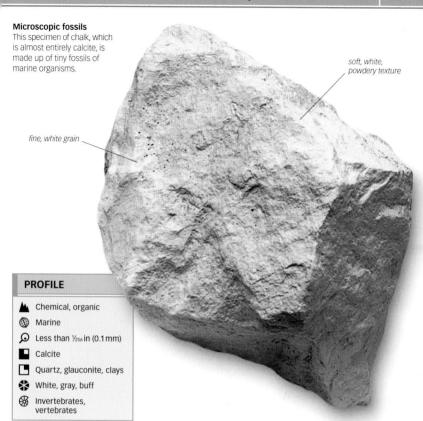

PROFILE

▲ Chemical, organic

⊕ Marine

🔍 Less than ½₂₅₆ in (0.1 mm)

■ Calcite

▢ Quartz, glauconite, clays

✸ White, gray, buff

⊛ Invertebrates, vertebrates

VARIANTS

Red chalk A specimen of chalk that takes its color from incorporated hematite

Marine chalk A specimen of chalk pitted by the boring of marine animals

CHALK

A soft, fine-grained, easily pulverized, white to grayish variety of limestone is known as chalk. It is composed of calcite shells of minute marine organisms. Small amounts of other minerals, such as apatite (p.148), glauconite (p.196), and clay minerals, are usually present. Silica from sponge spines, diatom and radiolarian skeletons, and nodules of chert (p.332) and flint can also be present.

Extensive chalk deposits were formed during the Cretaceous Period (142 to 65 million years ago), the name being derived from the Latin word *creta*, which means "chalk." Chalk is used to make lime and cement and as a fertilizer. It is also used as a filler, extender, or pigment in a wide variety of materials, including ceramics and cosmetics.

Blackboard chalk
One of chalk's longstanding uses has been compression into sticks for writing on blackboards.

Green marl
Marls differ in color depending on their mineral content. Green marls, such as this one, are colored by either glauconite or chlorite.

green color

fine grain size

curved fracture

PROFILE

▲	Detrital, from lime mud
🌐	Marine, freshwater
🔍	Less than 1/256 in (0.1 mm)
■	Clays, calcite
□	Glauconite, hematite
✳	Various
⊛	Vertebrates, invertebrates, plants

VARIANT

Red marl A specimen colored red by iron oxides

MARL

Calcareous mudstone or marl is a term applied to a variety of rocks that have a range of compositions but are all earthy mixtures of fine-grained minerals. In some countries, marl is referred to by the German terms *mergel* and *seekreide*, both of which mean "lake chalk." Marls usually consist of clay minerals and calcium carbonate. They form in shallow freshwater or seawater. The calcium carbonate content is frequently made up of shell fragments of marine or freshwater organisms or calcium carbonate precipitated by algae. The high carbonate content of marls makes them react with dilute acid.

Marls are whitish gray or brownish in color but can also be gray, green, red, or variegated. Greensand marls contain the green mineral glauconite (p.196), and red marls, iron oxides. Marl is much less easily split than shale (p.313) and tends to break in blocks. Specimens are often nodular, and the nodules are usually better cemented than the surrounding rock.

iron-oxide impurities

massive habit

Massive rock gypsum
This specimen of rock gypsum is from the Marblaegis mine in Nottinghamshire, England.

VARIANT

boleite crystal

Gypsum with boleite Blue crystals of boleite seen in a matrix of gypsum

ROCK GYPSUM

Also called gyprock, rock gypsum is the sedimentary rock formed mainly from the mineral gypsum (p.136). Although it is commonly granular, it can also occur as fibrous bands. Rock gypsum occurs in extensive beds formed by the evaporation of ocean water, in saline lakes, and in salt pans. It also occurs in some shales (p.313), limestones (p.319), and dolomitic limestones. Rock gypsum is commonly interlayered with other evaporites, such as rock anhydrite (p.133) and salt (p.324).

Most of the gypsum that is extracted—about three-quarters of the total production—is calcined (heated to drive off some of its water) for use as plaster of Paris. Unaltered rock gypsum is used as a fluxing agent, fertilizer, filler in paper and textiles, and retardant in Portland cement.

Mesopotamian seal
This ancient cylinder seal, with engravings of stags and scorpions, is made of alabaster gypsum.

orange color from iron-rich clays

crystalline salt

Crystalline rock salt
This specimen of crystalline rock salt is colored orange by iron-rich clays incorporated during deposition.

VARIANTS

Pink rock salt A specimen colored pink by traces of iron oxides

Massive rock salt Rock salt with coarse, white and blue crystals

ROCK SALT

Familiar as common table salt, rock salt is the massive rock form of the mineral halite (p.110). It occurs in beds that range in thickness from 3 ft (1 m) or so to more than 990 ft (300 m). Rock salt forms as a result of the evaporation of saline water in partially enclosed basins. It is commonly interlayered with beds of shale (p.313), limestone (p.319), dolomite (p.320), and other evaporites, such as anhydrite (p.133) and gypsum (p.136).

Rock salt often occurs in salt domes, which consist of a core of salt surrounded by strata of other rock. The domes can be 1 mile (2 km) or more thick and up to 6 miles (10 km) in diameter. They can occur with petroleum deposits: oil from oil-rich shales migrates up and gets caught on the underside of a salt dome.

Natural salt
Many people prefer natural salt for their cooking. Much of it comes from evaporating brines.

Porous diatomite
This specimen of diatomite exhibits its typical porous structure and rough texture.

loose, porous structure

rough texture

PROFILE

▲	Detrital
🌐	Accumulation of silica-rich organisms
🔎	Less than ¹⁄₂₅₆ in (0.1 mm)
■	Opal
▢	None
✽	White
✾	Diatoms

DIATOMITE

Also called diatomaceous earth, diatomite consists of about 90 percent silica; the remainder is made up of compounds such as aluminum oxides and iron oxides. Diatomite is easily crumbled into a fine, white to off-white powder. It is made of the fossilized remains of organisms called diatoms. A form of algae, diatoms have hard shells made of amorphous silica (opal) and containing many fine pores. Most float on the surface of the sea. Occasionally, large quantities are deposited in ocean sediments, eventually forming diatomite. A few significant deposits of freshwater diatomite are also known. Diatoms are so small that diatomite specimens may contain millions of diatom shells per cubic inch.

An important industrial rock, diatomite is easily mined. It is used for the filtration of beverages, liquid chemicals, industrial oils, cooking oils, fuels, and drinking water. Its low-abrasive qualities find use in toothpastes, polishes, and nonabrasive cleaners. It is also used as a filler and extender in paint and paper.

Red-brown laterite
This specimen shows the intermixture of iron and aluminum oxides with sand or other rock detritus characteristic of laterites.

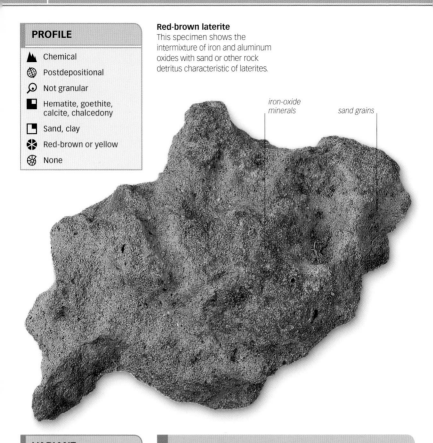

iron-oxide minerals

sand grains

Desert-varnished laterite
A variant of laterite with a polished surface

LATERITE

Laterite is nodular soil rich in hardened iron and aluminum oxides and resembles bauxite (p.101) in composition. Nodules of laterite are red-brown or yellow and contain grains of sand or hardened clay. The rock forms in hot, wet tropical climates, where it develops by intensive and prolonged chemical weathering of the underlying rock. Evaporation and leaching of minerals from rock, loose sediment, and soil leaves behind insoluble salts. This results in a variety of laterites, which differ in their thickness, grade, chemistry, and ore mineralogy.

Laterite is a source of bauxite, which is an ore of aluminum and exists largely in clay minerals and various hydroxides. Laterite ores have also been a source of iron and nickel. Many laterites are solid enough to be used as building blocks. An example is the laterite seen at the famous temple in Angkor Wat, Cambodia. Crushed laterite has been widely used to make roads. Laterites are also being increasingly used in water treatment.

oxides and
hydroxides of iron

Bog iron nodule
This nodule of bog iron shows
varied coloration, which results
from the various iron oxides
and hydroxides it contains.

gray mudstone

VARIANT

Bog iron ore Gray mudstone
with oxides and hydroxides
of iron

BOG IRON

Impure iron deposits that develop in bogs or
swamps are known as bog iron. Bog iron is typically
a brown-yellow mudstone with yellow, red, brown, or
black concretions of iron oxides and hydroxides. In
general, bog ores consist of iron hydroxides, primarily
goethite (p.102). Bog iron can contain up to 70 percent
iron oxide. It often contains carbon-rich plant material,
which is sometimes preserved by iron minerals. Bog
iron typically forms in areas where iron-bearing
groundwater emerges as springs. As the iron encounters
the oxygen-rich surface water, it oxidizes, and the iron
oxides precipitate out.

Bog iron was formerly used as an ore and was widely
sought in the preindustrial age. The Romans and the
Vikings made extensive use of bog iron as a source of
iron. Bog iron was also the principal source of iron in
colonial USA. Although it is still forming today, the iron
requirements of modern industry demand much larger
sources of ore.

PROFILE

▲ Chemical

🌐 Marine, terrestrial

🔎 $\frac{1}{256}$–$\frac{1}{16}$ in (0.1–2 mm)

◼ Hematite, goethite, chamosite, magnetite, siderite, limonite, jasper

◻ Pyrite, pyrrhotite

✳ Red, black, brown, yellow

🕸 Invertebrates or plants

red color from iron

rounded oolith

Oolitic ironstone
This specimen of ironstone is made up of small, rounded oolites, which are cemented by hematite.

VARIANT

Sandy ironstone A specimen of a leaf fossil beautifully preserved in ironstone

IRONSTONE

The term ironstone is applied to sandstones and limestones that contain more than 15 percent iron. Ironstones are rich in iron-bearing minerals such as hematite (p.91), goethite (p.102), siderite (p.123), and chamosite. These minerals give ironstones a dark red, brown, or yellow color.

Ironstone no longer appears to be forming; partly because of this, the process by which it forms is something of a mystery. Some ironstones seem to have formed early in Earth's history when oxygen was not as abundant in the atmosphere as it is now. Precambrian ironstones, which are more than 500 million years old, as well as slightly later ones, formed prior to 240 million years ago, are common. Many of the later ironstones consist of oolites (small spheres) of hematite and contain fossils. Although historically used as an iron ore, ironstone is too limited in quantity to be an economic modern source of iron.

Banded ironstone
This specimen of ironstone shows prominent banding of alternate chert- and iron-rich material.

hematite-rich layer

chert layer

PROFILE

▲	Chemical
✪	Marine
◉	Neither granular nor very fine
■	Siderite, hematite, chert
▯	Magnetite, pyrite
✸	Red, black, gray, striped
✸	None

BANDED IRONSTONE

Also known as banded iron formations, banded ironstone is made up of thin layers of alternating red, brown, or black iron oxides, which may be hematite (p.91) or magnetite (p.92), and gray or off-white shale (p.313) or chert (p.332). It is a very fine-grained rock that breaks into smooth, splintery pieces. Particularly abundant in Precambrian rocks, which are more than 500 million years old, banded ironstone can form very thick sequences, such as in the Hammersley Range of Australia, where it is an economically important iron ore.

Banded iron layers are found in some of the oldest known rock formations, dating from more than 3,700 million years ago. These layers are believed to have formed in the seas as a result of dissolved iron combining with oxygen released by the green algae that flourished in the oceans at that time. This was then precipitated into oxygen-poor seafloor sediments that were forming shale and chert. The banding of ironstone is assumed to result from cyclic variations in the oxygen available.

PROFILE

- Chemical
- Terrestrial
- Less than 1/32 in (1 mm)
- Calcite or silica
- Aragonite
- White
- Rare

Calcareous tufa This specimen of calcareous tufa is full of holes and irregular shapes. It was formed by the evaporation of water.

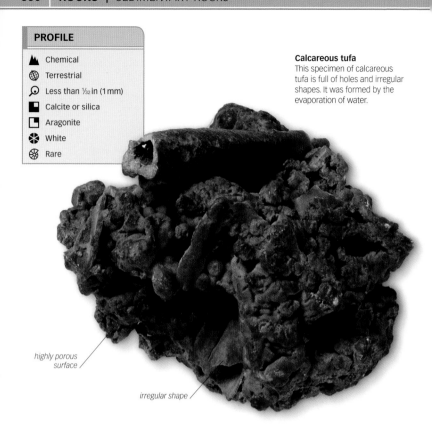

VARIANTS

Yellow tufa Irregularly shaped tufa that lacks bedding

Fossilized tufa Tufa formed around plant remains

TUFA

Two different sedimentary rocks that precipitate from water are known as tufa. Calcareous tufa, or calc-tufa, is a soft, porous form of limestone deposit composed principally of calcium carbonate (calcite) that precipitates from hot springs, lake water, and groundwater. Calc-tufa is often stained red by the presence of iron oxides.

Siliceous tufa, which is also called siliceous sinter, is a deposit of opaline or amorphous silica that forms through the rapid precipitation of fine-grained silica as an encrustation around hot springs and geysers. It is believed to have been partly formed by the action of algae in the heated water. The term "sinter" means that it has several hollow tubes and cavities in its structure, which are often a result of organic matter that has decomposed later.

Stone Wedding This pink tufa formation is in the Rhodope Mountains, Bulgaria. It is locally called the Stone Wedding.

PROFILE

- ▲ Chemical
- ⊕ Post-depositional
- ✿ Fine
- ■ Pyrite, marcasite
- ▢ Silica
- ✳ Various
- ⊛ Occasional plants and animals

Flint nodule
This nodule shows a variation in color due to differences in the extraneous material enclosed while the silica making the rock solidified.

compact silica

sharp edge

conchoidal fracture

VARIANTS

Melanterite A nodule of hydrous iron sulfate

Pyrite nodule A nodule of radiating pyrite crystals

Marine nodule A nodule of manganese oxides

NODULES

A rounded mineral accretion that differs in composition from its surrounding rock is known as a nodule. Nodules are commonly elongated with a knobby irregular surface and are usually oriented parallel to the bedding of their enclosing sediment. Most nodules are formed by the accumulation of silica in sediments and its subsequent solidification. Nodules containing manganese, phosphorous, titanium, chromium, and other valuable metals develop on the seafloor but are uneconomical to mine. Other nodules form around plant and animal remains as part of the fossilization process.

Pyrite (p.62) is commonly found as nodules. It occurs as spheres, rounded cylinders of radiating crystals, and flat, radiating disks, or "suns." Clay ironstone, a mixture of siderite (p.123) and clay, sometimes occurs as layers of dark gray-to-brown nodules overlying coal seams. Chert (p.332) and flint often occur as nodules of nearly pure cryptocrystalline quartz (p.168) within beds of limestone (p.319) or chalk (p.321).

Grainy chert
This specimen of fine-grained chert shows the way the rock breaks along flat to rounded surfaces.

rounded fracture surface

fine-grained texture

VARIANT

Fossiliferous chert
A specimen containing fossilized primitive plants

CHERT

A rock composed of microcrystalline silica is known as chert. It is commonly gray, white, brown, or black and may contain small fossils. Traces of iron (p.39) may give chert a light green to rusty-red color. Chert occurs as beds or nodules. It breaks along flat to rounded, smooth surfaces and has a glassy appearance. The rock forms by precipitation from silica-rich fluids and colloids.

Flint is chert that occurs in marly limestones (p.319) or chalk (p.321). It is generally gray in color. Flint is found as nodules, often in bands parallel to the bedding planes, and breaks with a conchoidal fracture. The nodules are irregular but rounded. Flint resists weathering, so it can form thick pebble beds on beaches and accumulate in soils that are derived from chalk.

Flint ax
A prized material for tool making, flint was one of the earliest rocks to be mined and extracted.

PROFILE

- ▲ Chemical
- ⊕ Postdepositional
- ⌀ Crystalline
- ■ Calcite, silica
- ▢ Celestine
- ✹ Gray, brown
- ⊛ Invertebrates, plants

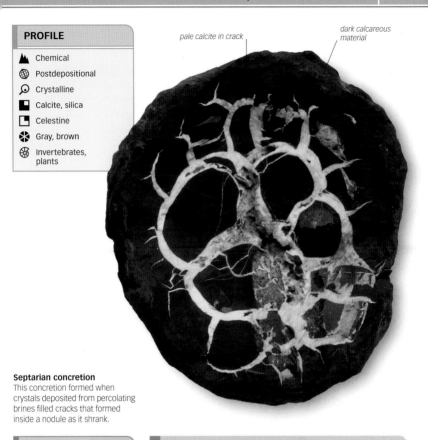

pale calcite in crack

dark calcareous material

Septarian concretion
This concretion formed when crystals deposited from percolating brines filled cracks that formed inside a nodule as it shrank.

VARIANT

Ironstone concretion
Pteridosperm (seed fern) fossilized in an ironstone concretion

CONCRETIONS

Nodules and concretions are distinctly different geologically, although they have some visual similarities. Unlike nodules, which are of different compositions than their hosts, concretions are made of the same material as their host sediment and cemented by other minerals, mainly calcite (p.114), iron oxides, and silica. Concretions are often much harder and more resistant to erosion than their surrounding rock and can be concentrated by weathering. They usually form early in the burial history of the sediment before the rest of the sediment is hardened into rock.

Concretions vary in shape, hardness, and size. They can be so small that they need to be seen under a magnifying lens. Specimens can also be huge bodies 9¾ ft (3 m) or more in diameter and weighing several tons. In some localities, fossil collectors seek out concretions that have formed around plant and animal remains and perfectly fossilized them. The largest fossil from concretions was an almost complete hadrosaur—a type of dinosaur.

METEORITES

Meteorites are rocks that formed elsewhere in our Solar System and orbited the Sun before colliding with Earth and falling to its surface. The fragments most likely to survive are either very large (weighing ⅓oz/10g or more) or very small (1mg or less).

STRUCTURE

There are three basic types of meteorite: irons, composed mostly of metallic iron and varying amounts of nickel; stony-irons, composed of a mixture of iron and silicate minerals; and stony meteorites, which are further classified into chondrites and achondrites, depending on the presence or absence of small igneous, silicate spheres called chondrules. The most common type of stony-irons are pallasites, which are iron meteorites with centimetre-sized, translucent, olivine or pyroxene crystals scattered throughout.

OCCURRENCE

Meteorites are found on every continent. They are often found in environments where they are highly visible—ice caps and deserts being examples. They range in size from microscopic specimens to masses that weigh many tons. Rocks that have been melted by meteorite impacts called tektites, are also widespread.

THE ORIGIN OF THE SOLAR SYSTEM

Meteorites are of particular interest in the study of the origin of the Solar System. Nearly all meteorites are thought to be fragments of asteroids—rocky bodies that formed in the solar nebula at about the same time as Earth. Radiometric dating puts the age of most meteorites at about 4.5 billion years, the same age as Earth.

Pallasite section
The stony-iron meteorites known as pallasites are usually one part olivine crystals to two parts metal. In this specimen, olivine is more abundant.

small to medium grains

iron-nickel matrix

olivine crystal

Achondrite
This stony meteorite found in Haryana, India, lacks chondrules, the small spheres of igneous minerals that would make it a chondrite.

Lunar discoveries
Over 100 meteorites are now believed to be material dislodged from the Moon, providing a more representative sample of the lunar surface than those brought back by astronauts.

Barringer Crater
This well-preserved impact crater is in the Arizona Desert, USA, and is ¾ mile (1.2km) in diameter. The meteorite that created it fell about 50,000 years ago and was about 165ft (50m) across.

Iron meteorite
The kamacite and taenite crystals in this iron meteorite occur as fine, crosshatched lines, forming what is known as a Widmanstätten pattern.

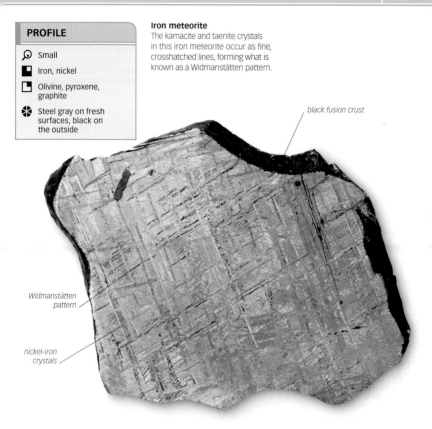

black fusion crust

Widmanstätten pattern

nickel-iron crystals

IRON METEORITE

These meteorites are believed to be the shattered fragments of the formerly molten cores of large, ancient asteroids. As the name suggests, iron meteorites are composed mostly of metallic iron (p.39) and up to 25 percent nickel, to produce two minerals, kamacite and taenite, which are otherwise rare on Earth. Other minerals present in minor amounts in iron meteorites include troilite, graphite (p.46), phosphides, and some silicates—most commonly olivine (p.232) and pyroxene. Iron meteorites are divided into a number of subgroups based on their chemical makeup.

Since iron meteorites are so different from most terrestrial rocks, they are recognized more often than other kinds of meteorites and tend to be over represented in meteorite collections. It is estimated that only about 6 percent of meteorites are iron meteorites. Chemical and isotope analysis of a number of iron meteorites indicates that at least 50 distinct parent asteroids were involved in their creation.

GLOSSARY

ACCESSORY MINERAL
A mineral that occurs in a rock in such small amounts that it is disregarded in the definition of the rock.

ACICULAR HABIT
A needlelike crystal habit of some minerals. See also *habit*.

ADAMANTINE LUSTER
A type of bright mineral luster similar to that of diamond. See also *luster*.

AGGREGATE
An accumulation of mineral crystals or rock fragments.

ALKALINE ROCK
A class of igneous rocks abundant in potassium- and sodium-rich minerals.

ALTERATION
The chemical, thermal, or pressure process or processes by which one rock or mineral is changed into another.

ALTERATION PRODUCT
A new rock or mineral formed by the alteration of a previous one. See also *alteration*.

ALUM
Any of a group of hydrated double salts, usually consisting of aluminum sulfate, water of hydration, and the sulfate of another element.

AMYGDALE
A secondary in-filling of a void in an igneous rock. Minerals that occur as amygdales include quartz, calcite, and the zeolites.

ASSOCIATED MINERALS
Minerals found growing together but not necessarily intergrown. See also *intergrowth*.

AUREOLE
The area around an igneous intrusion where contact metamorphism has occurred.

BASAL CLEAVAGE
Cleavage that occurs parallel to the basal crystal plane of a mineral. See also *cleavage*.

BATHOLITH
A huge, irregularly shaped mass of igneous rock formed from the intrusion of magma at depth. See also *magma*.

BLADED HABIT
A crystal habit in which wide, flat crystals appear similar to knife blades. See also *habit*.

BOTRYOIDAL HABIT
A mineral habit in which crystals form globular aggregates similar to bunches. See also *aggregate*, *habit*.

BRECCIA
A sedimentary rock made up of angular fragments. See also *igneous breccia*.

CABOCHON
A gemstone cut with a domed upper surface and a flat or domed under surface; gemstones cut in this way are said to be cut *en cabochon*. See also *cut*, *gem*, *gemstone*.

CARAT
A unit of gemstone weight, equivalent to 0.007 oz (0.2 g). Carat (also spelled "Karat") is also a measure of gold purity, the number of parts of gold in 24 parts of a gold alloy: 24 kt is pure gold; 18 kt is three quarters gold. See also *gem*, *gemstone*.

CHATOYANCY
The cat's-eye effect shown by some stones cut *en cabochon*. See also *cabochon*.

CLAST
A fragment of rock, especially when incorporated into a sedimentary rock.

CLASTIC ROCK
A sedimentary rock composed of cemented clasts. See also *clast*.

CLAY
Mineral particles smaller than about 0.00008 in (0.002 mm).

CLEAVAGE
The way certain minerals break along planes dictated by their atomic structure.

COLLOID
Any substance that consists of particles substantially larger than atoms or molecules but too small to be visible to the unaided eye.

COLOR DISPERSION
The separation of white light into its constituent colors.

CONCHOIDAL FRACTURE
A curved or shell-like fracture in many minerals and some rocks. See also *fracture*.

CONCRETION
A rounded, nodular mass of rock formed from its enclosing rock and commonly found in beds of sandstone, shale, or clay.

CONTACT TWINNING
The phenomenon of two or more crystals growing in parallel contact with each other and sharing a common face. See also *twinned crystals*.

CRYPTOCRYSTALLINE HABIT
A mineral habit that is crystalline but very fine-grained. Individual crystallized components can be seen only under a microscope. See also *habit*.

CUT
The final shape of a ground and polished gem, as in emerald cut. See also *gem*, *gemstone*, *gem cutting*.

DENDRITIC HABIT
A type of habit in which crystals form branching, treelike shapes. See also *habit*.

DETRITAL ROCKS
Sedimentary rocks formed essentially of fragments and grains derived from existing rocks. See also *sedimentary rock*.

DIATOMACEOUS EARTH
A sedimentary rock composed of the siliceous shells of microscopic aquatic plants known as diatoms.

DIFFRACTION
The splitting of light into its component colors. See also *x-ray diffraction*.

DIKE
A sheet-shaped igneous intrusion that cuts across existing rock structures.

DISCOVERY/TYPE LOCALITY
The site where a mineral was first recognized as a new mineral.

DOUBLE REFRACTION
The splitting of light into two separate rays as it enters a stone.

DRUSY COATING
A sheet of numerous, often well-formed, small crystals covering a mineral.

DULL LUSTER
A type of luster in which little or no light is reflected. See also *luster*.

EARTHY LUSTER
A nonreflective mineral luster. See also *luster*.

EQUANT
A mineral habit that refers to a crystal that is of equal size in all directions; a rock composed of grains of equal size.

EUHEDRAL
A term describing crystals with well-formed faces.

EVAPORITE
A mineral or rock formed by the evaporation of saline water.

EXTRUSIVE ROCK
A rock formed from lava that either flowed onto Earth's surface or was ejected as pyroclastic material. See also *intrusive rock*, *lava*.

FACES
The external flat surfaces that make up a crystal's shape.

FELDSPATHOIDS
Minerals similar in chemistry and structure to the feldspars but with less silica.

FELSIC ROCK
An igneous rock with more than 65 percent silica and more than 20 percent quartz. It is also known as acidic rock.

FISSILE TEXTURE
A rock texture that allows the rock to be split into sheets. See also *texture*.

FLOW BANDING
Layering in a rock that originated when the rock was in a fluid, molten state.

FOLIATION
The laminated, parallel orientation or segregation of minerals.

FOSSIL
Any record of past life preserved in the crustal rocks. Apart from bones and shells, fossils can include footprints, excrement, and borings.

FRACTURE
Mineral breakage that occurs at locations other than along cleavage planes. See also *cleavage*.

FUMAROLE
In volcanic regions, an opening in the ground through which hot gases are emitted.

GARNET
A member of a group of silicates with the general formula $A_3B_2(SiO_4)_3$ in which A can be Ca, Fe^{2+}, Mg, or Mn^{2+}; and B can be Al, Cr, Fe^{3+}, Mn^{3+}, Si, Ti, V, or Zr.

GEODE
A hollow, generally rounded nodule lined with crystals. See also *nodule*.

GEM, GEMSTONE
A cut stone worn in jewelry, valued for its color, rarity, texture, or clarity. It may even be an unset stone cut for use as jewelry. See also *cut*, *rough gemstone*.

GEM CUTTING
The process of shaping a gemstone by grinding and polishing. See also *cut*, *gem*, *gemstone*.

GLASS
A solid substance showing no crystalline structure—in effect, a very thick liquid. See also *glassy texture*.

GLASSY TEXTURE
The smooth consistency of an igneous rock in which glass formed due to rapid solidification. See also *glass*, *texture*.

GRANULAR TEXTURE
A rock or mineral texture that either includes grains or is in the form of grains. See also *texture*.

GRAPHIC TEXTURE
The surface appearance of some igneous rocks in which quartz and feldspar have intergrown to produce an effect resembling a written script. See also *texture*.

HABIT
The mode of growth and appearance of a mineral. The habit of a mineral results from its molecular structure.

HACKLY FRACTURE
A mineral fracture that has a rough surface with small protuberances, as on a piece of broken cast iron. See also *fracture*.

HEMIMORPHIC FORM
A crystalline form with a different facial development at each end.

HOPPER CRYSTAL
A crystal whose incomplete growth has created a hopper-shaped concavity on one or more faces.

HYDROTHERMAL DEPOSIT
A mineral deposit that is formed by hot water ejected from deep within Earth's crust.

HYDROTHERMAL MINERAL
A mineral that is derived from hydrothermal deposition. See also *hydrothermal deposit*.

HYDROTHERMAL VEIN
A rock fracture in which minerals have been deposited by fluids from deep within Earth's crust. See also *hydrothermal deposit*, *pegmatite*, *vein*.

HYPABYSSAL
A term describing minor igneous intrusions at relatively shallow depths within Earth's crust.

IGNEOUS BRECCIA
An igneous rock made up of angular fragments. See also *breccia*.

IGNEOUS ROCK
A rock that is formed through the solidification of molten rock.

INCLUSION
A crystal or fragment of another substance within a crystal or rock.

INTERGROWTH
Two or more minerals that are growing together and interpenetrating each other. See also *associated minerals*.

INTERMEDIATE ROCK
An igneous rock that is intermediate in composition between silica-rich and silica-poor rocks.

INTRUSIVE ROCK
A body of igneous rock that invades older rock. See also *extrusive rock*.

IRIDESCENCE
The reflection of light from the internal elements of a stone, yielding a rainbowlike play of colors.

LAMELLAR HABIT
A type of crystal habit in which plates or flakes occur in thin layers or scales. See also *habit*.

LAVA
Molten rock that is extruded onto Earth's surface. See also *magma*.

LITHIFICATION
The process by which unconsolidated sediment turns to stone. See also *recrystallization*.

LUSTER
The shine of a mineral caused by reflected light.

MAFIC ROCK
An igneous rock with 45–55 percent silica. Such rocks have less than 10 percent quartz and are rich in iron-magnesium minerals. They are also known as basic rocks. See also *ultramafic rock*.

MAGMA
Molten rock that may crystallize beneath Earth's surface or be erupted as lava. See also *lava*.

MAMILLARY HABIT
A mineral habit in which crystals form rounded aggregates. See also *aggregate, habit*.

MASSIVE
A mineral form having no definite shape.

MATRIX
A fine-grained rock into which or on top of which larger crystals appear to be set. It is also known as a groundmass.

METAL
A substance that is characterized by high electrical and thermal conductivity as well as by malleability, ductility, and high reflectivity of light.

METALLIC LUSTER
A shine similar to the typical shine of polished metal. See also *luster*.

METAMORPHIC ROCK
A rock that has been transformed by heat or pressure (or both) into another rock.

METEOR
A rock from space that completely vaporizes while passing through Earth's atmosphere.

METEORITE
A rock from space that reaches Earth's surface.

MICA
Any of a group of hydrous potassium or aluminum silicate minerals. These minerals exhibit a two-dimensional sheet- or layerlike structure.

MICROCRYSTALLINE HABIT
A mineral habit in which crystals are so minuscule that they can be detected only with the aid of a microscope. See also *habit*.

MINERAL GROUP
Two or more minerals that share common structural and/or chemical properties.

MOONSTONE
A gem-quality feldspar mineral that exhibits a silvery or bluish iridescence. Several feldspars, especially some plagioclases, are called moonstone.

NATIVE ELEMENT
A chemical element that is found in nature uncombined with other elements.

NODULE
A generally rounded accretion of sedimentary material that differs from its enclosing sedimentary rock.

NONMETAL
An element, such as sulfur, which lacks some or all of the properties of metals. See also *metal*.

OOLITHS
Individual spherical sedimentary grains from which

oolitic rocks are formed. Most ooliths comprise concentric layers of calcite.

ORE
A rock or mineral from which a metal can be profitably extracted.

OXIDATION
The process of combining with oxygen. In minerals, the oxygen can come from the air or water.

PEGMATITE
A hydrothermal vein composed of large crystals. See also *hydrothermal vein*.

PENETRATION TWINNING
The phenomenon of two or more crystals forming from a common center and appearing to penetrate each other. See also *twinned crystals*.

PHENOCRYST
A large crystal set in an igneous rock matrix, creating a porphyritic texture. See also *porphyritic texture*.

PISOLITIC HABIT
A mineral habit characterized by pea-sized grains with a concentric inner structure. See also *habit*.

PLACER, PLACER DEPOSIT
A deposit of minerals derived by weathering and concentrated in streams or beaches because of the mineral's high specific gravity.

PLASTIC ROCK
A type of rock that is easily folded when subjected to high temperature and pressure.

PLATY HABIT
The growth habit shown by flat, thin crystals. See also *habit*.

PLAYA DEPOSIT
A mineral deposit formed in a desert basin that is intermittently filled with a lake.

PLEOCHROIC, PLEOCHROISM
The phenomenon of a mineral or gem presenting different colors to the eye when viewed from different directions.

PLUTON
A mass of igneous (plutonic) rock that has formed beneath Earth's surface by the solidification of magma.

POLYMORPH
A substance that can exist in two or more crystalline forms; one crystalline form of such a substance. See also *pseudomorph*.

PORPHYRITIC TEXTURE
An igneous rock texture in which large crystals are set in a finer matrix. See also *phenocryst*, *texture*.

PORPHYROBLAST
A relatively large crystal set in a fine-grained matrix in a metamorphic rock.

PORPHYROBLASTIC TEXTURE
A texture characterized by relatively large crystals in a fine-grained matrix. See also *texture*.

PRECIPITATION
The condensation of a solid from a liquid or gas.

PRIMARY MINERAL
A mineral that has crystallized directly from an igneous magma and is unaltered by rain, groundwater, or other agents. See also *secondary mineral*.

PRISMATIC HABIT
A mineral habit in which parallel rectangular crystal faces form prisms. See also *habit*.

PROTOLITH
A rock that existed prior to undergoing metamorphic transformation into a different rock type.

PSEUDOMORPH
A crystal with the outward form of another species of mineral. See also *polymorph*.

PYRAMIDAL HABIT
A crystal habit in which the principal faces join at a point. When two such pyramids are placed base to base, the crystal is said to be di- or bi-pyramidal. See also *habit*.

PYROCLASTIC ROCK
A rock consisting of airborne material ejected from a volcanic vent.

PYROXENE
A member of a group of 21 rock-forming silicate minerals that typically form elongate crystals.

RADIOMETRIC DATING
The determination of absolute ages of minerals and rocks by measuring certain radioactive and radiogenic atoms in them.

RARE-EARTH MINERAL
A mineral containing a significant portion of one or more of the 17 rare-earth elements, principally ytterbium, gadolinium, neodymium, praseodymium, cerium, lanthanum, yttrium, and scandium.

RECRYSTALLIZATION
The redistribution of components to form new minerals or mineral crystals; in some cases new rocks form. It occurs during lithification and metamorphism. See also *lithification*.

REFRACTIVE INDEX
A measure of the slowing down and bending of light as it enters a stone. It is used to identify cut gemstones and some minerals. See also *cut*, *gem*, *gemstone*.

RENIFORM HABIT
A mineral habit with a kidneylike appearance. See also *habit*.

REPLACEMENT DEPOSIT
A deposit formed from minerals that have been altered. See also *alteration product*.

RESINOUS LUSTER
A shine having the reflectivity of resin. See also *luster*.

RETICULATED
Having a network or a netlike mode of crystallization.

ROCK FLOUR
Very fine-grained rock dust, often the product of glacial action.

ROUGH GEMSTONE
An uncut gemstone. See also *cut*, *gem*, *gemstone*.

SALT DOME
A large, intrusive mass of salt, sometimes with petroleum trapped beneath.

SCHILLER EFFECT
The brilliant play of bright colors in a crystal, which is often due to minute, rodlike inclusions.

SCHISTOSITY
A foliation that occurs in coarse-grained metamorphic rocks. It is the result of platy mineral grains. See also *foliation*.

SCORIACEOUS
A term for lava or other volcanic material that is heavily pitted with hollows and cavities. See also *lava*.

SECONDARY MINERAL
A mineral that replaces another mineral as a result of weathering or alteration. See also *alteration*, *primary mineral*.

SECTILE
The property of a mineral that allows it to be cut smoothly with a knife. See also *fracture*.

SEDIMENTARY ROCK
A rock that either originates on Earth's surface as an accumulation of sediments or precipitates from water.

SEMIMETAL
A metal, such as arsenic or bismuth, that is not malleable. See also *metal*.

SILICA-POOR ROCKS
Rocks containing less than 50 percent silica. See also *silica-rich rocks*.

SILICA-RICH ROCKS
Rocks containing more than 50 percent silica. See also *silica-poor rocks*.

SLATY CLEAVAGE
The tendency of a rock, such as slate, to break along flat planes into thin, flat sheets. See also *cleavage*.

SOLID-SOLUTION SERIES
A series of minerals in which certain chemical components are variable between two end-members with fixed composition.

SPECIFIC GRAVITY
The ratio of the mass of a mineral to the mass of an equal volume of water. Specific gravity is numerically equivalent to density (mass divided by volume) in grams per cubic centimeter.

SPHEROIDAL HABIT
A crystal habit in which numerous crystals radiate outwards to form a spherical mass. See also *habit*.

STALACTITIC HABIT
A mineral habit in which the crystalline components are arranged in radiating groups of diminishing size, giving the appearance of icicles. See also *habit*.

STRIATION
A parallel groove or line appearing on a crystal.

SUBLIMATION, SUBLIMATE
The process by which a substance moves directly from a gaseous state to a solid state. A sublimate is the solid product of sublimation.

SUNSTONE
A gemstone variety of feldspar with minute, platelike inclusions of iron oxide oriented parallel to one another throughout. See also *gem*, *gemstone*.

TABULAR HABIT
A crystal habit in which the crystals have long, flat, parallel faces. See also *habit*.

TERMINATION
Faces that make up the ends of a crystal.

TEXTURE
The size, shape, and relationships between rock grains or crystals.

TWINNED CRYSTALS
Crystals that grow together as mirror images with a common face (contact twins) or grow at angles up to 90 degrees to each other and appear to penetrate each other (penetration twins).

ULTRAMAFIC ROCK
An igneous rock with less than 45 percent silica. It is also known as an ultrabasic rock. See also *mafic rock*.

VEIN
A thin, sheetlike mass of rock that fills fractures in other rocks.

VESICLE
A small, spherical or oval cavity produced by a bubble of gas or vapor in lava, left after the lava has solidified. See also *lava*.

VITREOUS LUSTER
A shine resembling that of glass. See also *luster*.

VOLCANIC PIPE
A fissure through which lava flows. See also *lava*.

WELL-SORTED ROCK
A sediment or sedimentary rock with grains or clasts that are roughly of the same size.

X-RAY DIFFRACTION
The passing of x-rays through a crystal to determine its internal structure by the way in which the x-rays are scattered. See also *diffraction*.

ZEOLITE
A group of hydrous aluminum silicates characterized by their easy and reversible loss of water.

INDEX

Page numbers in **bold** indicate main entries.

ACKNOWLEDGMENTS

Dorling Kindersley would like to thank the following people from Smithsonian Enterprises at the Smithsonian Institution in Washington D.C:

Carol LeBlanc, Vice President
Brigid Ferraro, Director of Licensing
Ellen Nanney, Licensing Manager
Kealy Wilson, Product Development Coordinator

The publisher would like to thank the following people: Frances Green for helping to plan the profile sections; Janet Mohun, Miezan van Zyl, Lizzie Munsey, and Martyn Page for editorial work; Steve Setford for proofreading; Jane Parker for the index; David Roberts for database work; and Sophia Tampakopoulos, Jacket Design Development Manager.

DK India would like to thank Neha Chaudhary, Jubbi Francis, and Suefa Lee for editorial assistance; Vaibhav Rastogi for design assistance; and Mahima Barrow, Nidhilekha Mathur, Swati Mittal, and Neha Samuel for picture selection assistance.

The publisher would like to thank the following for their kind permission to reproduce their photographs:

(Key: a-above; b-below/bottom; c-center; f-far; l-left; r-right; t-top)

6-7 Corbis: William James Warren/ Science Faction. **8 Corbis:** Roger Wood (tr). **8-9 Corbis:** Ludovic Maisant (b). **9 Corbis:** Kevin Schafer (t). **14 Science Photo Library:** Steve Gschmeissner (b). **24 The Bridgeman Art Library:** Ashmolean Museum, University of Oxford, UK (cr); Egyptian National Museum, Cairo, Egypt/Giraudon (cl). **Corbis:** Jack Fields (bl); Bernard Bisson/Sygma (br). **26 Corbis:** WildCountry (br). **Dorling Kindersley:** Neil Fletcher (cl). **27 Corbis:** Momatiuk – Eastcott (t). **28 Dorling Kindersley:** Neil Fletcher (b). **Getty Images:** Keith Douglas (t). 29 Getty Images: John Elk III (t). **32 Corbis:** Jim Sugar (cr). **Getty Images:** American Images Inc (cl). **33 Corbis:** Philippe Eranian (t). **34-35 Getty Images:** National Geographic. **36 Corbis:** Ricki Rosen/SABA (cl). **FLPA:**

Silvestris Fotoservice (b). **39 Dorling Kindersley:** Peter Anderson © Dorling Kindersley, Courtesy of the Danish National Museum (br). **40 Dorling Kindersley:** Colin Keates, Courtesy of the Natural History Museum, London (br). **41 Dorling Kindersley:** Clive Streeter, Courtesy of The Science Museum, London (cl). **42 Dorling Kindersley:** Harry Taylor, Courtesy of the Natural History Museum, London (cl). 43 Dorling Kindersley: Judith Miller/Woolley and Wallis (br). **44 Dorling Kindersley:** Colin Keates, Courtesy of the Natural History Museum, London (cl). **45 Dorling Kindersley:** Colin Keates, Courtesy of the Natural History Museum, London (cl). **47 Smithsonian Institution, Washington, DC:** (br). **48 Corbis:** Eric and David Hosking (t). **Science Photo Library:** Ben Johnson (b). **60 Smithsonian Institution, Washington, DC:** (cl). 61 Smithsonian Institution, Washington, DC, USA: (bl). **65 Dorling Kindersley:** Alan Hills and Barbara Winter © The British Museum (cr). **Tony Waltham Geophotos:** (b). 69 Corbis: Heritage Images (br). **72 Dorling Kindersley:** Neil Fletcher (bl). **73 akg-images:** Rabatti – Domingie (br). **74 Corbis:** Steve Parish/Steve Parish Publishing (t). **Dorling Kindersley:** Courtesy of Dream Cars (br). **75 Corbis:** Klaus Lang/ All Canada Photos (t); WIN-Images (cl); Jim Reed (b). **77 Dorling Kindersley:** Neil Fletcher (bl). **81 Smithsonian Institution, Washington, DC:** (br). **83 Corbis:** Bettmann (br). **88 Dorling Kindersley:** Neil Fletcher (bl). **100 Corbis:** Vince Streano (b). **105 Corbis:** Michael S. Yamashita (br). **106 Corbis:** Stevens Fremont/ Sygma (cr). **Tony Waltham Geophotos:** (b). **109 Dorling Kindersley:** Courtesy of the Oxford University Museum of Natural History (br). **113 Dorling Kindersley:** Judith Miller/333 Auctions LLC (cr). **Tony Waltham Geophotos:** (b). **114 Corbis:** (br). **118 Getty Images:** (bl). **119 Dorling Kindersley:** Neil Fletcher (clb). **121 Smithsonian Institution, Washington, DC:** (t). **126 Tony Waltham Geophotos:** (b). **131 Corbis:** Gallo Images (b); Larry Mulvehill (cr). **134**

Smithsonian Institution, Washington, DC: (clb). **140 Dorling Kindersley:** Neil Fletcher (clb). **141 Dorling Kindersley:** Neil Fletcher (bl). **145 NASA:** Marshall Space Flight Center (br). **147 Corbis:** David Muench (b). **Science Photo Library:** Hank Morgan/University of Massachusetts at Amherst (cr). **151 Smithsonian Institution, Washington, DC:** (clb, b). 159 Dorling Kindersley: Judith Miller/ Mark Laino (br). 162 Dorling Kindersley: British Museum Images (br). **167 Alamy Images:** Pavel Filatov (b). **Dorling Kindersley:** Michel Zabe © CONACULTA-INAH-MEX (cr). **168 Dorling Kindersley:** Judith Miller/Private Collection (br). **169 Dorling Kindersley:** British Museum Images (br). **170 Dorling Kindersley:** Judith Miller/Wallis and Wallis (br). **173 Dorling Kindersley:** Judith Miller/Sylvie Spectrum (br). **175 Dorling Kindersley:** Judith Miller/Dreweatt Neate (br). **178 Dorling Kindersley:** Colin Keates, Courtesy of the Natural History Museum, London (br). **179 Alamy Images:** Piotr & Irena Kolasa (b). **181 Science Photo Library:** Joel Arem (b). **182 Dorling Kindersley:** British Museum Images – DK Images (br). **184 Dorling Kindersley:** Judith Miller/N. Bloom & Son Ltd. (br). **185 Alamy Images:** RF Company (cl). **Science Photo Library:** Joel Arem (b). **190 Dorling Kindersley:** Neil Fletcher (cl); Clive Streeter, Courtesy of The Science Museum, London (br). **191 Dorling Kindersley:** Neil Fletcher (bl). **193 Dorling Kindersley:** Judith Miller/ Cooper Owen (br). **194 Corbis:** Scientifica/Visuals Unlimited (bl). **196 U.S. Geological Survey:** G.R. Mansfield (cl); E. D. McKee (cl). **198 Dorling Kindersley:** Neil Fletcher (cl). **200 Dorling Kindersley:** Judith Miller/David Rago Auctions (br). **Dreamstime.com:** Gelyngfjell (bl, cl). **206 Dorling Kindersley:** Judith Miller/Dreweatt Neate (br). **209 Alamy Images:** Andre Joubert (t); RF Company (bl). **214 Getty Images:** DEA/C. Bevilacqua (cl). **Science Photo Library:** Scientifica, Visuals Unlimited (bl). **215 Smithsonian Institution, Washington, DC:** (clb). **217 Dorling Kindersley:** Judith Miller/

Blanchet et Associes (br). **Getty Images:** DEA/Photo 1 (cl). **218 Getty Images:** Mark Schneider (clb); Scientifica (cla). **222 Dorling Kindersley:** John Chase, Courtesy Of The Museum of London (br). **223 Dorling Kindersley:** Judith Miller/Lesley Craze Gallery (br). **226 Alamy Images:** Alan Curtis (bl); Greg C Grace (cl). **230 Getty Images:** Mark Schneider (cl); Visuals Unlimited/Scientifica (bl). **231 Dorling Kindersley:** Judith Miller/Woolley and Wallis (br). **232 Dorling Kindersley:** Judith Miller/HY Duke and Son (br). **241 shutterstone.com:** (cl, bl). **243 Dorling Kindersley:** Judith Miller/Joseph H Bonnar (br). **246 Dorling Kindersley:** Martin Strmiska (c) Alamy (b). **248 Dorling Kindersley:** Judith Miller/Beaussant Lefevre (br). **249 Dorling Kindersley:** Judith Miller/Wallis and Wallis (br). **252 Dorling Kindersley:** Colin Keates, Courtesy of the Natural History Museum, London (cl). **254-255 Corbis:** Chris Harris/All Canada Photos. **257 Corbis:** Gary Braasch (b). **259 Dorling Kindersley:** Neil Fletcher (bl). **261 Dorling Kindersley:** Judith Miller/N. Bloom & Son Ltd. (br). **Smithsonian Institution, Washington, DC:** (bl). **264 Corbis:** Visuals Unlimited (bl). **Getty Images:** Mark Schneider/Visuals Unlimited (cl). **269 Dorling Kindersley:** Judith Miller/HY Duke and Son (br). **270 Dorling Kindersley:** Neil Fletcher (cl). **Getty Images:** DEA/A. Dagli Orti (bl). **272 Alamy Images:** RF Company (t). **274 Alamy Images:** Susan E. Degginger (bl). **Getty Images:** DEA/R. Appiani (cl). **275 Dorling Kindersley:** Image Plan (c) Corbis (br). **276 Alamy Images:** Phil Degginger (t); Susan E. Degginger (b). **281 Alamy Images:** Photo resource Hawaii (clb). **Corbis:** (bl). **283 Dorling Kindersley:** Neil Fletcher (cl). **shutterstone.com:** (t). **286-287 Alamy Images:** Daniel Dempster Photography (b). **291 Dorling Kindersley:** Judith Miller/Ormonde Gallery (br). **293 Dorling Kindersley:** Courtesy of the Blists Hill Museum, Ironbridge, Shropshire (br). **294 Alamy Images:** Susan E. Degginger (clb); RF Company (cla); geoz (bl). **296 Alamy Images:** geoz (cl); RF Company (bl); Fabrizio Troiani (clb). **297 Alamy Images:** The Art Archive (b). **300 Alamy Images:** Leslie Garland Picture Library (cl). **Corbis:** Scientifica/Visuals Unlimited (t, bl). **Dorling Kindersley:** Neil Fletcher (clb). **305 Corbis:** Ric Ergenbright (cr). **307 Dorling Kindersley:** Peter Hayman/The Trustees of the British Museum (br). **309 fotoLibra :** Brian G Burgess (b). **316 Dorling Kindersley:** Colin Keates, Courtesy of the Natural History Museum, London (cl). **317 The Bridgeman Art Library:** Detroit Institute of Arts, USA/Gift of Lillian Henkel Haass and Constance Haass (br). **319 Dorling Kindersley:** The Trustees of the British Museum (br). **320 shutterstone.com:** (bl). **323 Dorling Kindersley:** The Trustees of the British Museum (br). **326 Dorling Kindersley:** Neil Fletcher (bl, t). **327 fotoLibra :** John Cleare (t). **332 Dorling Kindersley:** Courtesy of the Pitt Rivers Museum, University of Oxford (br). **333 Dorling Kindersley:** Colin Keates, Courtesy of the Natural History Museum, London (cl). **334 Corbis:** (cr). **Smithsonian Institution, Washington, DC:** (c). **335 Dorling Kindersley:** Neil Fletcher (b). **336 Dorling Kindersley:** Colin Keates, Courtesy of the Natural History Museum, London (cl); Courtesy of the Oxford University Museum of Natural History (t). **337 Dorling Kindersley:** Neil Fletcher (bl)

All other images © Dorling Kindersley
For further information see:
www.dkimages.com